# *Move Past Your Past*

A Process for Freeing Your Life

Alice Parker

"Updated Version"

# Move Past Your Past

*A Process for Freeing Your Life*

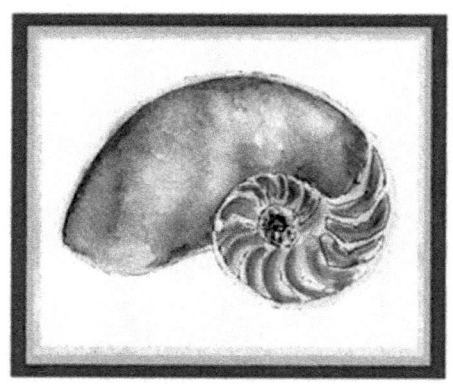

Alice Parker

EXPLORA BOOKS
700 – 838 West Hastings St. Vancouver, BC V6C 0A6
www.explorabooks.com
Phone: (604) 330 6795

*Original Nautilus shell watercolor and artwork by: Cheryl McDonald - www.cherylmcdonald-art.com*
*Author photo by: Suad Bejtović - www.suad.com*

ISBN: 978-1-998394-20-3 (Paperback)
978-1-998394-18-0 (Kindle)

# Table of Contents

# *Dedications*

To Cheryl McDonald, my so very creative friend
and cohort in discovery
www.cherylmcdonald-art.com

For my son David - I wish I had known
more earlier for raising you.

And, to so many other friends and supporters of me and
my work.

The Nautilus Shell symbolizes our Past lives as we grow
from each one, accumulating what we have lived and
learned. Yet, also letting go of any negative experiences
from those Past lives. Each life is for learning anew,
creating and receiving our joy and happiness, so promised
to us by God-Source, as we are all worthy of it. Colors are
for the top four Chakras: Crown - Violet; Third Eye -
Indigo; Throat - Blue; Heart - Green - Universal
Connection - Communication - Love.

**Artistic design by Cheryl McDonald.**

# *Prologue*

I have been told from my Akashic Records, that almost all of my numerous Past lives I have been a teacher/trainer. So, beside what parts of the information in this book that has been given to me by my Angel Guides, the rest has come from the teachers, guides, books I've read and those of my Past life experiences, as well as this one as a teacher/trainer.

There is no telling how many miles
you will have to run while chasing a dream.

I believe that there are only two emotions - Love and Fear. All other emotions and feelings are derivatives of them, with love being the all powerful positive and fear being the negative. I also believe that the opposite of love is not hate, but apathy. Hate - a word I try not to use - still has emotions attached to it, but apathy means not caring or absence of any emotions. I also believe that love is always more powerful than hate, and can overcome it when the love is honest.

What I feel I have learned in my studies is that probably more than 90% of most of our problems, pain and unhappiness comes from our Past experiences. Then, to reach that point of being happy means to explore and learn how to release and let go all of that Past stuff. That is what this book is all about. While I will repeatedly say that change and everything else is a choice, most people will not accept that. They have rationalized or believe that their obligations or whatever will not allow them to do so. Perhaps as they read through the different directed parts and try some of the various exercises, they will see how wonderfully freeing from their Past change can be.

This is not about any organized religion, it is about Spirituality. While one may find Spirituality within some religions, religion is not within Spirituality. Spirituality is generally considered a singular, personal connection to Mother/Father God/Universe-Source, since that power is within each individual to have and use as promised through the Holy Spirit. While some people may enjoy meditating together or having group sharing, one's own path has only personal rules or guidance which can be changed as needed, or preferred through Choice. We have been given Freewill from God, and should give it to others to choose their path to enlightenment and Spirituality.

The Great Enlightened beings did not intend to establish forced, rigid religions on our Earth. They did not seek followers, or to be worshiped. They simply shared what they had learned about the path of awakening and left it open for those who may choose it. To travel the path these wise-ones laid out, there are few rigid rules to follow. The approach of this path is not linear, as you may sidetrack, retrace steps, have speed bumps or even stop for periods of time. It is not a path with a set destination, or involving a timeframe you can force with your human will, as if competing in a marathon. It is truly about the experiences of the journey and the roads you take on it.

Tools helpful to one's path are unique to each person for the changes/growth they desire in their life. A person may need to be exposed to a certain guide, teaching, or life lesson and may ask for help from whomever they choose. The helpful catalysts will vary, depending on the person, the stage of awakening, and your timing involved. These lessons are purely self-chosen and may be ended or expanded on your decision. Trust that Divine intelligence within you, that can guide you along the path of enlightenment to joy. This wise part of you can connect you with insights, about the various baggage you will want to let go of, from this life and others. It can help you to prioritize your energies, your focus and your actions in the world, so you don't repeat lessons. It can lead you to the people, teachers and personal help you want, to view yourself and your life differently.

**Caveat:** For those of you who have been working diligently toward the integration of your full-human potential, I am sure that by now you wholeheartedly agree that the path of Spiritual growth is not all rainbows and butterflies. The sobering-reality of the choice to activate your divine-blueprint and integrate it fully into your physical life. It duly requires a sufficient amount of naïveté, more energy than you may have to expend, deliberate sacrifice, a dash of masochism, relentless determination, a mammoth sense of humor, isolating solitude, freakish patience and above all else, the super-human will to trust in something you can't see. Most times this boils down to feeling like your being dragged feet-first across a rocky terrain . . . face down.

When we come from Love, all things are brought into harmony and balance, as well as acceptance, compassion and Peace.

We are all One from the same Source/God.

You can make a difference through your love.

# *About Me ~ My Background*

Those of you who have read my Memoir, *Choices, Changes & Friends: 1970s After Divorce*, know this, but for others: I'm originally from Chicago, have degrees in psychology and marketing, bilingual–bi-cultural studies in graduate school. I have traveled to 36 countries and 40 states –lived in six and wrote for an international business-travel magazine, as well several in-flight magazines. In Japan for seven years, as a corporate business trainer, then ten years in human resources management with 200 to 1000 employees in San Francisco. I've been a student of metaphysics/spirituality for over thirty years and wrote this book in 2009, as requested from followers of my blog. Then as a Life Coach, I used it for numerous presentations, workshops and classes, as well radio/TV interviews. I've been in Dallas since 2013, continuing to teach my memoir writing classes and help my students edit their books for publishing. I moved to be near my two grand-children, then joined the Poetry Society of Texas, where I won first place in State several times in their annual poetry contests. I live passionately about everything I've written, so I feel qualified to write with satirical humor regarding life, heart, soul and Love. My blogs and poems are on my website: www.a-wonderland.com. You are welcome to contact at alice@a-wonderland.com or apinsf@gmail.com.

I was not raised within a Spirituality belief system, it was definitely more the framework of organized, protestant religious content controlled by the rules of its context. Years later, I was glad I had that Bible-base to springboard from, in other words, I could speak of it, because I had tried it and it didn't work for me. Even before my slow, steady move into Metaphysics, I believed things happened for a reason and all people were connected. I read and studied Mary Baker Eddy and

Christian Science, the Mormons, Baha'i Faith and extensive study of Judaism. Finally, being guided into Unity, I also discovered Buddhism and touches of the new discourse - Spirituality. I admit that during most of the nine years following my divorce at twenty-six, I rarely studied religions per se, though often into astrology - hypnosis, yet unknowingly reading spiritual-oriented books.

After my second divorce, still living in Japan, my success soared as my travel continued to foreign and even exotic places, escaping from my workaholic-self, as well as Japan. When I stopped long enough to think about it, I had made so many of my dreams come true and was absolutely satiating my quests of knowledge with much curiosity. I was finally that person, on that plane going to so many interesting foreign places. And, while I spent sporadic spare time studying Buddhism, more was spent getting to know so many people from so many countries, who came to Japan to teach or learn. Studying people was my new religion and I slowly released myself, as I began to study myself, as I needed to change in how I related to men, if I wanted to become more happily involved with them.

After seven years, and tremendous success, I knew it was time to return to the States. I needed to get to know me in a less distracting, quiet surrounding. The last years in Japan, I had spent much of my free time writing separately about Japan and Australia's Aboriginal cultural-history. With Japan, it was in regards to American Occupation there and with Australia, their modern relationship with Aboriginals, of whom I'd learn a lot in my five extended visits there.To me, the Aboriginals had an innate Spirituality, that the Japanese, in contrast, had so many strict cultural precepts that controlled them, in even the most minute-facets of their lives. I had presented to me numerous case studies, and my Psychology degree ran rampant with exploring them.

I was beginning to understand how Belief Systems and our indoctrination in them from childhood, kept control of us in the most personal and broad experiences. Even with both of my parents now deceased, their differing influences would bounce in my face, or blip through my brain with some past deed or statement. Finally, with some available time in exploring me, living in San Francisco I took classes of every sort from New Age, Metaphysical, Spiritual and all kinds of relationships. I became the quintessential-onion peeling myself and then surprising myself with each layer discovered, explored and often discarded. It took years to learn *not to* 'throw the baby out with the bath water,' as I was an accumulation of my past and knew I simply could not invent someone else's life as me. It is an ongoing process still, with every negative or positive situation that I now know I bring in, or brought into my life was for a purpose, reason or lesson.

After only two years in San Francisco, I allowed a former teacher of mine who convinced me into moving to Hawaii with him to set up a training company - very long, arduous story that turned into a financial-disaster-nightmare. The main lesson I learned from that was: though one may speak of Spiritual-things and seem to have almost mystic-abilities and knowledge, they may not have learned to use them in a positive, Spiritual way *for the greater good.* He was quite brilliant, though unfortunately, a most manipulative, egotistical and insecure man, who also later we discovered, was unbalanced by his bipolar disability. Yes, it was a costly experience, I know I learned so much more about me in my three and half years there. For one thing: perception - positive or negative - can be a very dangerous thing. I am, and always have been, a very trusting person, which basically comes from personally being a very honest person, thus expecting it in others. Obviously, I also had not learned as much as I thought I had about relationships. On a positive note, I learned to start trusting my intuition - if I had followed it several times, rather than him, it would have made a big difference in several outcomes. Again, most importantly I had the opportunity to learn about many other cultures, that I would not have connected with directly in San Francisco.

I moved back to San Francisco in late 2000, with the promise of a job and the interview seemed almost too good to be true. In the aftermath of the Dot-Com bust-ripples, the job was gone before I could start it. Obviously, not quite there yet with the intuition. Now, that I feel my intuition is directly connected to my angels or Source, I follow it with conviction and rarely question. I guess that actually means "my" intuition still needs additional support - kind of funny, but works for me. Back in my beloved San Francisco, I was lost and afraid of competing with so many much younger than me, accompanied by computer skills that had fallen behind in in Hawaii. Though I had money, I couldn't get an apartment without a job, so had to settle into a semi-tacky residential hotel with my twenty some boxes in storage - a revelation within itself.

After several temporary jobs, I finally got a long-term contract and met up with several people who guided me back to my studies, which I wasn't calling Spiritual yet. One of the first big jumps was when a co-worker mentioned to me about the book *Conversations with God*, by Neale Donald Walsch. I believe I almost recoiled, as I had become quite adamant about "Bible-bangers" and organized religion the past few years. He agreed, but also quite brilliantly said, "This was quite the opposite, as it was about our direct connection to God - Spirit, and rather counter to organized religion's controlling how we related to God." Today, I'd say it is similar to comparing Spirituality to being clean, healthy and purely Organic - direct from Source, and Organized Religion as being heavily fertilized with chemicals and dogma for their Belief Systems, as marketed products.

We talked several more times before I literally stumbled across the book at the library. I think my intuition does get some credit here. I had been at the library a couple of hours looking up agent contacts for my books I'd written, when I needed to get up and walk around a little. The moment I stood up, I felt drawn to the book shelves across the room and never noticed the heading until I glanced at the books. Right there, just below eye level, the third or fourth book I saw was truly *Conversations with God*. I'm sure my mouth dropped open as I reached to pull it out, automatically opening it up to read passages. I then flipped back to read the inside covers and intro, then simply taking it over to the table to continue to read before gathering my stuff up to check it out. It ranked right up there with a dozen or so other books that I could say changed my life, to the degree of the shift they made in my thinking. I feel it was the fact that Walsch most admittedly considered himself to be an ordinary man, who had obviously screwed up more than once in his relationships and life in general. Yet, he felt the audacity to question God, and God - to his shock and absolute questioning-surprise - answered him.

A lot of it, and I think Walsch recognized this, he was ready to listen to God, as he had nothing to lose and everything to gain, as his life was not going anywhere, fast. I think more than anything was Walsch having the courage - though I understand he was strongly pushed to do so by God - to have the "conversations" published. The majority of it was quite counter to what organized religion, or the 'powers to be' preached - dictated on this Earth plane. This resonated with me and popped back in my head in early 2008, when I felt compelled (forced actually by my Angel Guide's voice that wouldn't leave me alone until I did it) to start writing my blog - Move Past Your Past - precursor to this book. While excited and remarkably fulfilled by writing the blog, I was amazed how the words absolutely tumbled out of me. I did not and do not consider myself to be a Channeler, Intuitive or even an Empathic-type person. With any of my previous writing, and especially the poems, as with many writers, it's just inside and has to come out. Usually, it would only take a read-word or phrase to set me off writing on and on. I was sometimes shocked when I would see similar statements or thoughts in famous others' writings, as I continually read more and more Spiritual stuff.

I eventually learned that within our Spiritual-topic-spectrum, many of the same themes were presented in various forms. After much reading and writing, in my mind I realized that my dealing specifically on the Past and its core controls, was the whole key of being able to make the journey of individual change. Still, the idea of sharing it beyond a select set of friends, much less actually publishing it, was not within my realm at the time. So, while I could relate to Walsch at first, I did not feel at his level.

I was working a contract job, soon to expire and began to meet many other people very 'openly' into Spirituality and very supportive about suggesting things to me. That kind of support from people I didn't know well, often stopped me in my tracks momentarily. In looking back months or years later on these synchronicities, I could acknowledge that I had been guided to them to learn. Unfortunately, being a workaholic, it was only during my unemployed times that I had and took time to continue, or actually get back to my self-studies. I was still referring to them as Metaphysical teachings until I met an Intuitive guide in late 2006. After a personal reading, meditation classes and an opportunity to meet so many others along their path, did I finally realize that I was on a Spiritual journey myself.

I accepted also, I'd have to change myself more and learn so much before my Divine Destiny was brought into fruition. With part-time employment came time, as unbelievable manifesting experiences of money, people and other things into my life for learning. I actually lived adequately, for over a year and a half after my last full time job, with support from the most unfathomable places. I accepted that my time had not yet come, as I realized part of me was not yet ready to accept fulfilling my dream, so that had to be worked on and passed. I also had learned to listen to my intuition, especially when repeated until I acted, which included writing a blog on the effects of one's past on the present. Still, I was constantly studying more Spiritual writings of various types, which guided and supported me in understanding my worthiness in being chosen to also write. I was changing and many of my long time friends noticed the 'softening' of my speech and actions. I had a long way to go, as obviously I thought I needed to be able to walk and talk like a person of Spiritual understanding and practice.

Acceptance of my Self and who I was becoming was huge, as I reminded myself that it was thirty-plus years from my first O'Hare Airport dreams of crossing the ocean, to crossing many of them on a regular basis. Divine time is not linear as man's time - it is fluid, and happens when it is best for all to happen. The Universe/God/Source does not have or need a Rolex or even a Timex. When we are ready - meaning it is *for our best and highest good and the highest good of all* - our dreams will manifest. "We are never given a dream without also being given a way to make it come true" - Richard Bach. God speaks to us all, sometimes we just need to get some things like our past out of the way, so we can open our ears, our hearts and our minds to truly listen and hear what S/He is saying to us. You can make a difference, and nothing is impossible if you believe you can do it.

# *How to Use this Book*

Only you know, what you need to have joy and love in your life. Only you know, when you can no longer settle for the *illusion* of happiness, or what other people tell you will make you happy. With the awakening process to no longer repressing your true feelings and desires, you learn to live in the present - not the unknown future or faulted past. It is as much about changing yourself, as changing your surrounding life. There are many effective key statements that I will give you repeatedly and some you have heard before. It is how you choose to use them or not, that make a difference, or not. The most important that will be said frequently is that *everything is a choice* - your choice. There are no *real* rationalizations, excuses of any kind accepted regarding everything being a choice. It is, period, accept it, or you will never change to know true happiness. Yes, a choice may be a process or step-plan, but you need to know you can choose what you want in your life and have it. You chose where you are - health, job, relationship, etc. - yes, you did - and you can choose to change it.

Choose whatever works for you, as it is your life that you are changing. I will share with you what worked for me and other people, but if you want success you will have to decide what best works for you. It may be multiple things changed or just bits and pieces to begin with - which is fine. The changes you want will come when you are ready and choose to use them. It's your life and your choice. No one can do this for you. You may have guides, supporters, etc., and you are never alone, as always connected to God/Source, but it is your personal journey and path. You do it, it is sometimes painful and you can not phone it in. It may be sometimes exhausting and you may stop or even quit. But, you will not be able to go back to the life you had, once you've experienced the personal freedom of truly making your own choices. This does not mean you must be a rebel or anarchist - we all have to adapt, pay our taxes and follow the laws. It will be amazing how your stress levels will lower, when you no longer put yourself into drama situations. Your whole physical-self changes with this awareness of what you are doing with your body. The process of deep breathing alone, heightens the senses while increasing your energy.

Look at this as a reference book to help you along your way with your process of changing your life to make you happy, joyful and even find your bliss. You may or may not change after having read this book, it is obviously not a panacea and wasn't meant to be. It is a true guidebook for your travels on your different paths, for your individual journey. If you've ever used a travel book as a tourist, then think of this as that. Some things will interest you and they will work, while some ideas are not of interest, maybe you will read to practice, simply because you have not thought of such before. Many similar subjects will be repeated from different directions, as they may be acceptable to you one way, rather than another. Also, you may not have been into listening before. Not all museums are alike - the Louvre is very different from the Uffizi, though they both hold magnificent paintings and sculptures. You go through enough Twelve Step programs, then eventually they work, if you haven't relapsed into self-destruction. You have to be ready to change. Don't throw the book away because it doesn't work, it does work, you just may not be ready for it to work. While I would hope that you are more of a participant than a tourist on your Spiritual journey, approaches, detours, side-trips and backtracks are all experiences which you may learn from to grow.

You might want to think of this as the Domino Affect - each thing, no matter how small that you change in your life, will change your life. Assessment isn't a one-time-thing, or a simple reassessment. It needs to be rather continuous, but not obsessive. Who, where, what and when may be changed in steps and adjusted to or let go. You learn that chaos is a good thing, as it brings out many elements and energies together, which actually releases clarity of which things to keep hold of and which to let go. Fear is usually the biggest and often the most continuous reoccurrence. The amazing thing is in chaos, you see and recognize new potentials within that, which were never realized prior. With family - which can be parents, relatives, spouse/partner or even children and siblings - it is usually about controlling - who's telling you what to do or not do. How much you choose to continue to have them in your life is unequivocally, multiple decisions over time as you grow and change. Yet, you can be your own worse enemy. This book is definitely not about looking in the mirror, to be critical and finding any fault. That accomplishes no forward movement and is not positive to any extent. You'll actually learn to look in the mirror to say "I love you," to yourself and mean it.

Basically, you can read this book and do the practices either in order - which they weren't really written in a real step-order. Or, you can skim through the Table of Contents to pick and choose which parts resonate with you, or you feel you need to read and hopefully practice. You may feel a little lost, as I do work from a knowledgeable base of which is somewhat laid down in the first few parts. The basic truth principles of Spiritual Law or Metaphysics are few and sometimes slightly interpreted differently by various channelers, *intuitives* or guides. There is an Appendix that goes into more detail and exercises. Basically it is all about love - unconditional love - being positive and being of service to one another. Other things naturally fall into place - awareness, responsibility and acceptance that we are all One. You may or may not, understand or accept that you are a Spiritual Being having a Human experience. In knowing and accepting this, you can realize the power that you have within you, to control and change your life experiences you are having here on Earth. God/Source loves you unconditionally, is within us and wants us to have all we desire, to be happy in this game that we are playing. As humans, we all have Pasts within this life and prior ones, so forgiveness is a large part of moving past the pain. God has given us Freewill, and we need to learn to give it to each other - that is what choice is all about.

There is a Reference section at the end that gives you some reading suggestions which may support you and help you to learn many other facets of developing yourself. Since new books are coming out all the time, and I do not claim to have read them all, so it is obviously an incomplete list. I encourage you to scour and search new and used bookstores for those gems that draw you to them. They may feed you with the knowledge and strength to become true guides or Lightworkers, Pathfinders and Truthseekers. I have also listed many websites, which generally have connections to others of like-mind.

Remember, there is no right or wrong regarding what you may have done in your past, there is only the experience to learn the lesson. There is no need to give up your dreams just because your parents did not have their dreams fulfilled. There is also no need for you to feel guilty being happy, if your parents weren't. You and you alone are the co-creator with God and designer of your life - every day and every moment in it. Think of yourself as the writer, painter and actor - you choose the words, sentences, colors, brush strokes and performance on your choice of stages with whom you choose. This means you are also the director-producer, so you can change anything and everything that you want at any time you are no longer happy with the results or even audience. You are truly powerful because God/Source has given you Freewill to experience your life as you choose. Choose wisely, play well together and be happy as God/Source truly wants you to be. You are always loved, never alone, as Guidance is always available to you.

Love and Peace to you all on your journey.

# *Ten Rules of Being Human*

#1 - You will have a body.
#2 - You will be presented with lessons.
#3 - There are no mistakes, only lessons.
#4 - The lesson is repeated until learned.
#5 - Learning does not end until you've passed over.
#6 - "There" is not better than "here."
#7 - Others are only mirrors of you.
#8 - What you make of your life is up to you.
#9 - Your answers lie inside you.
#10 - You will forget all of this at birth.

Your profound journey within, reaches deeply into the various corners of your soul. There are highs - lows, jolts backwards, leaps forwards, with upward shifts and sometimes scary downward falls, beyond any amusement ride. Speaking or writing about it does help process and make sense of it, yet finding the words to really capture its essence, can be difficult. Think of it sometimes as a gift, hidden in a thorny bush, which takes getting some scratches, or bloody to retrieve and learn how to use it appropriately. Still, it's worth your tumultuous experience, earned by diligence of one foot in front of another.

You may believe that you are surrounded by complex choices, but it's truly simpler than that. Look carefully at the choices of where you are to where you want to be. Now, choose which one will move you forward into the light, joy and creation of all that you want in your life. Awakening - self-awareness - puts you into your intentions and keeps you moving forward, until you bring them into full fruition of all that your heart truly wants for you. Never forget that You Must believe that you do deserve all that you ask for.

# *Changing Yourself - Part #1*

I am not a Psychologist, though Psychology is one of my degrees. Nor am I a Counselor, per se, yet did Life Coaching in San Francisco and Michigan for years. I also have more than twenty years assisting people as a professional trainer with various businesses, as well my Human Resources Management experience in Employee Relations for almost ten years. Then, there is my own erratic quest, since the 1980s of understanding myself and others - as previously mentioned. I have learned much from the interactions of giving numerous workshops and presentations on various topics, then continuing to share all with many others.

In this process of new lessons learned, I've followed my own advice to change some of my personal beliefs over the years. And, compelled from within by my Angel Guides to share these things, those pertinent experiences gleaned from multiple sources, regarding the process of moving forward to freeing one's Past. You may have read some of these ideas before, but I feel I've gathered them together in one book. So, I've tried to use the most basic, but straightforward learning steps for a novice that worked for me. Also included are quotes, affirmations and other supportive suggestions to inspire or cushion the difficulties of change - letting go of one's Past.

Areas of this information are repeated from various different perspectives or ways, since we sometimes need to have things written to have them sink into our brains. Each one of us can be a source of inspiration to others, so they can see the choices available for them to access, then to shine their light for more people. Know that sometimes the answers and solutions to your most dire problems are simply you making a choice to live freely, be happy, create peace, know love - especially for yourselves. Take every opportunity to be in joy and access your unlimited abundance in all things - including financial. That choice shifts your energy into new frequencies, to move you out of any Karma and into the creation of self-awareness.

Your individuality, your own thoughts, beliefs and ideals are woven together as a part of the rich tapestry of Your life. Yet, it's your inter-connectedness of the Universal-whole that's necessary, so there are others more experienced who stand firm and support each of you, so you don't become lost. While you may walk alone through life, every thought, breath, action and non-action sends ripples through space and time, as one soul breathes out, another breathes in, allowing the flow of life to continue. Most of us are at a different progression in our growth and so support is there to guide - direct you when you ask for Divine Assistance for clarity or direction. The choices - decisions are still yours to make, so awareness is the requirement of the day. Yes, it takes courage, but you are never alone, so do NOT allow fear to come in. These are the choices to live a more connected and awakened life, even when times get challenging. Never forget that you're human, and perfection is not expected, nor required - love yourself as you are.

The whole letting go - Moving Past Your Past - is a step process, but one that is more linear than bottom to top. In other words, it is as if we progress in a continuum, adding and deleting as we learn what works for you or doesn't, as time goes by. As the first major step - dissolving or replacing of an old belief system or your conditioned -response negative. This sometimes takes either a trauma to bring it to the forefront of the brain, or simply getting tired of repeated negative results. Emotionally, you can usually only work on one at a time, but sometimes one is directly connected to another. Once this happens, your awareness and acknowledgment needs to examine the old belief/conditioned-response - where did it come from? Why it doesn't work anymore? etc. Then, a decision has to be made as to how to replace it, and with what.

Sometimes, simply going for the opposite response works for a while. Like most things subconscious, or in the brain, it abhors a vacuum and you don't want another negative thought put in there, so it may be time for something new or at least positive.

> **Example 1:** Someone accidentally steps on your foot, you: a) say "ouch"; b) punch the person; c) apologize - as you were raised amuck stoicism, so constantly apologizing for your occupying space or taking oxygen from a more worthy person. Which response is positive?

> **Example 2:** A close friend/relative dies in a plane crash when you are a child; you overhear mixed things that planes and flying is dangerous, so conclude if you fly you will die. You: a) never fly in a plane; b) restrict your life to what you can get to by car, train, bus; c) look at the statistics and choose a safe carrier. Simplified, but typical also.

Since some of your negative beliefs may have been with you for longer than you can remember, they are usually reviewed gingerly or one at a time, as the revelations they bring up can be painful, and embarrassing, or simply scary that you still choose to follow them. As you let go of one, there may be an opening up of others and you feel pretty good, so maybe confident to look at more misconceptions. There will be those that, as we examine them we see the hurt that created them, or the hurt we have brought on others by perpetuating them on those around us. This may slow the release process down, or even stop it for a while, as pain is no fun. Many people - especially those with the same beliefs - will tell you that leaving old sores in the Past is best, and not to open up Pandora's Box.

But there was something freeing and positive once you got over the last few revelations and eventually you may be ready to continue the process. For some it may take days, months or years and others will never be able to let go of all of their Past, or maybe just leave it for another lifetime. They may rationalize (can't live a day without a rationalization) or justify, as they have learned - grown enough for this time. Others can't wait to have more positive love and freedom come into their lives, to start living a full and joyous life. It is all a choice and part of your fulfillment of Freewill, which God/Source and the Universe has given to us, along with the Pursuit of Happiness, which we are taught is ours in the United States.

There are major steps which have to be done for any kind of realization of success; key are: Awareness, Acknowledgment, Honesty, and True Desire to have Change as part of your life. There is no timeframe for the process, as everyone's path is different. For myself, I got lost several times, took detours, back peddled and even just gave up, because I did not think I had the time or energy to put into what was needed to do it. Sometimes resuming, I could continue on, other times I had to go back several steps to get my momentum back. Often, it was the times between jobs that I could concentrate on me, since I was a workaholic, usually too stressed-out on the job.

Generally speaking, most people will only consider real life changes when they have been put through some trauma - life/death, divorce, bankruptcy, addiction wipeout, etc. It usually takes more than just an "Aha" moment, it is more like walking backwards over hot coals - you certainly didn't see that coming. Though the rewards vary from person to person, most will say as I do: I am Now a new person everyday - free and clear of yesterday - if I choose to let it all go. Whoever I thought I was yesterday, I do not have to be that person today. The Past is only a blip - take from it what you need to learn, or want to remember and let the rest of it go. Its negative weight truly increases everyday, that baggage you hold onto, or any mistakes that you think you may have done. There are no mistakes, if you have learned something positive from it, expect to not repeat it, then let it all go. Have no regrets, that's what forgiveness of Self is for. You don't need that weight pulling you down. Letting go of the Past is Your own powerful act. Purging, releasing and alignment can cause stress, but at least there is something accomplished when it's done.

**Note:** Pride is a good, positive thing, ego is a negative control.

**Exercise:** Frequently exercise your Deep Breathing, so it is important to understand how to properly do the process. Practice by standing up or lying down, to know you are getting the full results. You can later do it sitting, when you know you are doing it correctly. Place your palm of either hand over your bellybutton. Spread your fingers wide open, so your thumb is almost vertical to your little finger and perpendicular to your middle finger. In this way, your Solar Plexus and diaphragm are just above your thumb, so what you are looking to feel is the movement of your breath. Start with taking an 'In Breath' as to a slow count of five, slight hold and an 'Out Breath' count of five, also. If you did not feel your thumb or little finger move, continue to practice increasing the number count until you do feel movement. Like any daily-practiced exercise, you should with time be able to reach a count of ten, going in and ten coming out. This is one of the healthiest things that you can do for your body! Google to see what all your deep breathing does for you.

Now, to get the full experience of the Deep Breathing, you add your Key Words - what you want to go into your body - the positive, and what you want to come out of it - the negative. So, you might start with - "Positive in - ten count - Negative out;" move on to "Love in - Fear/Anger/Ego out;" "Healing in - Pain/Disease out;" "Abundance in - Lack out," etc. Eventually, you will learn to direct the Breath to all different parts of your body to release and let go of pain, or send White or Golden Light/Love to your heart or other areas of distress or pain. The Breath is your personal-power energy-source and one physical thing that connects you to God/Source. It is also your own personal, unconditional love of yourself, because no one can do it for you.

**Note:** If you smoke, you will not be able to receive the full power of your breath, so you might want to consider quitting. NO, it's not easy.

Positive thinking is acknowledging each of your individual feelings, and not just repeating rote affirmations to soothe over what you're feeling underneath it all. To really change them for the positive action to take place, you must examine them and, most importantly, where they came from. As you process each step, stay with a feeling until you know it has begun to change. If it does not improve fully, then go ahead to begin the next step. Deep-seated negative feelings are usually not resolved or dissolved in the first round of the removal process. Sometimes you need to take stronger or repetitive action, but don't give up or ignore your feelings, either way. They are your internal-compass of letting you know that you are going in the right direction for positive changes. Just try it again another day.

**Awareness:** Many of the following exercises have to do with releasing the ego, as it houses and controls your identity as a human being. Especially, it controls your reactions when you experience an emotional pain - someone lets you down, hurts you, or reflects you so accurately, that it allows you to truly see your own flaws. This will crack, or destroy your idea of you that your ego has surely created and protected, so it hurts you to your core. This pain usually hurts deeper and longer than any physical pain. Part of the whole process in this book of releasing 'yourself' from your past, is to teach your ego to be more flexible, not so controlling of all that you are, or want to be. The ego is a necessary part of you, but it does keep you from playing well with others, or trying new things to expand your experiences.

Your ego can be like an overprotective-mother, smothering you with a facade, that says over and over again that you are perfect and don't need to change. It is *Not* concerned with the fact that you are *Not* happy the way your are. It is simply and totally against change of any kind, but especially the kind that limits *its* control of you. Which is what freedom and independence does. Never forget that this is step process, so earlier on your Spiritual path, you will probably expend a great deal of energy covering your eyes to avoid seeing your deepest problems. While further along your journey, you will genuinely seek to see the Truth wherever you find it, and work through it to release it, as it will set you free. You will also have learned to do this without judging it, or punishing yourself for having had it within you.

\* \* \* \* \* \*

Here is a test to find whether your mission on Earth is finished: If you're alive, it isn't.

We all have a light inside; and if we don't let it shine, we might not influence someone who is more shy to shine theirs.

# A New You - Part #2

**Exercise:** Make a list of all of your good points - skills, talents, qualities, characteristics, even your physical ones - smile, eyes, etc. There must be at least ten good things about you that others have mentioned or complimented you on having. Keep this list, not only to reread when you're down or questioning it all, but also to add to it, as you grow and accept yourself more. Next, make a list of friends, close acquaintances and group them: Close, very good, good, email-phone, work, social network and even family. Rank them with stars - decide which ones are supportive of your changes and which are not, or you're not sure either way. You will have to decide soon, which you will have to drop, or really limit your involvement with, if they are negative toward your growth and new changes.

Sometimes *your* letting go will be very difficult, other times they will make the decision themselves and release you. People come into your life as lessons - for you or them. When the lesson is learned, they often leave or you do. Keep this original list to note the changes, as well additions, since you will be bringing more positive, like-minded people into your life as you change and grow. These are your Support-people, not people who want to rescue you, or think they can do the changes for you. How much, if anything, you want to share with them about your life-changes is totally up to you, but to begin with, less-is-better. Be prepared, some will respond as you expect, others will even surprise you - totally.

**Note:** As said, Pride is a good positive thing, ego is a negative controlling thing. The ego sometimes feels that it must be worn like battle scars, or metals you've won for surviving. No one actually lives in Disneyland, and it is not a Disney world. Why waste your time repeatedly commiserating with others, as to who had the worst or toughest childhood or past. It is only the ego needing recognition and people being stuck in their Drama-Lives. Stoicism, rescuing and martyrdom are not usually seen in the same company as happiness, joy, whereas passion for life is. When one is truly passionate about life, one lives in the moment for the enjoyment of today. The past should be like fallen drops of rain. Letting go of them serves their purpose of feeding the Earth. To try to catch them in your hand is futile and against the natural process. It is as sleep refreshes the body, lets go of each day in your dreams and you awake a new person on a new day. Letting go of the past also gives you a chance for love to come in - all kinds of love. But if you are filled up with your past, no new anything can come into your mind, heart or body - so no new creative thoughts, ideas, experiences, friends or love.

Life is meant to flow into you and through you, bringing new things to make your life grow and expand, so you can learn how to fulfill your destiny. When you're holding onto your Past, it's as if you are shielded by an impenetrable encasement. More than anything, it is the ego and its fear of change, that keeps you sealed up with your Past. The question is - who is the stronger one - your soul and your mind or your ego? Breaking free of the past is really letting go of your ego's control - which is fear-based. Nothing related to the ego is truth, for it is not related to unconditional love or giving.

Some may see or believe there is love related to the ego, but it is only a negative perception that is fed like a facade. Those ugly aspects that some think are related to love: control, obsession, possession, objectifying, are things that dehumanize another to simply boost the ego's power. When the heart is open, the love flows through - giving and receiving limitlessly. But the ego keeps the heart shrouded, saying it is protecting it from pain, hurt, abuse and those undeserving of its love feelings. Yet this is a protection a truly, open heart does not need, for unconditional love flows free, without emotional fear of any of these things, as it is pure, positive energy. When living with an open heart, it is embracing truth as Light. When the heart is open there is no lack, as there is no fear. With an open heart there is a giving-love with acceptance. We cannot truly call it love without this unconditional acceptance as you are, not "I will love you if …" Something many of us had in the past, from whomever may have said that they loved us.

Love with acceptance is "Warts and all." Love me as I am, or not at all. If the heart is open, then the acceptance is a real foundation of the love. "I Am What/Who I Am." So love me as I Am. We can do that Only when the heart is open, as it has no fear of being hurt. "I am an Open Heart. I have no fear, I am accepting of people how they are."

When sharing this basic information with others, it is their choice in how they choose to fulfill their destiny. You can give them ideas and suggestions, but it is their choice to let go and love all. There is no doubt that it is scary and we have all been hurt by what we thought was love, but they may have only spoken of love. The emotional Fear, Ego, for whatever reason, stopped it. When you're not feeling great, be aware that a lot of the conversations in your head, center around not being loved, or liked, or appreciated by others. Know, sometimes, it's actually you, you are the one that is not appreciating yourself and you're not aware of your negative thoughts. Sometimes, you then surround yourself by others who also feel this way. Eventually, you'll learn to recognizing this negative habit, then catch it and even change those thoughts, those negative, mental self-conversations. It is truly, the most important first, big step to realize and accomplish, in what you can do to change your life for the better.

**Note:** When you want more for the other person, than they want for themselves, you will be disappointed. No matter how much you truly love someone, they still have to accept their worthiness to allow themselves to be loved, to return it.

\* \* \* \* \*

You are led though your lifetime by the inner learning creature, the playful Spiritual Being that is your real Self. Don't turn away from possible futures before you're certain you don't have anything to learn from them. You're always free to change your mind and choose a new, different future, or a different past.

# *Anger ~ Part #3*

**Exercise:** Anger is a secondary emotion - something or even someone must trigger it to come out. Why that person? Who did they remind you of from your past? Where does it come from? What is it trying to tell you? Catch yourself as soon as you get angry, breathe deeply 3 - 5 times, (In Harmony - Out Anger) with a ten-count breath, if you can. Then, back in control, ask yourself those questions slowly, while you keep breathing deeply. You must be honest and answer these questions for yourself, or you will not be able to let go of the anger. If your ego has it blocked, it may not work the first time, but keep trying. It will work if you really want to know what/who makes you angry. As you become more in touch with your various anger reactions - your conditioned responses - you may want to write down all of those emotions, to thoroughly release them. Then for dramatic affect, burn the paper or tear it up to be resolved and released.

**Note:** Pushing anger down is not releasing it or letting it go - it is turning it into *poison.* Research has shown that old, accumulated anger sits like a bitter-pill causing pain and illness. You may not remember what all the anger was related to, yet it still can destroy your life. You will not make the changes you may want, if you don't deal with the old anger, as it is usually synonymous with past situations you need to release. It is all about the forgiveness process - which is truly about you, not the other person - but start with the deep breathing.

With your open heart, love flows to you and through you, so you can give love to other people, as you are accepting of them *as they are.* Many people are totally oblivious of what they say or do, truly. Acceptance does not mean *Agreement* regarding anything about them, nor does it mean that you *must* have this person in your life. You can simply accept them as they are, and let them go their own way. I say: "God/Source loves you and I'm working on it!" You can learn to have no judgment, resentment, jealousy or envy of any part of their life or success, or whatever. You know you can a make your own success with your open heart, as it creates Miracles for yourself, as well as other people - if they want you to do so for them.

It is more than *just* positive thinking, because with an open heart you are at-One with your purpose. As you are on the path of least resistance, you are in the flow. This path will get you to your goal, because you no longer need to struggle to learn your lessons to become your destiny. You no longer need your ego to fight your battles, believing that only through *struggles* will you really, really learn your lessons well. That is Not true now, because with an open heart you have no emotional fear, and with no fear, your heart is surrounded by unconditional love.

You can see now that with awareness you have let go of your life-long conditioned-response of anger in not getting what you wanted. With processing your anger, you can know where all of the disappointment and all of the unmet expectations came from. These things may have not been fulfilled because *subconsciously,* you believed that you were not worthy, or good enough, or unlovable, or deserving of what you wanted. Think about *who all* told you or just insinuated that - they were wrong! We are ALL worthy to receive in Abundance. On your new path, you have let go of your ego restrictions with your open heart and thus, there is no chaos. You have *no need* to show how strong you are. You have *no need* to suffer to show how brave you are. You have *no need* to be angry with those who once controlled you, as you no longer believe or let them control you.

With unconditional love surrounding you, there is no hurt or pain, there is only joy. When the heart is open and the past is let go of, the ego no longer has power over us. Suddenly, there is nothing left that needs vindication. We are free to move forward to learn and do, what we need to do, to fulfill our destiny. It is quite amazing how this process works. But no one said it would be easy letting go of the past, and definitely untangling oneself from one's ego. It is like giving up and throwing away a pair of old, comfortable shoes, or sweats or a robe. The ego is something that knows us so well and fits so comfy. How can we let it go, when it has worked so well for us for so long? And yet, the day comes when we see that the routine has become a rut, and *the rut is only six feet from a grave.* We are obviously no longer moving forward when anger pops up. Our happiness quotient has been dropping for some time, but suddenly it is all too clear that changes have to be made. It is definitely time for a clean sweep - out with the old and in with the new.

But replacement therapies, or band-aides just don't seem to work any more. Simply new clothes, or residence or job is not even enough. It is all, so much deeper than that. It is no longer the outside world that needs to be changed, but our inside-Self that needs the overhaul. We need a thorough vacuuming, as the sweeping is only a surface cleaning. Of course, it's not as if there is anyone but ourselves making us make these changes. Some people tune-out all of the signs and signals of the need for real change - marriage, loss of job, health, financial woes, etc. It is always a choice to change. There are pills for that depression you put yourself in, when you refuse to change and there may be agencies to help, when your life has just about been destroyed. Or, you put it off and get your act together in your next life!

No, letting go of an angry past is not easy with all of its many encumbrances of the ego, parents/family/partner, friends, et al. Truly, what does one have to gain from all of this detachment? An open heart is free of emotional fear, with allowing happiness, unconditional love abounding and even joy of a passionate love of life, that's all. But then again, you are not alone in how comfy you are in your lifestyle being run by your ego, because everybody else is the *one* who is wrong. *Procrastination?* But that's the way you've Always done it! It never ceases to amaze how we hang onto ego-invested things, long after they have served their stoic-purpose. If they ever did, not wanting to make that admission of being wrong in your ways or decisions. Agencies do it, companies do it, even Governments do it, - why can't you?

**Note:** Can't live a day without a rationalization - join the martyrs!

*  *  *  *  *  *

If you always look for the Positive in all things and all people, you will find some. And, it will make your life more positive - even joyful.
Like attracts like, so if you are walking thru a big pile of 'cosmic dung,' do not blame the holy cow or the farmer. Clean up your own act!

# *Open Heart ~ #4*

The last part of the first step of letting go, if this has not been made clear, is to *totally* Open Your Heart. Granted, I know there are no switches installed in your chest, so you can just flip your heart open. But, you can learn to do it mentally-visualizing, *believing you* will be happy - physically-emotionally. (If you are not familiar with the basic Seven Chakras, you may want to do some study of them - see below.) Unfortunately, when people's hearts are closed, they are not open to hear us tell them this, or accept love inside. It is more than a Catch-22, but less than a vicious circle, as it can be corrected - a choice. Ego has a protective, emotional fear that permeates and controls a closed heart, that will not allow it to listen and receive the information, or steps of how it can open. Most people, as said, have to go through some major trauma or multiple minor ones to get the message of a change being needed. The ego-fear thinks the wall it has put around the heart will protect it from getting hurt, but it needs human interactions to be and feel alive. It is truly not a self-contained system - *we need others.*

Once the heart recognizes that negative feelings are results of conditioned-responses, to these traumas or situations, it will start to listen. When you've been slapped up-side the head often enough by how your life is going, you may even question if it's working for you anymore to continue this way. The Truth is like a time-bomb, but once it's finally revealed, the healing can begin. Then we face the process of getting the heart and head together, to learn what steps are needed to stop the pain. Most people don't believe that they have the skills to change, using their "feelings" rather than the pushing-power the ego used. It is a transitional period, that can go back and forth while you learn that your feelings have power, just a different, softer kind that's more gentle, but creates successful results. Like the competition fable between The Wind and The Sun, as to who can make the man remove his coat. The Wind - ego - tries to blow it off, while the Sun - feelings - warms your bare-soul with love, and people will open up to you.

Many people during this time of learning how to open-up will feel stuck, as they are losing their ego's control, but not understanding how to use your love-power. While some of your inward-journey has been fascinating and revealing, other parts may be embarrassing or shocking that you had held on to, or practiced a certain belief. Some of these revelations, when painful have made you strong, but you may begin to punish yourself for what you did in the past, or allowed to have been done to you. This also may bring anger up with yourself, as is so often said in Zen - "You take yourself wherever you go." Those quick fixes of new job, partner, etc. doesn't fix the problem as it lies within. It may be painful, but the change has to come from within, or no other outside changes will work. So, as you grow to love yourself more, there is no need for any anger or self-punishment. Believe not all of what happened in your past needs to be forgiven, let it all go. Learn to just appreciate the Past as *lessons learned*.

The Soul whispers to your heart on a regular basis - most of us call it *Intuition*. The only problem is the heart and mind doesn't always take heed. When the chosen results turn disastrous, then you need to acknowledge what had been said inside, but *not* followed. This is where the Love Power comes from. Each time you do follow that inner voice and it is correct, you are empowered. You begin to become a believer and trust yourself, not the false-shell the ego had built around you. So, then you may even be saying, "Tell me more, tell me more," to your intuition. You may even acknowledge that you made the changes without struggling/pain, as your ego had wrongly justified creating the fear, or no that change could come without pain.

As you build a sense of accomplishment with your positive changes, you may see that you are not as angry, or some things don't frustrate you the way they did. Things then seem to be flowing your way, while you may not have discovered the mother lode, but life is certainly looking up. What you may, or may not realize is that anger, or any other negative presence, cannot stay where your love's positive energy exists, as they cannot coexist in the same space. Your positive "Beingness" is helping you to do your thinking differently now. This new, positive energy works for you, to direct or guide you to better choices. These are often choices that you would never have made with your ego in control. Funny about that, as the heart opens, you detach all the negative tentacles that your ego penetrated into so many parts of you. Look at yourself with total acceptance and love now.

**Exercise:** Go into your 3 - 5 deep-breathing set with your eyes closed. Now visualize a heart - big, red, beating - as if happy, joyful, contented and wanting everyone to know how good life is. Visualize that heart in your chest, with little heart shapes all around it glowing, as if celebrating how many other hearts love your heart. Continue to deep breathe saying with each breath: Intake-Love and Output-Fear. You will feel more relaxed, and definitely more unconditionally-loved for who you are. Repeat this on a regular basis, several times a week until you are totally comfortable with this concept.

If you are not aware of the basic Seven levels of your Chakras, you need to be. They are seriously important for supporting and contributing to the balance - harmony of your Mind, Body and Soul. Thought-Mind is based in top 3 chakras - Physical Emotions in bottom 3 -

and All brought together in the Heart-Soul center chakra - true feelings. Your Mind-Thought brings together the conscious and sub-conscious, and eventually Super-conscious. Your open Chakras are involved in assisting your Soul-Heart, as it rises to a higher level with the clearing of the negative past and subconscious. Of course, the Physical Body receives all the results of the invisible transformations, or processes of the Mind and Soul. So tangibly, with all clear, open Chakras, you see the accessing and acceptance of higher truth - cosmic consciousness, creating this happy person who no longer contains old, outmoded or negative - restrictive beliefs. Progressing along your path, with clear chakras, you will have become incredibly intuitive to avoid allowing negative ego to return. Another work result is that your left and right brain become more balanced, so you become both very creative and analytical melded-together. You have the capability of wisdom, as you thoroughly learn from all of your life experiences-lessons or knowledge.

Detailed explanations of each chakra and its purpose within us can be easily researched - simply Google - Seven Chakras.

* * * * *

**Extra Exercise:** Monitor your emotions, thoughts and body. Each will give you very helpful clues about what is out of balance and why. Begin and end each day with some positive and loving thoughts. Loving thoughts include those of gratitude. Remember that your inner state will determine how you experience your day, as well as your sleep state. Therefore, be as loving as you can towards yourself. Now, allow that self-love to grow over time, creating an energy field inside of you and around you, effortlessly broadcasting from you in all directions.

This love will begin to attract fortunate circumstances, opportunities, and the love you seek from others and your world.

Things do not change, we change. Thoreau

Nothing endures but change. Heraclitus 540 - 480 BC

The Universe is change, our life is what our thoughts make it.

Marcus Aurelius Antoninus 121 - 180 AD

When you change *the way* you look at things, The things you look at change. Einstein

# *Our Ego - #5*

Since we are only human, many of us think that we need to prove things to others. Like the fact, for some reason, that we think we are better than others - whether it is socioeconomic, intelligence, race, sex or whatever. Our ego, along with its built-in foundation of many insecurities, requires this so, we always feel good about ourselves. We thus need to put others down, or constantly criticize them. The ego does not just shrink, as the Love-Power moves in. The ego continues to throw blocks, or try to trip you into falling. And then, the moment any insecurity of action slips in, the ego is right there feeding it with anger and frustration. These things can free its power, so it tries to take back control. This is when it's really helpful to have learned the power of your breath, as breathing deeply can clear almost anything within your realm. It may not work the first time, but it does the more you practice it. Immediately use it when any back-steps happen, and they will. You also need to learn protection, by surrounding yourself with Golden Light and keeping the White Light as guide. But all this does take faith in the transition process, into your New Self. Just remember to keep repeating with your deep breathing - "I can do this!"

Much of the ego's strength comes from the power of fear, which is fed by doubt, and all of it is false. Remember the acronym for **Fear**: *False Emotions Appearing Real.* It is a restricting prison of your own making, if you believe what the ego is telling you. Before you can escape, you must remove each shackle of emotional fear that is controlling you. Sometimes, the easiest way to handle this is to sit in private and write down each one of your fears. Some may be related because of jealousy - you don't have what another has; or revenge because you didn't get what you wanted; or maybe it is simply greed, or the need to be 'king of the mountain,' whatever your mountain is. After you've written your list, take them one at a time, for they may have been with you for a very, long time. In fact, you may only be able to dissolve one at a time. You begin by saying that, "This fear is not real, and it is no longer true of the New me. This was created by my negative-ego to limit and control me, but no longer is true of me. It is a figment of my imagination and not something I believe any longer. My ego has cheated me by believing this and thus, I have cheated myself of happiness or satisfaction." You can accomplish anything you want with positive energy, not by negative energy or blaming others, or in looking for a short cut. It may take many steps to clear your list.

**Reminder:** This emotional fear may come from old negative words said to you, but you know they were not true, so now you do not need to believe them any more. Just because your ego repeatedly fed you negative thoughts and you took them to heart, doesn't mean they were true. You may have once been ignorant of your true self and guilty of not knowing, or acknowledging your true worth. In essence, you have allowed your ego to hold you back, and that is a personal offense to who you really are. You are no longer in a prison of fear, surrounded by darkness. You are free to choose positive work, to bask in the the Power of Love, which is unconditional in its acceptance of you. You are free from everything connected to your past, of which this fear is a large part. The past is gone, you have let go of it and all of the fear that your ego controlled you with. You are standing tall in the Light of Love as a Divine Human Being that is totally loved Unconditionally, for you are worthy of it. *Do Not forget to replace each emotional fear with some positive belief* - often the opposite word is effective, but think about it. You must fill that vacuum before your ego digs up some other fear-based insecurity. Forgiveness is a good tie-in here, but we'll go into that later.

**Exercise:** The above paragraphs are something that you may want to copy and reread as is necessary. Do this with each emotional fear and cross it boldly off the list. Again, there is no time-frame here, so do them as you feel ready to process them out. If you have any at all hesitation or inner feeling that you have not completely and totally eradicated a fear, come back to it later, to do the process all over again. Many of these fears have been with you a very long time - more than one life time, so they are well indoctrinated - usually by people who were very powerful in your life. Do NOT concern yourself now with who said what or why. We are not intended to have perfect lives, yet you were never promised a bed of roses. It is in the ups and downs of life that you grow, learn lessons and move on. If more time and energy is spent on those things that are not exactly as you want them, even when they are good, then you are wallowing in all the imperfections. Think about how much your ego likes to keep you in the "woe is me" category, rather than "Is this a great life or what?" group.

Sometimes a thing and its significance is all in what you make of it. Again, detaching or letting go of the little hurts or problems, can keep them from mounting into bigger things. It may be that bringing joy back into your life merely means appreciation of who and what is around you. The whole Universe can be mind-boggling, *if* you stop to look at it, how little we all are, and how truly small most problems are. Part of the growth is learning how to move on, not dwell on things. Remember, only an open-mind and heart can receive new ideas. When they are closed, they are filled with pre-conceived or recycled old ideas. This is why routines are repeated and the results remain the same. When living in the present or now-moment, the heart and mind have an opportunity for expanded consciousness. We each have our own individual paths to follow, and lessons to learn. While you may help or guide each other, the journey is your own - no one can do it for you. You are responsible for your own Spiritual growth - side-tracks, yes, short-cuts, no. In order to make the journey and be successful in all you do, you must first have Unconditional love for yourself.

This is another thing where the negative-ego held you back, for it is always finding fault in all you did, then feeding your insecurities with criticism. If you do not love yourself Unconditionally - "Warts and All" - *you can not truly love another.* And, you can not thoroughly know joy until you've experience sorrow, for you would have no comparison. Love is a natural state of being, that you were born to give and receive it - Unconditionally. Only as fear was introduced, love became limited or conditional. Fear *is* created by the absence of love, but cannot exist when love is the radiating force in one's life. Fear is only an imbalanced frequency, a state of mind which the ego plays-on to manipulate and control us. As love moves back into your heart and mind, that energy it creates brings miracles to you and all things in your life. Again, the more of the negative that is let go of: anger, pain, fear, frustration, etc., the more love that can come and flow through your total being. Once the negatives are replaced by love, compassion, forgiveness and acceptance, then joy abounds.

**Exercise II:** Find one or more simple practices to help you open your awareness. These can be straightforward Spiritual practices like deep breathing, moments of silent contemplation, or just being as loving/kind as you can in each moment with your words and actions. The important thing is consistency - finding something to do daily. You will want to have your "practice" in your mind and awareness during the day, allowing it to become a part of your routine.

\* \* \* \* \*

Life is not an accident, there is a purpose to be fulfilled.

The life which is unexamined is not worth living. Plato

Life shrinks or expands in proportion to one's courage. Anais Nin

Only those who dare to fail greatly can ever achieve greatly. Robert F. Kennedy

# *Breathe Deeply ~ Part #6*

When all of the changes are moving too fast for you to comprehend or absorb, before the frustration overcomes you, take a moment to do your deep breathing once again. Deep breathing is your private sanctuary, that you can go to no matter where you are - in a group of people, driving your car - any location or situation you can breathe. You simply concentrate on your breath and breathe deeply at least three - five times, having it come from as deep, down inside you as possible. Hold one hand over your chest and the other over your Solar Plexus - belly button. Whether standing, sitting or lying down, you should be able to feel your belly swell, as you breathe in through your nose, hold momentarily, and then feel your belly descend as you breathe out of your mouth or nose. If your shoulders are pulled up and it is only your chest moving, you are not breathing deeply enough. Build to a count of ten in and ten out with each deep breath. If you can close your eyes, do so, as you can actually take yourself away to relax and let go while you are still present.

**Exercise:** Repeat mentally or under your breath, whatever mantra or words that you use, or basically repeat any of the following: "Let it go; I can do this; I AM loved; I Am worthy," etc. The first few times you may not feel a lot of relief, but when your ego has realized that it is not getting control of you again, it will be as if touched by a magic wand. You will not only be able to carry on with whatever has to be done, but your energy level will have risen and you're ready to go on to handle whatever you have to do. Before an expected stressful situation or especially travel, I often use along with the deep breathing, affirming a Golden Light around me and a White Light ahead of me, guiding and protecting all, that I am doing with positive energy from the Universe. There is no limitation to the abundance of 'Divine Assistance' and support that you can ask for regarding positive light energy to go along with your deep breathing. Choose whatever Positive Key Words for your In-Breath - Love, Healing, Forgiveness, Harmony, Relaxation, etc. and then whatever Releasing Words for your Out-Breath - Fear, Pain, Anger, Confusion, Stress and so forth to feel better in control of you.

Always remember that the more you let go of from the Past, the more room you have to receive new positive energy. This means more that just love, though it must come first. The Universe exudes abundance in all things and always wants to share with us, to give us whatever we want. As your Soul Essence grows strong and confident in its positive love, you will be more accepting of receiving all the Universe offers to you. As your self-worth also grows, you will ask for specific things, and as you are able to believe that you deserve them, they will be given - sometimes even if you hesitate about deserving, they are given! Repeat your mantra of love and worthiness as often as you need. An important reminder is that showing appreciation or being grateful, as well as sharing your abundance, increases all that you do receive. You are learning to be a vessel by letting all flow through you. You can visualize this along with your deep breathing. Give/Receive - Receive/Give and always say "Thank you" for both steps. You are as grateful for being able to give, as grateful to be able to receive. Soon the joy increases more from the giving than the receiving. Amazing!

If you ever question the positive energy that is in you or coming to you, do not hesitate to re-energize it by affirming a Golden Light around you and a White Light ahead of you. When you ask, it is there guiding and protecting all that you do with positive energy from the Universe. You can always do your deep breathing to give you some clarity and balance, as you process to let go of more and more of your Past. Again, this is not something that happens quickly, as things will pop up that you have not thought of in years, that you can now easily let go of. The important awareness is your realization of having more peace in your life and within yourself, as you expand in your growth process. It is a contentment that you may have rarely, if ever felt before. It is another one of those wonderful by-products of love, the Unconditional kind of love flowing in and through you, at such a high volume. Breathe deeply to thoroughly enjoy this sense of peace, as it is also giving you a feeling of being complete. See, you always were complete and perfect to the Universe, but it is your opinion that had to be convinced here.

The deep breathing has many other benefits - scientifically proven - beside the major one of reducing stress, that helps harmonize your nervous system. It can also lower your blood pressure, release problems ranging from panic attacks to digestive disorders. Many people use breathing in conjunction with their biofeedback or behavior modification programs, to control chronic pain or headaches. Since the practiced deep breathing increases your lung power, it also increases your energy for exercise, as the feel good endorphins are released. When your breathing is full and deep, the diaphragm moves oxygen downward to massage the liver, stomach, other organs and tissues, then upwards to massage the heart.

This whole process can detoxify your inner organs, promote blood flow to pump the lymph more efficiently through your whole lymphatic system. This is an important part of your immune system, which depends on muscular movements, including those of your deep breathing. This is always a positive impact on your overall health. Deep breathing is often used as part of a meditation program to bring you into calm, mind-clearing, or the presence of Now. As you may have heard, even when young, deep breathing and counting to ten are helpful for keeping your anger in control. Of course, once you become a regular practitioner of deep breathing, anger will become a lot more deflected before you can react negatively. The deep breathing helps in awareness on how to *respond,* instead of reacting from emotional pain. Love yourself and Breathe!

* * * * * *

Learning is finding out what you already know. Doing is demonstrating that you know it. Teaching is reminding others that they know just as well as you. You are all learners, doers, and teachers. Richard Bach

# Letting Go ~ Part #7

**Exercise:** Part of the process of letting go of your Past is not only beliefs and things, but also people. Once you've gotten to a point of clarity and peace, as well as confidence in your Soul Essence, you may want to look around at those people who are within your life - either passive or active - and their level of direct involvement. In other words, how have they handled your transition-changes? Do I need to say that this is really important to continued success? If they have supportive and encouraging, or even joined you, then you definitely still want them on your team. If the opposite has been true, to any level at all, it is now time to sit down with them to have a talk. You need to be aware, unfortunately that for many of them, a Soul to Soul talk will not be accepted. To many of them, this purposed-life change may not be taken seriously, as you've talked of things-changes before - maybe a diet, vegetarianism, or even stopping some addiction without the right support of some kind. You talk, you do the change for a while, you slip and you may stop - we all have. But, once you're on your true growth-path of freedom and independence from your Past, you can never fully go back to all of the negative. You may have even taken a long hiatus - I did, several times - yet eventually, you are ready again to do the hard work of letting go of your Past.

Most of you know many people come into our lives for a limited purpose/reason, and once that has been satisfied for either of you, they or you move on. Whatever the situation that brought you together - long term or short - you need to be sure to express profound appreciation, even if they benefited more, you still learned from the experience. If they stop growing and do not leave on their own, you need to begin a slow-distancing from them for release. They may have gotten to a point that is comfortable for them, so they don't want any more change. People who are not into change, or their existence has been fed by your energy, whether prior when negative or now the positive; you are not doing them a benefit by continuing this unhealthy relationship. If these other people do not understand fully what has happened or why you changed, this lack of comprehension will bring in fear, frustration and, of course, anger on their part for you changing. Love may be blind, but real friendship needs to be *clairvoyant*. Their ego may make them feel rejected or unwanted, yet you need to know, if you find yourself gravitating back into *their* old repetitive behaviors and thoughts of "I'm not okay," you will relapse.

How much you can talk, explain or even demonstrate the new you, will directly relate to how open they are to listening and hearing what they do not want to accept. As much as you may have resisted changing at the beginning, some of your 'friends' resent it more. You may need a physical and emotional separation from these people, with the option to get back together. You can talk again, once they want or have more understanding of who you are now, and that you are *not* going back to who you were. When you can do this, truly you have gotten Past your Past! Letting go of those negative people - and they may be directly related to you - is probably the hardest, most testing of all of your steps to you becoming a totally whole, totally new, positive person. They may not have seemed that negative, but if they are - consciously or unconsciously - following a list of neurosis or behavior controls: rescuing, passive-aggressive, blaming, jealousy, etc., even in the name of love, or what *they think is best for you,* escape is best for your continued growth. It is the only way that you will be able to have emotional, spiritual, mental and physical freedom to develop to your Highest

Good, and fulfill your Divine Destiny - and you do have one.

Some people do eventually come around, especially when they recognize the positive life changes you've made as demonstrated by the happiness, peace and joy within you. They may decide to jump on the band wagon, but you do need to remember that though they may have joined your parade, the trip or path they take is *totally their own* to do and be responsible for. It is always their choice, should they decide that they want to make the transition also. One thing you can reiterate to them, is how much their relationship and support has meant to you in the past. So, you will be there to support and guide them.

But, and we all must remember it is a big but, the change process has to be *their choice for themselves,* not for you or anyone else. There will be no judgment on your part, as to their progress or lack of it, or even their choice to drop out. This is not a competition, race or date-oriented success-goal thing. Everyone will get something different out of their moving past *Their Past.* It is totally private, therefore the personal choice of each as to what they hope to achieve, if they even know.

Just like any new life-changing program one undertakes, it will only work or succeed if the person is *completely vested* in doing it for themselves. Fortunately, or unfortunately, there will be others who will slowly drift away, or continue to cause friction in your relationship until it has to be ended. When we can choose to release and let go of "old world" burdens, old relationships that make us feel heavy and drained; we will then find ourselves in a brand new reality filled with lightness, ease, joy, laughter, fun, light, peace, love and wonderful like-minded - similar-vibrating companionships. You are never alone, as God/Source is within, yet you will be surprised how quickly you will begin to meet others who have a positive vibration. One of the greatest things you can do in life, to ensure your success is to be with those other successful people who are further along their journey than you are. The lessons learned in these encounters can be magnetizing.

It matters not how advanced anyone is on a Spiritual level, they usually can share some experiences that may be useful to you. Even for a few minutes, they can be a great teacher. They don't need to be a guru with all the metaphysical, esoteric and spiritual knowledge of the world inside of them, if it is what *you need to hear* at that moment. It is the psychological-emotional maturity that is the central core point of maintaining balance and being ready when the right teacher for you does appear. Being aware, listening and always being open is the core stabilizer of every soul choosing to walk the path of the New Spiritual Warrior. No one person knows it all and the best teachers will tell you that. Someone who says they are the *only* true guide, *is not.*

Part of the purpose of the path is to bring you and so many teachers into contact with each other. This is not a correspondence course for which one gets a diploma, it is a *life-process of growth.* Some *may think* they are helping you because they've some key experience that was good for them. Wrong! It is not a cookie cutter-process, what worked for them may have no interest or assistance to you. They are obviously ignorant of the process and steps needed. A Lightworker may think they are being helpful, but are sometimes more dangerous than the average ignorant man or woman on the street, that knows nothing about metaphysics, esoteric philosophy or anything else. It is always, about how one lives one's life, as the best example. Do not ever try to convert those who are not ready, you are fighting a losing battle. Just be an example by living your truth, speak it, be it and everything around you will fall into place. Accept as much of what I offer you, as works for you. As, I also do not pretend to have any, nor definitely, not all the answers. I have barely formulated my questions.

\* \* \* \* \* \*

A man is but the product of his thoughts. What he thinks, he becomes. Gandhi

We are what we think. All that we are arises with our thoughts. With our thoughts, we make the world. Dhammapada 1 BC

He who controls others may be powerful, but he who has mastered himself is mightier still. Lao Tau

# *Unload Stuff ~ Part #8*

It is amazing how as we unload the old stuff inside of us - ugly words, thoughts, left-over comments of/to others - our bodies react as well. Coming to terms and sifting through the layers, causes shifts in your emotions, your immune system and everything inside us. It is like going through withdrawal from any addiction, or fog to sunshine. You are used to carrying that baggage, it has been a part of you for a long time, yet your body feels not a loss, but a lightness, when you let it go. So, you must prepare for some reaction to keep your balance.

Do you know that when you feel that you are ugly, unlovable, unattractive, fat/skinny, or all the other labels you may give yourself, you are being distracted and being played with like a pawn? Because the worse you feel about *the Self* the more *dis-empowered* you are, the less love you feel for yourself the stronger your fear becomes. Then. the minute you feel unattractive, unlovable and downright disgusting, remind yourself that you are being *toyed-with*. The real beauty of your soul, your heart and the light that you emanate-out is so much more powerful than the looks of a physical body. Yes, we are all working towards reversing the aging process. How long that will take, or be strived for is debatable. In the meantime, you must nurture that inner-Spirit, that inner-quality of light and of true inner-beauty.

**Exercise:** To perform this, I suggest you request people - probably Not some one related - you trust to seriously assist you, as we usually believe others more than ourselves. Ask them to sincerely write down everything about you that is beautiful, nothing to do with your physical body, *the you*, that inner-soul quality - behavior. What is it about you that attracts them, that keeps them in your space? You can offer to do the same with them, if they want to know the truth, in what you see. In the twelfth-week of an extended metaphysical class I took, each member was to write down three positive characteristics of each member. The last week, the facilitator then gave personalized sheets to each of us with those positive traits listed. I was totally amazed. I still have that sheet framed and hanging in my bedroom. The more you feed the Light of Self, *not the ego,* the stronger you become, as that true inner-glow shines through. You have felt it in yourself, you have seen it in others - there is just something about them, that is what you want to connect with, to focus on. That is what will nurture the love within and amongst you.

I assure you when you move beyond the surface-exteriors, you then penetrate the depths of the true essence, wisdom, light, power and love that exists within every soul. These realizations - transformations are usually beyond your grandest imaginings. Your energy will shift, as you change the way you feel about yourself and life, for you will change dramatically. The way you see yourself, the way others see you will also be very different and by that, I mean in your frame of mind. Yes, we all have bad days or times when being around you-yourself can be difficult, to say the least. This is where having those friends that have seen the 360 degrees of you. They still love the you they know is deep inside, whatever exterior you may be showing some days. As we grow, you need constant positive energy from the inside, as well as the outside, as this is not an easy journey.

So, another step in the growth process of letting go of the past is what we would call physical issues, that are emotionally connected and rather challenging. Two big ones are physical pain and body weight. Both things are factors of your past tendency to hold on to something, partly because it fed your negative-self. You believed you were not worthy of being pain-free - it may have been rationalized by age or weight. You may also have felt the need to take on the pain of others around you. This could be either from empathy or being part of their suffering program, as in joining their commiseration. Amazing isn't it?! As growing older, I've added suggestions when someone speaks of their ills, rather than adding mine to them in support.

Drama Kings and Queens do not want to suffer alone, so if you are a "real friend," you will join their chorus on whatever topic they are ranting today. These can often be those people who have the deep sighs - "Oh, woe is me," and they want to suck up *your energy,* so they feel better. I've heard them referred to as "Emotional Vampires." Get away from them as quickly as you can, whether in person or on the phone. If anything can possibly go wrong, their negativity will attract it to them! They learned from an early age, that if they could not get attention for doing something positive, then they got it in sympathy for their "bad luck." They have rationalized-away most of their life.

While you may indeed have incurred some physical injuries over your life time, how you handled your pain-control may not have benefited you, or at least not the New You. There are many different venues for physically releasing pain from basic stretches, yoga, or simply getting a massage, chiropractic or acupuncture treatment. A new source remedy that was brought to me has been pure and natural Essential Oils or Hemp lotion. These are amazing in that they work almost magically with our senses for relieving pain. These sources will help, if you are open to allowing them to do so. But, reaching in to the core-cause of the emotional connection is required to actually know *exactly* what all you need to release and let go of, for the pain in your body. There are many excellent books that list all sorts of physical maladies and their corresponding emotional/psychological cause.

Think about it, research has proven that 90% of ALL illnesses and disease are psychosomatic or brought on by your negative-mind when filled with fear. Nowadays, there are so many Natural elements - *not pills* from the 'Big Pharmies' that are preventatives, boosting your health - Turmeric, Krill oil, Red Yeast Rice and more. Just Google your problem with 'natural preventative' and be amazed. Coconut oil is one of those that the help-list is almost endless. Yes, much you can control naturally, as you go through your other steps to balancing your life in a positive light. But, if the physical maladies have been with you a long time, then sussing out their origin, along with remedying them. This is then your major prospect for letting go of the pain, for total health recovery. Notice, I did not mention long-term prescription medications, as they are also addictive, or become ineffective over use in time. Check the research, placebos are still 90% effective in treating almost all pain and illness, because *you believed* in a magic pill.

**Exercise II:** Use your breath, your affirmations, light energy and whatever else you can to recapture your vital, energetic health. Visualize the area or spot that is painful and send it healing green or pink light, love it and ask it to heal; then let go of the pain. As usual, it may not work the first time, but repeated daily efforts will get the positive response. This is like Bio-Feedback, which has a very high success record. It is important that you connect with a resource that is most comfortable for you and don't go over board with any exercise program. I do water aerobics 4-5 days a week, as I only weigh about 25 pounds in the water, so no stress on bones or joints! Check with your doctor, or one that is open to alternative therapies, if you have questions. But as with everything, start slowly and see what works best for you. Breathe deep and feel the vibration in your body, then follow your intuition. Trust yourself - that is part of this whole process of believing in yourself, whatever it is that you are involving your-Self with. You brought the pain to you, now you can take it away. Always, most importantly, you must be able to look in the mirror and say loud and proud: "I love me Unconditionally - Warts and All." This is the most important daily exercise you can do. Weight is another situation and will be next.

\* \* \* \* \* \*

There is no passion to be found in playing small – in settling for a life that is less than what you are capable of living. Nelson Mandela

Integrity is not about being perfect, Spiritual Beings. It is about true motivation and commitment to doing the best one can.

# *Human Weight ~ Part #9*

Here's the answers I have learned and they are all actually Good News: I am not who I thought I was. I am not my body. My body is mine, but not the most important part of me - my mind and soul are. The "me" that I am, lives with and within my body and uses my body as a tool or vessel to move. The "me" that I am, lives by being surrounded by my body, encasing and protecting me. I need my body to move me around, so I must exercise it to keep it moving. I must also fill it with good food and water, for all of my organs to keep me alive. Therefore, how much I exercise it, what I feed it and how much I water it, is very important for my basic, Earthly experience. I am well aware that I am a Spiritual Being having a Human experience, but I cannot have that without my body. My body may or may not play a major role in my transition back to my Soul-etheric self. So, in other words, if I keep it healthy and disease free, unless I choose to pass by way of an "accident," I could live to a very ripe old age! That's the logical part of it all, but the emotional is a whole other story.

**Again:** "Argue for your limitations and they are yours!" Think about what restrictions you put on yourself - "I can't do that ..." etc. The emotional connection to weight is legendary and touted by many, but processed by few. It is so typical it has been called by the media to be 'epidemic.' While numbers are growing in disease areas of anorexia and bulimia, the obesity-factor is of greatest concern with the majority of all ages in the U.S. population. However, the main concern is with those of you who have made letting go of your Past, your life changing program. As with physical pain, many of *us* have carried or added to our weight while we were stuck in our negative, ego-controlled lives. Scientific studies have proven repeatedly that 95% of overweight is emotionally stimulated - no joke. Who do you see when you look in the mirror? You see a human, yet do you know that body is merely the temporary housing for your eternal Spirit?

It is usually a conditioned-response, which only builds as the negative ego criticizes us, and then we punish ourselves. "Have a cookie little girl, you'll feel better! But why did I eat a dozen?!?" It is a billion-dollar-industry, telling you how to get the weight off. But, rarely will it be kept off, if you are not totally changed and living in a New positive light, minus the negative ego. You must be totally filled with love, compassion, forgiveness and acceptance to get the weight off and stop *the need* to put it back on. It is all about filling up that "emptiness," and sometimes just one cookie won't do.

It is usually not so much what one eats - though we all know to stay away from the fast foods, fatty foods and fried foods for health. It generally is the quantity of the food we take in, to fill the *"void"* and then lack of exercise, that is typical with our society. I can honestly say, this is one continuous-adjustment for me. I am so passionate about life, so when I get 'rocky' - practicing what I preach escapes, then the weight zooms back on me, until I notice my clothes getting snug.

**Exercise:** Just as with the pain, you need to first get in touch with why are you over-eating - what is the key, the insecurity - there may be more than one thing that sparks you - does for me. This may be a long or continuous process, that may be more painful than you expected. So, you may need to work on it in short increments. To begin, you need to observe and write down what makes you want to snack, or put more on your plate than you know you really *need* to eat. Again multiple triggers, so you may discover them over a long period of time. You also need to remind yourself that food is your friend - savor it and enjoy every scent, aroma and your tastebuds-blooming.

Put the food in a positive light as healthy, enjoyable and feeding your body. If you go the opposite and put it all in a negative or 'evil temptress,' it will continue to go right to your belly, hips or thighs! Love your food for all of its goodness, then visualize it as positive energy into, around and within you - down to cellular level as making you healthy and fit. This may not be easy to begin with to look in the mirror and repeat: "I love my beautiful, healthy, fit body." You may want to write out a full "My Perfect, Healthy, Fit Body" affirmation, and tape it on your bathroom mirror or any other place that you will see it, to repeat it often.

**Sample:** "My Perfect, Healthy, Fit Body": "I can see in my mind's eye the perfect, healthy body for me. What it looks like, and the size of clothing I am wearing - a blank-blank. My New Healthy Body feels great, wonderful and perfect for me! I am over flowing with positive energy into, around and within me, into each and every cell in my healthy, fit body. Now, I feel so proud of what I accomplished - feeling confident with my New, healthy fit body. My positive energy level is with me everywhere I go and no matter what I do. I created this body through positive strength and positive energy flowing into, around and within me, for a long, happy, healthy life.

It feels absolutely wonderful to do everything that I've always wanted to, as I am now confident and healthy enough to pursue it all. I see the faces of my friends and family as they look upon my new healthy, fit body with pleased happiness and pride for me. Even one year later, after my initial weight reduction, I can picture in my mind's eye easily maintaining my newfound weight. In fact, it is simply happening automatically, without any effort of control on my part at all. My body on its own wants to be healthy, fit and full of energy - all of it positive in all I do. I know it will be easy for me to stay healthy, and fit all my years from now on for life. I'm positive and filled with positive energy flowing into, around and within me, into each and every cell in my healthy, fit body."

Other addictions I had over my life were easy compared to weight, since we need to eat to live. But really exploring your Past history with food and its hook on you is the key, I believe. For myself I knew it was in part wanting to get "my fair share." This went all the way back to childhood and competing at the dinner table with my brothers and father. It was not that we did not have enough food, we had plenty. I simply felt being the youngest and smallest, I was the last to have a choice, as the plates of food were being passed around. In my eyes, the best pieces had already been taken. In reality, there was still plenty of food, I felt rejected being *the last* to make my choice. Then to build my equality to the others, I put as much on my plate as they put on theirs. While we were never restricted on how much we could take, *we were required to eat it all and not waste.* Thus, over and over I set up the habit of over eating, because emotionally I had to get my 'fair share.' Later, when overweight, it subconsciously *'assisted'* me in limiting men in my life, as I had not always made good choices.

In my latter teen years, my chubby body was a limitation to many things especially boys, though I did have many as friends and a few as boyfriends, because I was very physically active, a tomboy and into sports with them. With love-emotional feelings limited in its/my expression, from my mother being very controlling of my dating, my realizations of being really liked were limited. After dropping pounds, I became aware of my curvaceous figure and the male attention I could get. Unfortunately, I supplanted this for the lack of love I felt from my mother, and consistently made bad choices in men. My weight became a yo-yo in that while shapely I could have the men I wanted, then I'd gain weight to keep them away, along with the pain of failed romance.

After two divorces and too many involvements, I put a solid fifty-plus pounds around me, to protect and limit my being tempted in making bad choices in men. Of course, this was ridiculous, but I have to add that every time I'd drop significant weight, men did come into my life. Usually by then, I was starving for more than food and repeat my same pattern. It didn't change until I finally began to let go of my past, loved and accepted myself as I was. It is a continuous work-in-process, to finally let go of the weight without the fear of attracting men who are only there to hurt me. As a 'woman of a certain age,' as they say, there really isn't the plethora of men to choose from, as I once had. Ironic, how the Universe plays those games with us. I do not regret my age, as I have developed much wisdom when it comes to relationships, as well acknowledgement of my sometimes negative-participation in those past relationships.

**Further Exercise:** So, as you traced back and realize what your key receptors that trigger your eating patterns, or what past situations created or added to your weight gain or if anorexia - bulimia are your fears - you process them out. Again, do the breathing, use your affirmations and especially have forgiveness, compassion and unconditional love for yourself. Key words to use - though you may want to create from your Soul Presence what resonates for you: "I AM filled with my own Divinity, with Light energy, with Love energy and I do not need to fill myself with food when I am not hungry; I AM filled with my breath and my breath balances me and fills me with Love Energy, so I have no need to fill myself with food when I am not hungry; I AM eating the things I want without gaining any excessive weight; I AM only eating to satiate hunger, as I am filled with Love energy." As mentioned with the letting go of the 'pain process,' weight will begin to drop-off simply as you become more loving of yourself, and positive of living in happiness with a balanced lifestyle.

Excess or over-control in anything is negative energy, for it is trying to fill a gap-void-emptiness that has been created by some emotional-lack feeling about oneself. There is no lack in the Universe, it is pure abundance, especially regarding love. I now know I receive more than "my fair share" of love from the outside and the inside, as I process no longer the need to fill myself with food. Yes, unexpected or unprepared for stuff still happens and food may be the first thing I use. Still, I eventually process that there is no gap or lack in who I am, or how I feel. Of course, some people may need to fill this gap - feeling of lack with other things - drugs, alcohol, cigarettes, television, shopping or whatever. The process is the same in letting go of the addiction when you are filled with love and abundance of positive energy. I know, as food wasn't my only problem. It takes practice to constantly visualize yourself, as that person you want to look like in the mirror. In the United States especially, we live in a very critical, negative-media atmosphere against fat and age. At least your have the power to change the weight and then not care about your age.

I AM Unlimited in what I can do!

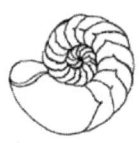

# *Dogma - Part #10*

This continual rebirth process that you have in letting go of the Past moves you into a new circle of *like-minded* friends, who have also successfully made the journey, or are on the path. A new positive language has developed that brings you together to share your many thoughts and experiences, as your life comes more alive everyday and you are supported. As your moments of joy expand, the ego can not limit you again with its negative definitions or restrictions, as long as you are true, and your love is a constant expression of your life. You know with truth-security, that you walk with Grace surrounding/encompassing you, as in your acceptance that *we are all One.*

It will amaze you how people begin to notice how you've changed and some will ask how they also can make the journey. It is as if what you have is contagious - in a good way, so more people will want the freedom and love that you exude. It will be part of your job, as a vessel to spread this Light by example to those who want it heart to heart. Remember, that not all people will succeed and that is not your burden, for some people just are not ready to let go of their fear, routine, or their ego controlling their lives. As more people are freed of their Past, a balance in the world builds, as anger and other ego-based contentions leave. Harmony can only be among those who have let go of their ego and love *all* unconditionally. We will all be tested to speak up, from time to time as powerful people, unfortunately even 'leaders' come to the forefront, spouting prejudice and discrimination of others.

The basics to review on all of your behavior change is that it's devised from thoughts, ideas and beliefs. Most of those beliefs came, unfortunately, from your childhood experiences or memories of them. Again, unfortunately the most powerful were the negative ones. They are, of course, what set up your conditioned-responses to let your ego take over controlling your life. But, as we've seen, as an adult you can undo - change those negative beliefs and your behaviors. Whatever crises or major life-changing experience that made you realize your behavior was no longer working for you, the letting go of it brought more happiness into your life. Being open to new ideas comes with the change in your routine to spark things up. When simple changes barely take more than a nano-second, we might look closely to see how our routine was actually so stuck in such *dogma* for so long.

Ideas and behaviors turn into dogma as they become more restrictive and controlling - back to that negative ego again. This is comparing it to any zealot - religious or otherwise - who truly believes in totality of the ideas that are pushing them to behave as they do. As most are aware, being able to show zealots or tell them their beliefs are misguided, much less wrong, is practically impossible to do. But, as a singular-individual having experienced negative trauma/drama, you had the choice of awareness and acknowledgment to change, to free yourself from your own negative dogma. Releasing and letting go of such basic ideas that 'people have hurt us and that we must get back at them,' is an unfortunate mantra of many people.

As a matter of fact, the whole idea of being disrespected, "dissed" - ignored or discounted is a first rule of gang violence. It's coming into another's turf, verbal or physical behavior or action that does not acknowledge or recognize 'who I am.' How basically insecure is that? It is more than the child's game of "King of the Mountain." It is road-rage, as much violence is thus created simply by the reaction to *real or unreal* verbal or even non-verbal action. *The worst emotional thing one human can do to another is ignore them,* as if they are not even there.

Think how often on a crowded city street you ignore a panhandler or someone wanting your attention. It truly fills their negative space. Now, multiply this a few zillion times and you get why countries go to war, or have major uprisings. Another big dogma is often: "Why do you get that, and not me? I'm a good, deserving person!" This is deeper than jealousy or envy, it is a feeling of true *unbalance* in the Universe, an *unfairness* where they are the target to NOT receive. It is the major cause of violence in that, "I'm going to take what you have" - entitlement or you owe me. "I must be more powerful than you, so you cannot control or limit me."

You - We are part of one another and are meant to learn from one another. So, set your *Intent* - what you want - for a real multi-dimensional experience - see your life from a different point, *from another's point of you.* This is how you'll learn to treat each other with respect and nurture each other at every opportunity to work at getting along, even have fun together. It is all about *cooperation,* instead of *opposition.* Most of us have some doubts and fears, we don't need them filled by the way others treat or react to us. It is a very "Past" concept that reinforces in your mind the mistaken belief that you must 'do something' in order to "Be" who you already are. No controlling of others, just knowing you are accepted and loved unconditionally - likewise, show and give that to others. **Basic:** God/Source gives you Freewill - try to allow - give it to others as well.

Your ego-self sinks you to the depths of familiar, old, deeply-embedded behavioral patterns of speaking of another's Past actions. This is a form of gossip, that for some it is gleefully received. Make no mistake, your words are weapons you choose to use against another's soul - to judge, pull down, or disintegrate another. These verbal knives are rampant, cutting through the memory, reliving a Past incidence in an attempt to make it as negative, as attention grabbing as possible. All the while verbally reducing another soul's honor to shreds. Think of the last time you ridiculed another, perhaps through unacknowledged jealousy, you sought to destroy another's efforts. You may have called it a joke or a tease. To what extent of thoughts and words you judge another and seek to pull them down with your lower judgments, then you fall backwards, you place yourself in the lower levels. You allow your ego-self a negative victory.

**Exercise:** Take a look at your habits - those things you do of choice in your spare time - TV, hobbies, eating, drinking, etc. Have they changed as you have? Do you have some new ones? Are you letting go of those that no longer really satisfy you? Which ones are or were negative? What new positive things can you do for you? How can you sincerely compliment another to make them feel good about themselves? Do you need rewards for your progress - what makes you happy, even if it is frivolous? Just getting out in nice weather for a walk is positive. It does not have to cost money - the park, a favorite place you never tire of, or something new to experiment and treat yourself. These are not "should" or to impress anyone, this is to make your heart and soul happy. It is your path and journey, be aware of the part of your life still stuck in dogma. Do something new, even trivial.

Whenever your life is not moving, it is because you have cemented your feet *again,* in the Past. Your Past does not serve you, but as a reminder of what failed. Live in the present and look to the future with a heart that goes beyond words or expectations. Stand up to see the truth and your true reflection of the Cosmic Spirit you are!

\* \* \* \* \* \*

In the 4th century the Catholic church edited our Biblical writings - 45 books condensed - *20 removed*. This was revealed when the Dead Sea Scrolls were discovered and the true untapped potential of our Human Empowerment understood. We are Divinely connected to God/Source - no intermediary is needed. Jesus gave each of us the power of the Holy Spirit to be Divinely connected, but it is still your choice to use.

Your belief in me is not needed for me to be who I am. It is only truly necessary *for me* to believe in myself and my beliefs, which I live by every day.

The Universe is change, our life is what our thoughts make it. Marcus Aurelius Antoninus 121 - 180 AD

The process of release is letting go, *so that change may occur*—just as you must *exhale* to continue breathing.

# *Forgiveness - Part #11*

What we learn from making the minor changes to the major ones is a jump-process, or quantum leap of becoming the New You. But once you're there, you will have the awareness/acknowledgment that this is a *return* to *who you were,* for all of us, as being God's children. We were born perfect in Light and Love. It is all about the journey, as you always were welcomed and loved unconditionally by Source. There should be great satisfaction of accomplishment of your success, besides the wisdom you learned along the way. Remember, it is the ego that wants you to believe that there are people lesser than you, so your insecurities can be pampered. The ego must judge and put others down, but as you come into your own realm of confidence and acceptance of who you are, it then expands over to the *inclusiveness* of more and more people, no matter who they are. *We are ALL One.* As you open your heart and mind to let go of the little, limited thoughts and beliefs, your world also opens to so much more. When you no longer have niggling-insecurities, you no longer need to put others down, then you are ready to start the Forgiveness process.

**Definition:** Forgiveness is the mental, emotional and/or spiritual process of ceasing to feel resentment, indignation or anger against another person for a *perceived or real* offense, difference or mistake, or ceasing to demand punishment or restitution.

**Exercise:** *Do not start this unless you have time -* several hours and total privacy, so you won't feel rushed or being exposed. One of the enhancements of your letting go process is the forgiveness of yourself and others that you may have felt 'done you wrong.' Forgiveness of Self may have to do with realizations of what you *allowed* to have done to you, or things you *actually did* to others.

While this is in some ways similar to a Twelve Step program, as it is more necessary for some than others, and as always a choice. I have always found that the physical writing of Forgiveness Letters - Dear Self or Dearly Beloved Self, or if to others, Dear So & So - *whether living or dead*, as many of us - myself included, have issues with one or both parents, are a tremendous release. The physical act of writing is releasing within-itself and whatever works for you - pen in hand or computer will do. The magical thing is that once the process is begun, the flood gates are opened and stuff comes pouring out - pages and pages - from the back, deep crevasses of your mind. Things that have been weighing you down, or eating-you-up subconsciously for years.

Of course, unlike Twelve Steps, there is no need to mail, email or share these letters with anyone. Your whole letting go process is private, so if you start sharing intimate details, you may actually start editing it, or doing it to please another person. This counters the whole release purpose. I actually sent a Forgiveness letter to my sister and I got a letter from her attorney saying I was harassing her. She missed the message obviously, but I didn't. Remember each path is singular, while you may guide or give direction to those others who wish to make their changes, fine. But you do not need to share anything really personal, as an example to them, it may have an adverse affect on them - trying to live up to your raw experience. You may later have regrets that you shared something so revealing with a friend, even if they are on the path also. The letter to yourself can be done as often as you feel the desire to dump more out. As with most processes, it has that layering effect which reveals-up more on a regular basis.

For some *living-people*, that you now realize you may have treated wrongly, a verbal or written apology may well be useful. Something to think about, should you decide to ask them for their forgiveness, that is their choice to do or not, and in asking for it, you have added the burden (as well the power) to them to give it. If you simply and sincerely apologize, then they are free to handle it how they choose. This way you are truly giving them something without asking for anything in return. Also, there is the consideration of the unburdening your soul with something, which will *only hurt the other person.* In other words, *some people have no need of certain things - information which will only give them pain.* If you have gone this long without confessing to them, then they are happy in their ignorance. The unsent message is better to have been written and burned, to release all of the negative to dissolve into the Universe. Many people do this as a ritual at year's end to keep the build up cleared out.

Think about it, write it down, release it and forgive yourself. As you progress along your path, you will not repeat these negative actions or behaviors. If you do, you better go back a few steps, as you obviously missed some key things along the way. Also understand, there will be some people that you feel you 'wronged,' but they have NO clue or memory of what you did or didn't do. Accept that as their choice of memory, or perhaps you were not even on their radar.

Don't push for a resolution on some big things, if it is not ready to be brought forth. Deep breathe, take breaks or give yourself space. Focus on what you truly want from this situation and don't hesitate to ask for Divine Assistance from your Guardian Angels, or Higher Self and the Universe. The answers are out there, or actually inside us. If you simply ask the right questions and then be open to the response - which you may or may not like. Accountability and/or responsibility may not be a forte of others, but you may need to forgive or acquiesce to diffuse or release the situation. Also Key: *Acceptance regarding a situation is not Agreement* with it. Moral Rectitude: You do not have to alienate your principals to succeed. As always, everything is a choice - for yourself and others.

We all are human, at this point, so assume as much goodwill as you can as who knows, these Past things were used to dealing with an "old you." So the New You, filled with such positive energy, action and behavior could turn the whole thing totally upside down and be a benefit for you and the Universe. Again you are the positive one who needs to go into this learning experience completely open to the lessons offered. Mindfulness in the planning of this, will serve you incredibly well and may bring some enlightenment to you. Above all, accept and love who you are - 'warts and all' - and where you are in your life. If you, and only you, are OK and accepting of that, then don't worry what others think of you - crazy or not. You have and are changing, so don't beat yourself up for that other person you were before. This is forgiveness WITHOUT judgment of you or others!

Definitely, forgiveness is a gift you give yourself in its release and others - it is NOT something any one OWES you. There will be a wider opening of your heart with every forgiveness that you give, so keep free-flowing the love into you and through you for so many others. Think of these negative things as impediments that need to be removed, so more and more love, good and abundance can come in - Flow to you. Trust in the Universe and Karma. If someone has truly done you wrong, then they will be dealt with, *but not by you.* You are lowering yourself to another's negative level when you waste your time and energy to enact revenge, anger or hate upon them. Even if it is only verbalization - what goes around DOES come around to you. Negative Past anything has to be let go of, for *your good health*.

\* \* \* \* \* \*

The weak can never forgive. Forgiveness is the attribute of the strong. Gandhi

One of the gifts of facing death is to gain the appreciation of life.

God is *every where*, within *every one*. Respect that, no matter who you meet, or where you meet them. We are All One, from the same God/Source.

# Awareness ~ Part #12

It all starts with Awareness, at some moment becoming aware of who you really are, or what you have or haven't become. Whether you laugh, cry, scream or shout, it is the awareness that is the first step. It tells you either that you love who you are, or you definitely need to change. Continuous awareness is to live each day to its fullest and give thanks for all things that are given to you - small and large gifts, as well as the miracles graced upon you. Awareness lets you know how attuned you are in living your life in *real, live color*, noticing even the smallest of things and using all of your senses fully. Remember your sub-conscious mind is like a computer - it takes in EVERYTHING -Positive and Negative that you think or say. It makes no judgments, as it is subjective and simply receives whatever you feed it. And, then whatever is repeated many times, or fed into it with great emotion is kept the longest. You could say, emotion moves it to the top of the heap, as being the most important. This is then passed on to your conscious mind for you to take direction or action. In other words, the more attention or mindful-awareness you give to something, the quicker it comes into fruition - negative fears or positive affirmations.

This is what we usually refer to as being programmed into our belief system, or to extreme negative - brain-washed. While a portion of the sub-conscious can come from the collective consciousness of humanity, the strongest influence usually comes from *those groups directly surrounding and influencing* you. The most influential, usually being family/culture, friends, though education, near-community and religious-spiritual beliefs have various levels of influence. As you become aware of all that was *dumped* into your sub-conscious, you can choose what to keep and what to let go of. The self-examination of opening each little box of memories is not easy, even painful, as we realize what we have done with our lives. But forgiveness and loving ourselves is the *salve*. There is also the sweet-taste of Self-awareness and true freedom, as you know who you really are. One by one we can learn that awareness can change each one of us, so together we can, of course, change the world. It is not for the faint of heart, but for those who understand that growth comes from changes and we will do it.

The world is a book, and those who do not travel read only a page. St. Augustine

The more knowledge and experience you have in the bigger, world around you, then you'll be an aware of those things that are no longer acceptable within your Belief System. It is your choice to heal your imbalanced-unconsciousness through your learned lessons of what is valid/true or positive/negative for you. Some people are so resistant to change these rigid beliefs from fear, or outside pressure and influence. For this life time, they may be stuck in the illusion that their Belief System is working for them. You need to let go of people and things to move on, as you choose to evolve along a path of more enlightenment and peace with true happiness and joy, free of anger and fear. As you progress in your recovery from the Past and into a more Spiritual awareness, you bring in that balance of Oneness within yourself. This is truly connecting within your own energy and real awareness. It gives you the strength, sense and balance of being, as you move forward from there with a lighter, positive energy.

Awareness and listening to your own "Body Language" around other people, helps you be comfortable to the point that you can *be yourself* and not someone else *to please them or restrict yourself.* Your health and happiness will be affected by it. It will be amazing how your stress levels will lower, when you no longer put yourself into drama-situations. Your whole physical-Self changes with awareness of what you are doing with your body. The process of deep breathing alone, heightens the senses while increasing your energy. Sometimes you don't see the blessings that are right in front of you, whether they are things or people. Taking someone or something for granted is similar to ignoring it/them. And, especially ignoring a person is the worst thing you can do to them, as you are saying they are not there, they do not even exist, they are not worthy of your time.

Patterns of thinking and emotional responses are usually habits you allowed yourself to develop - without much conscious awareness. Now, that you have decided to take charge of your life, you no longer need to just muddle-through the day. Instead, you can deliberately control your thoughts, words, actions and feelings. It is a Universal, natural law that what you put your attention and energy into, *you draw* into your life. It is only logical, that you take the steps necessary to let go of any Past destructive-programming, to begin creating for yourself a fulfilling, happy, harmonious, abundant and peaceful life. The deeper level, or Spiritual dimension of that, is you will continue to understand the preciousness of your emotional life and your ability to live fully as a human being. Knowing you are of both Spirit and physical matter, raises your awareness, as does the preciousness of every human life, no matter how short-lived, or how distant from yours.

True Spiritual-guidance *never* involves solving someone else's problems. Rather, a role-model, a beacon of light and awareness to them, which mirrors their problems back to them in a way that enables them to take another look at it. It enables them to see meaning and value in the problem; it returns to them a sense of Freewill, as well responsibility. The term Super-consciousness has often been given to those who have moved more into this direction. They have learned how to control what is put into the sub-conscious computer-mind and thus passed onto their conscious mind. We could say the sub-conscious has been reprogramed - positive in - positive out. Something to strive for, as we move on our path to be living a more harmonious life.

**Exercise:** There is a survival, even sanity in paying attention to life going on around us. A comfortableness in the receptiveness of the seasons - leaves, buds, blossoms - coming and going. You miss the silence of birds, only when you hear one. It is beyond comprehension sometimes, how much you need to appreciate nature and yet we all take it for granted. The density of the rain by sound, tells you what it will look like visually. The devastation and destruction of property is only truly known, to those who paid attention to what it held for them prior. Awareness of the ebb and flow of life, gives you a continuity, like knowing the sun will soon return stronger, after the shortest day has past. Give your-Self (on your own if possible) an excursion to a park, even one you are familiar with and see how many things have changed since your last trip there. Drive a different way home, or a walk around your neighborhood. Be visual, as well as audio in having awareness of what is around you and perhaps, what you never realized before. Now, transfer this new awareness to your job, home, friends or favorite places. Absorb as much as you can about *all* around you.

\* \* \* \* \* \*

The world is a dangerous place, not because of those who do evil, but because of those who look on and do nothing. Albert Einstein

The Truth is the Truth, no matter who said it - God, Buddha, Mohammed, Jesus, Krishna, or Gandhi. Martin Luther King, Jr.

Life is not meant to be a painful struggle without hope. Allowing new possibilities into your consciousness will begin your opening process to full miracles. It takes *willingness* to have your life be happier and more satisfying, even if you don't know how to do it. This *willingness* allows the forces of the Universe to work for you. Shanta Gabriel

# *More Lessons ~ Part #13*

Physically most of you have just begun to get an idea of how wonderfully the body reacts and feels, as the negative is eliminated from the systems. Life is no longer just based on ideas or beliefs you were told, but on positive, concrete knowledge, a knowing because you experienced it. You felt the energy, you know it exists. It is more than a metamorphosis, you've lived with the vibration within you and know clearly what is love and how good it feels to be surrounded by it. It has made you invincible - impervious to any negative invasion. The Truth is the knowledge of knowing you are the Light - there is no question, only certainty of your positive power to energize others.

As you keep the Golden Light around you and the White Light in front of you, there may be times that you have let your shields down and like a lightening bolt, something or someone challenging suddenly comes into your life. These things happen, as they are there for your lesson to be learned. No one is perfect and when you no longer have lessons to learn, you will no longer live on this Earth-plane. That is a fact, *no one dies before their time, no matter how long or short their time is* and there are not any know-it-alls on this plane. If you are still here, you still have lessons to learn, period!

So, while this bolt from the Past may set you back on your heels, eventually you will be glad for the experience for a lesson was learned. How much drama you create from this is up to you. How much you ask why? or I thought I was past all of this? - is a waste of time and energy. Get on with it - what is it, work with it, what can be learned from this? These are the questions at hand to set up the action. Being calm may not always work, but do some deep breathing to get control, so you keep your mind and heart open for the experience. Your belief in your own goodness gives you a certain relief-factor.

**Exercise:** Remind yourself in your breathing that you will be growing from this and the Universe never throws you a challenge without also offering ways to handle it. You are not alone and for sure you are not unloved. Do take things as they are - no molehills into mountains - and remember to break it all down - steps, pieces, bites - whatever you want to call it, so you can handle it, to work through it to your solution as easily as possible. Be sure to keep the whole process positive, even if others involved in the situation are negative - keep the Golden Light around you *to always keep out the negative vibes*. And, Forgiveness is *always* your strongest ally, as well as apology, if that is involved. The weaker person never forgives or apologizes - they see it as admitting to a mistake, rather than taking responsibility for their action, *even if it was not intentional*. I learned the "Power of Apology" with living in Japan for 7 years, though they do take it a bit too far. Apology and forgiveness make you seen as vulnerable - honest and so very human.

A lot of your Past stuff really does have to do with acceptance, or the feeling that you're not accepted, thus you have to change, or resent those who don't accept you as you are. Don't waste time on these things, *consider the source of who* is saying these things. You don't need the tension, resentment, anger or dealing with their many insecurities or petty jealousies. You know who you are and are positive about that person, if you weren't, you wouldn't have all of the positive energy flowing through you. You would have blips of non-acceptance, or a need for a correction, or change in who you were or are to be. You have chosen to live your life in a certain way and you will know it is good for you, as your vibrational energy will let you know when it needs to be tweaked. It happens like a tune-up or alignment, and not to be made into a really, big thing, but a good thing as you are totally in touch with yourself. Part of the whole growth process is understanding that you may not be the same person today, that you were yesterday.

If you make such things into a big issue, then the Universe cannot bring the assistance or solutions to you. You set up a resistance to positive flow and clearing when you stop to question everything or why it has happened to You. Being open means not getting in the way of things that need to happen, especially if you have stated that you want them - they just may not appear the way you wanted or expected. Remind yourself that the Universe is here to basically serve you in what you want, because of you being a Positive Light Energy product, especially when as a beacon you are assisting others out of darkness-negativity. There is a serenity in knowing that to others you are a true symbol of love, peace and joy to all who encounter your presence - just being around you, can have a positive affect on others who would be open to your shared gifts.

As long as you keep in touch with your inner-self through your breath and meditation, you will have a compass guiding you through just about any storm, or from other inclement inner-outer weathers of life that can be thrown at you. You are who you are meant to be at this time. If the Universe feels changes are necessary for new lessons, then you will get them. Just remember there is no such thing as too much love and that is what is always available pouring onto, into, around, over you from the abundant Universe. It is a flow that never stops or runs out, *as long as you are open t*o receive it. Where there is love there is no fear, especially fear of the unknown. You do not have the need to know the future when surrounded by love. You simply love your Destiny as your chosen dreams fulfilled, whether you have been brave enough yet to dream them or not. Breathe deeply and receive the love knowing that you are quite worthy, as you do your part.

When unwelcome surprises come into your life, demonstrate some resilience for the challenges, by rising to meet them using your best ideas from whatever sources. I recently saw a most amazing photo collection of Bird Nests from around the world. We can look to nature to see a resiliency, as we are often only reminded of in mankind's bravery during disaster or war. Birds have the ability of flight and nest building may be instinctive, but precarious in the very best situations. Yet, dealing with enemies, weather or simply location, rarely stops the birds in their tenacious dedication to prepare a home for their eggs and forth coming babies. You have not fallen short either.

Birds don't reward each other for the "best built nests," so we must assume that they are done through desire to protect those future generations, much as they carefully choose their mates perpetuating their species. How passionate are you about doing the 'right thing,' much less to the best of your ability? Birds and other animals don't stop and complain, "Why me, why do I have to be the one who has to do this?" They know and accept their responsibility, they have an innate accountability to do whatever is expected for them to do - nest building, sitting on the eggs or continuously feeding those little, open mouths until their children can feed themselves. There is much we can always learn from nature. Yes, they may have a pea-sized brain that doesn't question, but they always have a song in their heart, that they happily share with all who care to listen.

\* \* \* \* \* \*

Every person, all the events of your life are there because you have drawn them there. What you choose to do with them is up to you. Richard Bach

There are great potentials even from negative experiences - Important lessons to be learned, so they don't have to be repeated.

Greatness is not a function of circumstance, it is largely a matter of conscious choice and discipline.

Great potential is a positive anticipation in young children. If you haven't developed it by the time you are a mature adult, you probably won't. Your actual actions are what count, not potential to have them.

What has procrastination kept you from achieving?

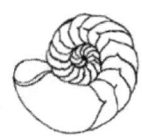

# *Stay Positive - Part #14*

It is not unusual during transition to the positive life to feel scattered, unclear in using or finding the right words to convey things, particularly your emotions. You may also get lost in your thinking and get unfocused, or dwelling on one thing. You are assimilating in an extension of Source Energy, which runs at a higher vibration than you were before. It can sometimes throw you off balance, as the vastness of Energy being absorbed within you. In response to what you see and interpret, you have an exposure to contrasts, which cause thoughts of desire to make your life better. You can get what you want, if you can manage to get out of the way of it working through you. You also sometimes might have what seems like expansions or jumps of time or space reality from this Energy. Deep breathing, as well visualizing harmony may help manage the vibration, so you can focus on alignment with the Source Energy, that is given to you. It may be a very confusing time until you are able to have congruence with what all is happening to you. I know the time-jumps really shook me.

**Exercise:** Practicing Positive thoughts keeps bringing in the Law of Attraction; Negative thoughts always block it. Managing your thoughts is an ongoing-process to receive your life-intentions as you expect and deserve. Keeping a Golden Light around you, usually helps protect these streams of positive-consciousness available from Source within you. Understand, accept and repeat to yourself - "I am more because of it and cannot make excuses for not receiving, or blaming others for holding me back. I am the *only one* who can hold me back. To be all I can be, I must *not* go into the negative at any time or for reason." I try to Never even utter negative words. I have often said that I work very, very hard on staying positive all the time. Living in the real world, among typical people, tolerance needs to be practiced, as others may not be as aware of their constant negatives put out into the Universe. I certainly don't want any of it to get attached to me, just because I'm surrounded by them.

Consciousness works with and helps stimulate energy, for it is the Master of energy. Do NOT push or force or battle or worry about things - there is no point, just a counter-point. The smoother your life flows, everything simply comes to you, naturally. If you question the process, and many of us control-type people do that (I'm a little OCD) - "Am I doing this right, maybe it's not working …" - then it doesn't work. You have stopped it by questioning. Just open up your heart with a deep breath and receive what the Universe wants to give you. Divine timing is NOT linear. It is fluid, it happens when it is best for it to happen. Think of Harmony in all things, unfolding with the process released through all parts to completeness. Fearless means believing ALL is in Divine Right Order for you.

Once you feel aligned or stable - no continuous revelations to deal with and let go of - you can use your new found intuition to bring a like-minded person into your life to share it. Remember to clearly project the like-minded characteristics you want, as you certainly don't want your chemistry to react to the physical alone and attract one who still clutches their Past baggage. Just as in AA, and as most recovery programs strongly suggest, you need about a year into your New Self before you can deal with the emotional-rollercoaster of a New healthy relationship. The advantage you would have in being solid within yourself is very well defined intuitive skills, so you actually prefer to have someone who is good for you, as their belief system is positive and loving. Any one with personal struggles or uncomfortableness that their life is not going right, is obviously *not* good for you.

Thought vibrations must only be strongly positive to fulfill your purpose by inspiration - Stream of becoming - life gives you an expanding experience and we need to go with it. Ask for what you truly, deeply, passionately want - do not tell or talk about the absence of *what you don't want*. It is the Art of Allowing in that loving yourself to receive. Let go of doubt, knowing that you deserve the very best partner who will love you as you are - "Ask and it is given." "Nothing is more important than my feeling good and being loved for who I truly am." Become the vibrational equivalent of the Source within. Feel eager, enthusiasm about those things you want, not what you don't want. DO NOT FOCUS ON WHAT IS WRONG!!!

AFFIRM: "My conditioned-responses from the Past to so many things have been amazing, as I'm learning to re-channel them all to the positive. I've reconnected and renewed my passion for my work, my life, my creativity and my relationships."

It is the flow of Creative Passion that will move you forward and upward into the next spiral of your ever unfolding potential. It is letting the Inner Child come through, totally engulfed in the passion for living life as the ultimate game to be played, as an ever-evolving exploration. When Passion is at play, there is only a knowing and doing, there are no questions, no doubt. Those negatives can not exist in the Positive atmosphere of Passion. You can prepare for setbacks by keeping a reservoir of positive beliefs - affirmations of who you are and can truly become. You can't always control what's around you, but you can control what's inside you. You will feel sometimes that you are being tested for how much you desire your dreams to come true. What or who will you give up, or how hard will you work to get what you truly want? Never forget that the big dreams are the ones that change you and the world around you the most. And, there is no reason you can't have them come true. Think about what may be holding you back: There is no need to give up your dreams just because your parents didn't have their dreams fulfilled. There is also no need for you to feel guilty being happy, if your parents weren't.

The best way to stay positive is to let go of all those negative thoughts holding you back. No matter *who* *t*old you them, they hold you back. They certainly hold you back from happiness. Accumulated negative thoughts are your problems, especially if you repeated them with belief. They got into your head, stuck there, as you bought into them and lived them. Think of giving yourself a clean slate. While you may have experienced many hardships to arrive where you are today, you can make positive choices to rise above *the need to recreate* the grievances of your Past. So, just be what you have learned and then watch what incredible new opportunities come your way! Be open to all that comes your way, but if it doesn't work out as to what or the way you wanted it, just go back and ask again with more clarity.

If there are no new lessons, then let it go for good. With practice, we learn to discern what information is in alignment for us and what is not. Sometimes, it is when we are ready to receive a later or better time. For most people, deep breathing or meditation helps the most in being open and receptive to guidance from Source. It is often interpreted that, for many people *prayer* is where we ask for help and *meditation* is where we receive it. Other people feel comfortable working through their chakras, various lights or vibrational energies. Simply said - whatever works for a positive you is what you need to do. I've been specifically requesting *Divine Assistance* with bringing forth whatever it is.

\* \* \* \* \* \*

What the caterpillar calls the end of the world, is what the Master calls a butterfly. Richard Bach

The world and everyone in it reacts to you - what are you putting out? What foot prints are you leaving? Will they last for the good things or the bad?

Bring something to the table - we cannot change the cards we're dealt, just how we play the hand.

Experience is what you get, when you didn't get what you wanted.

# *Old Belief Systems ~ Part #15*

Knowing the future is not necessary, just know that it will be good for you is what's important. Movie previews, as we all know, cannot tell the full story. The point of life is to live it with passion - to live it fully, completely using all of your senses and especially clearly looking it right in the eyes, so to speak. Sometimes it takes courage to go on, especially after realizing how much and how many times you screwed up. I know this too, well. Finally, knowing and accepting who you really are is not easy. Just as with verbalization - it is not always *what* you say, but *how* you say it. So, it is with how you live your life, once you've gotten through your growth-letting-go-transition.

It is not just the "Be all you can be," but be more than you ever were, or expected to be, in every aspect of this New-accepting and living of all life. Your slips, snags, back steps and mistakes are NOT sins. And, they've been forgiven by God/Source, the Universe and all your Guardian Angels, long before they are forgiven by yourself. Do not beat yourself-up, forgive, learn and have the courage to move on to your Divine Destiny and fulfilling it with your best ability. That's the point of not always seeing what is coming, because then you learn and grow how to *encounter life,* one step at time with love and acceptance.

Working in harmony with everything around you is a form of grace or synergy. Know, there is always a rainbow given after the rain. Discernment in what you do is determined by your intuition, so follow it, believe it and as your HigherSelf grows, it will give you the best direction. Creativity is equal to passion. When the heart is open, the ego is let go of, so you no longer need to compete with others. You only compete with and within yourself -

as sports-people say, "Your Personal Best." As without competition, there is no anger or negative towards others. You are only *now* concerned with improving yourself, or helping those next to you to improve, *if they ask*. Share your secrets or experiences, that worked for you in being your best.

There is no separation between us, as we accept and love all, unconditionally. The answers are always within ourselves, all we have to do is *listen* to hear them. So, on your own you have great creative, light energy. Yet, when you reach out to help another, and not separate yourself as your energies come together, the synergy will be more than just of the two of you. This is a key thing to remember - the more you give and share with others, the more you are given in return.

The flow of positive energy is everywhere, in every thing, as the abundance of life, of every *thing* good flows into you the more open you are. Life-Force energy grows with you to help you connect with everyone you choose to meet. Help whoever feels separate and let them know that we are all connected together, that is where the love is, for we are All One, from the same God/Source. There is no separation of any one of us for any reason. Old Belief Systems of your Past can get in the way of your growth and connecting. They must be re-examined and re-evaluated on a regular basis. Then released when they no longer work for the New You, who has grown to learn what it was saying is no longer true for you. Follow yourself, as you gather and create a New Belief System that is positive and true.

This is a great responsibility and will be your choice, though you can always ask for guidance from the Universe. But, much of this building of new Belief Systems comes from within you, as the Love and Light flows in and through you, for your new vision of your life.

Accept things as they flow through you, but do not let them get attached to you. It is totally OK to question your belief of your Beliefs, no matter how old they are. You are merely breaking the cycle of being a creature of habit, since you are no longer the same person. You now think - evaluate, all that you do and say from your heart solely, not what others have said you must do.

It is this Old Belief System that had defined who you were, your conditioned-responses that controlled you. You followed it *only* because you thought it was good for you, and it may have been at one time. But once you've had your epiphany, or your trauma that said this is not working any more, you began to see how limited your belief system - conditioned-responses were. One by one they must be let go of and replaced with positive ones, for you to grow. You then become that person to fulfill another layer of your Divine Destiny in this lifetime, or not - your choice. These, obviously, are challenges for most beliefs - automatic reactions that limit your creative process or conditioned-responses - go back to childhood family, friends, religion, education, neighborhood, etc. Some may even be sacrosanct. That part has ruled your life and will not go-lightly into disintegration. Be fully aware, your magnetic field around your body has been moving to a higher vibration and as you open up, the Universe sends you more and more positive energy with Love. Higher truths are out there, but the Old Belief System may try to limit one's access or acceptance of these truths, as you journey on your path to find and develop yourself more.

Choose every day to be on purpose for positive change. This keeps the Old Belief System at bay. Joy is a key factor for change, as from the love you receive. You no longer have a tolerance for the lower vibration - accepting what life throws at you as being *good enough,* as if you are not worthy of more. Your heart knows where you are going and your connection to your Higher Self, as you are filled with more Love-Energy, so the total realization will be revealed to your consciousness. This may create some difficulties as your releasing is replaced by New Truths.

**Exercise:** In the realm of getting to know who you have already become, write down each day 3 things that you are grateful for having in your life. This is another awareness-building exercise that can be done any time of the day or night. It is to keep you out of the rut or routines of life, that suck so much creative energy out of you before you know it, as such creatures of habit. There are no rules or limitations on those things that you are grateful for having. They can be totally mundane and ordinary, as you quickly forget how many people around the world do not have even a small percentage of what we continually take for granted. It can be people, places, clothing, food, sunshine, fresh air or water, etc. Absolutely anything and of course, everything that you as a human are grateful for having.

If you care to get more esoteric, you might think of having freedom of choosing your beliefs, freewill or the continuous choices you are given to accept or deny to do or have in your life. So, you see choosing only 3 things daily may take only seconds of your time. But, over the days and weeks, you will find that your awareness of who you are and what you have in your life has expanded. This has then made you a more positive person who sees those things, that so many others don't bother to notice. Life is good, but can always be better.

Again remember, you are not alone, and you do not have to experience it alone. You can always ask for Divine Assistance from God/Source or your HigherSelf to create the positive energy. Let go of old energy systems, for new energy knows no lack, only abundance in all things -

especially unconditional love. The ego's true divisiveness is to keep us separate from Love and Light. Some of you had a clear contract before you came to Earth and what you do is part of your life path, though you may not find or develop it until later in your life. It is always about being open, to receive the information and trusting what is given to you - believe that you do deserve it and you will receive it.

You must truly believe that you are the creator of your own experiences. No person has power over you, *unless you allow them to do so.* In the Past, others may have gained control over you, or even tricked you into feeling you had no power at all, through fear and guilt. These things blocked you from your inner knowing, but these elements have or are falling away. So, it is now necessary for you to rise into your own Empowerment, to become everything that you were meant to be. It is time for the creation of your New Belief System that allows you to be just who you want to be. You are God's perfect child, so there is no question as to your ability or creativity - just do it.

We can easily forgive a child who is afraid of the dark. The real tragedy of life is when men are afraid of the light. Plato

# *Destiny ~ Part #16*

Part of the whole awareness and acknowledgment of your conditioned-responses of your Past is to exactly understand how they had "made" you create the negatives in your life. Some of it, you now know, may have been part of what you needed to learn as your lessons. The key is, when you have been so stuck with them being repetitive, you lose any learning received or deduced good from them any more. They've lost their significance or purpose. Again, what you perceive to believe to be true, may not be the real truth, if it was founded on the negative and creates more negative. Love is only positive energy and Love is the real truth. Jump far ahead of simply yourself and see what this freedom could produce if practiced by others - dozens, hundreds, thousands, millions!!!

Nothing related to the ego is truth, for it is not related to love or unconditional giving. Anything-one that tries to control you is *Not* love, no matter what it/they say. Some may see or believe there is love related to the ego because of boasting, being protective or saying it is so, but it is only a perception that is fed like a facade. When the heart is open, the love flows through - giving and receiving - limitlessly. But the ego keeps the heart shrouded, saying it is protecting it from pain, hurt, abuse and those undeserving of your love. Yet, any open heart does not need this 'protection,' for unconditional love flows free without fear of these things, as it is pure, positive energy.

Eliminating the negative could bring an end to greed, or even oppression by governments and groups, an end of fear, an end of basic suffering of all kinds to all humans. Think about it. Unconditional love can do that, for again it is the most positive, powerful Love-Energy. You can not be even minutely negative to one person that you love unconditionally - they are two polar opposites. It is all that simple - start with yourself - the love of Self, forgiveness, acceptance, etc. As a living example, more people will want to be like you, or have what you have in peace and love. Extend yourself to them, show them, tell them, guide them, but remember the trip down the path is theirs, their choice - "When you want more for the other person than they want for themselves, then you will be disappointed."

When someone simply is whiney and complaining, but not quite ready to ask for help, just respond, "I know, yeah. I've been there, or I was there, too." It gives empathy, yet still puts the ball in their court to either ask for help, or continue to mull it over before asking. If they ever do ask, then they are ready for you give them the basic steps - not rescue. As long as you continue to be the example of how life can be, by letting go of the Past, they may continue on their path. The short answers are best, "I finally got tired of repeating the same scenarios; or being angry or frustrated all the time, my life as it was, just wasn't working for me any more." It is all about the other person being ready to receive your message. But, as you know, it is not always an easy journey, but the unlimited rewards can't even begin to be expressed, for it is the essence of true freedom. Still, you are never alone for Universal Love is with you always, and it will Never fail you for it is not an illusion, it is real Love. This is your Divine Destiny - follow it and live fully.

Many people are out of integrity/honesty when they wish for one thing, while doing another. There is a gap between what they do desire and what they actually manifest. They hope for change, but are afraid to create or commit to it. No one can live this way of being for long. The positive self-changes are putting pressure on everyone to step into their potential, to move past their fears and to be in integrity-harmony with their Highest Good. Everything in your life is an opportunity to manifest your Highest Good. The most difficult experiences occur when you are out of integrity, when you are not using your power to create, but are allowing yourself to walk the middle ground. There is no middle ground any more, everyone must be in the light *or not,* to be fully in their power, *or not.* You must now be willing to step into the flow, to follow Universal Law and to co-create with it. Everyone is then experiencing the full effects of their creative ability. When the results are difficult, it is a reflection of their level of integrity-truthfulness with their Highest Good, their power and their potential. I've seen people succeed and also others fail - it's hard.

If you work more with allowing yourself to feel loved and nurtured from within your connection to your divine essence, then you will be filled with a loving, nurturing, compassionate aspect. This in turn will begin to replace the aspect of yourself that sends you into depression, feelings of failure or memories of not being good enough. Whenever you wake up in the morning, before you get out of bed, or perhaps when you are taking your shower, whatever it may be; begin to create a daily routine in which you open and acknowledge bringing in your own Divinity, your own God/Source connection within you. Let it come into you or wash over you or fill you up; even if it's only for a few breaths, or a few minutes. What you will find is that you will then become much more comfortable with being within your Divinity, and from there it will then begin to fill your daily life up more.

**Exercise:** As you awake each day, consider that you have been washed of your Past. Certainly, each day is meant to be new, as it is new. It is a day that has never appeared before. Remember this. Intent says it all - the experience is *now* without a timeline and not what you think you *should* be doing. Know your Passion. Experience life as a passionate Spirit-Angel, as you smile to give light and joy to yourself and others. When you have the opportunity to live your full life from within your Divinity, you are then able to look at life and the world with discernment, without judging, with simply taking in, making choices, making decisions, without that sense of duality, without that sense of 'is this right or wrong?'

No one has less heart, nor more heart than another. No one. The difference is in the usage of the heart, or what you have filled it with - negative or positive. Definitely some use their hearts more than others. The heart has an infinite capacity. There is no end to love, and yet all too often, you cut off the love to or from others. You snip it off, believing that you have given or received enough. There is never too much love. You cannot overdo with the pure sending of love. Let love dispel everything in its path. Get yourself out of the way of love. Let loose the love in your heart. Rein it in no longer. The wiser you are, the more you have to let go of analyzing everything that is happening to you. The more that is out of the way, then your mind becomes a de-cluttered house. That is the same as to say the Past is behind you.

If you are NOT vulnerable — totally Open to your feelings for another person - because of your fear of being hurt, you are limiting yourself to fully-feeling the love they wish to give you. Yes, emotional pain sometimes comes with being human and loving someone fully. Put yourself in a shell, or Risk to live life fully. Even limited joy is better than none at all. There is a freedom in trusting - in yourself for making wise decisions regarding loving another and in the power of being free of Fear controlling your feelings.

Awareness - Acknowledgment - Acceptance -
Appreciation - Gratefulness - Forgiveness - Positiveness -
Unconditional Love - Joyfulness - Peacefulness -
Worthiness - Wholeness -
It All Starts Within You.

\* \* \* \* \* \*

Our chief want is someone who will inspire us to be what we know we could be. Ralph Waldo Emerson

It's never crowded along the extra mile. Wayne Dyer

There is nothing in a caterpillar, that tells you it's going to be a butterfly. Buckminster Fuller

Success ... The freedom to live life how you choose.

# Self-Sabotage ~ Part #17

It's something that goes back to when you were actually quite young. The usual is being told you are not good enough. Or, it is trying to make you fit into a particular family/cultural mold in which you did not feel comfortable. Therefore, it usually results in some constricting depression, or sense of failure in being unable to complete something. It is all interwoven with that feeling of non-acceptance, no matter what the task, so why bother attempting the job. Even if it just happened one time and everything else may have been a repeat performance. Criticism and judgment may be the expected from teachers and parents, yet everyone seems to feel they can jump on the bandwagon of the insecure child. Bullying does not come to children naturally, like most verbalizations, they are home-brewed and spewed from those who want to cover up their own insecurities. It is what real cowardice is all about.

You have to tell yourself absolutely, that you have the ability to complete this journey, or work with any project, see it through to full completion. When you get to that place that puts you into a depression or questioning space, that's when you need to go into yourself and release that negative Belief System that says you are not good enough to finish it. You need to say repeatedly, as strong as possible, "I can do this, I can see it through." It's a negative subconscious-act that no longer works in your best interest. This is a wall of procrastination that does not want you to take control of your life and successes. As the old systems begin to fall away, you will then be matched up with better supports of who you are and how your New Energy is vibrating. You can no longer utilize or team with negative energies, thoughts or people that are not in alignment with who you are. It does help if you choose to accept that a Universal force does exist - God/Source or whomever, as it supports you to be in the flow of your positive energy.

Once again, only you can stop the negative flow, whether it is from fear, doubt or shame - questioning yourself - "Who do you think you are?" Its real name is Self-Sabotage. This may come basically from your parents, "What will people say?" - "What will the neighbors think?" When insecure about anything, you question who you are and what you are doing, which can either stem from, or be a reaction of Past criticism. Critics are sometimes simply a grown-up name for the school-yard bully, or the bully-supervisor at work. It may be someone that sees your talent, intelligence, work or whatever, as a real threat to them. If you are "too good" at what you're doing, inept or insecure others will find ways of criticizing or putting you down. Once some people find your Achilles Heel, they never let up until You no longer let "it" control you. Warning, watch out for that sly, slick *passive-aggressive* person with the left-handed compliments that only wants to give you "objective" or "just being honest" criticism.

**Exercise:** Deep breathe what these people have said, releasing their negatives. Be open if it has any valid ideas or suggestions, but let go of the disparaging ridicules, which are only thinly-veiled jealousy.

**Behavior modification** - privately write down and read aloud any words that make you react uncomfortably, until they don't - repeat as frequently as you need. Keep the deep breathing and affirmations also going, so you don't get sucked into someone's negative vortex. Put the Golden Light around you to buffet-away the doubts of who you are, or on your way to be. It keeps the negative vibes out.

Creativity in whatever you do is a gift that cannot be denied, but if you stick it on a shelf after the first nay-sayer, it will never have time to grow into what it might have been. It does not have to be other people who are successful - it can be you. Useful criticism doesn't tear your guts out, it makes you see another approach or direction to do something. Everything is a process and there are missteps in all things. Awareness also is important, if the criticism or the critic reminds you of anything or one that happened in your Past. You may have found something new to dig up and deal with, or to let go of for your future movement forward. Most importantly you must try again, if you don't learn from your mistakes you may turn them into avoidances, which quickly become phobias and fears. We're looking to get rid of these, not add to them in a sabotaging way.

When I was in junior high school, we had cooking one semester and sewing the next. I had no problem with the cooking, I loved it. But my mother was an excellent seamstress and my older sister designed and made clothes - she rarely finished them, but that's another story. So, I felt I had something to prove and my teacher, as well as my mother, were very critical of my work. I actually didn't want homemade clothes then, as the other girls had store-bought. I had a real block and barely passed the class because of the blouse we had to make. That summer, through some circumstances, which I don't remember now, I became more determined in my skills. I bought a Vogue pattern, a type considered more difficult than the Simplicity that we did in school, and the material to make a blouse on my own. My mother was working and my sister married, so I had no one to hover over me with a critical eye. I made a lovely blouse and proudly wore it, showing them the pattern and my fine work detail. Neither believed that I had made it myself, but I knew I had, and wore it constantly telling everyone with pride. When I felt my point had been made to *my emotional satisfaction*, I donated it to the church rummage sale and never really sewed anything for myself again. I didn't need to.

The point being, that I passed a personal self-test, where what they thought, at least regarding the blouse, no longer had an affect on me. Those blocks we all create are not just a fear of failure, *but also of success.* You will have something to live up to and if you tell yourself it was a fluke, then of course, repeating the success, or another one, will be difficult. If you fail, you create excuses, or people feeling sorry for you, or thinking not to make such demands on you. But, if you succeed, then you have the responsibility of dong more and better. Bosses don't ask the slackers or inept ones to take charge and receive praise or raises on projects.

The capable people are the ones that are asked to lead, organize or do whatever others have shown that they won't or cannot do. It can be scary to be in charge. It is the same with happiness. Things that make you happy, or would present you with an opportunity to be happy, are things that speak of how highly you value yourself. Be aware of an internal dialogue of phrases such as "I don't deserve this," "it will never last," "don't worry about me" or anything else that puts you down, devalues or minimizes your importance. These are all indicators of low self-worth and signs that you will sabotage your happiness, or success when it appears. With awareness, you can then actively monitor your speech and rephrase your internal dialogue to maximize your importance/value, recognizing that you are worthy of experiencing happiness and success.

**Exercise:** Without blaming yourself or others, think about how you have sabotaged things in your life - trying out for something in school, job interviews, taking credit for something you did, etc. Now, write how you could have done it differently, if you had believed in yourself and not what others had told you. When finished, be sure to write about something more recent where you did 'go for it' and let your 'light shine.'

* * * * * *

Clear your mind of can't. Samuel Johnson

Only those who dare to fail greatly can ever achieve greatly. Robert F. Kennedy

Success seems to be connected with action. Successful people keep moving. They make mistakes, but they don't quit. Conrad Hilton

Most great success comes from having made some big mistakes or bad decisions. It is also the foundation of wisdom.

# *Judgment ~ Part #18*

Most of us on the path are evolving on a regular basis, which means any day in that process you may be doing things that are part of that lesson's progress. You must learn to release all judgment, for that other soul you judge may be in the process of lesson-learning also, and it may be an important 'life lesson.' Many of your Past behaviors are embedded in lifetimes endured in darkness and will require a great effort to release, or transform your thoughts, to lift them to a higher level. It will require you to be alert and watchful of your thoughts. They are the seeds which create blossoms or weeds through your thought creation. If you experience someone attempting to bring another person down, by reminding them of Past words and actions, then flavoring them with their own judgments, don't hesitate to call them on it. *"That is in their Past,* they're changing, don't judge on someone's yesterday."* Respect whoever you meet, wherever you meet them. Yes, it's hard work to have that awareness. No, it's not easy. I'm still very much working on it!

You cannot reach the summit of true peace within you, until you release judgment - of yourself and others. Further, many others do not do things the way you would, or complete a task as you would. While they may do it in a really different way, the completed result may be the same. Does it really matter that they accomplished the task in a different manner than you, as long as the end result is the same? So, why do you judge or think they cannot be right, because they did it differently? Just as we are all on our personal paths to ourSelves. We are not puppets, we have Freewill, and most of us choose to use it. You are not here to change the world by judging events around you, but by *expressing the living example of your life.* So, it's not about being superior and never using the word 'perfect' in any way. It's not about knowing more than any one else. It's not about preaching. It's simply about being grounded, a good example and offering your support.

You do not always have to be right. You do not have to be proven right, nor do you have to prove someone else wrong. What is changed, is whether you or *anyone* is correct or incorrect? Where did they do their research? Either way, it is a passing fancy, *only to an ego does it matter*. Count your mistakes as great steps on the path of learning. Pretty much, in the world you live, much of your learning has to do with unlearning - your ability and willingness to let go of an old idea, methodology or process. Let new ideas be new stepping stones, *not ignorance written in stone*. A free Being does not hold himself to the Past. He does not stick up for it, nor does he denounce it. He lets it go without judgment, as it no longer matters. There are so many lessons to learn that will help you change and grow, but the biggest one is knowing that Fear is an illusion. Even if you feel it, don't let it deter you.

**Exercise:** You are so much more than you credit yourself with, as your own worst critic. But, you hardly credit anyone, and this is another one of your patterns that will change. When you exonerate yourself from the Past, then you will begin to see yourself and others in the Positive Light. Reveal yourself to yourself - unmask yourself - get to know the real you with a sense of humor. Take off those old thoughts and you will reveal yourself in the same breath. Have enough Self-confidence and Self-esteem to only associate with people who are good for you, *and* to you. You have had your fill of toxic associations and are ready to sort through your address book, highlighting a list of names that you know have your true, best interests at heart. Anyone who does not fit the bill can be crossed out - erased, with no questions asked. As you have glimpses of who you can be, you let go of more judgment, as you return back to your path for continued growth. It is about keeping your sense of humor *and* biting your tongue. This may be as difficult as reframing from criticism, basic chastisement or hard judgment of your Self and others, if this was a common habit from your Past. It may be a main-challenge to keep your humor following you along on your journey. Let go and laugh more!

Being Joyful, Loving and Accepting without Judgments, are not just platitudes. They are positive results with consistent practice of keeping all criticism in check, along with giving Blessings and Gratitude for the strength to do so. It does work. So, don't miss the significant crossroads in your life, or your many opportunities to transform your reality, because you were distracted by judgmental details. You are in a constant process of transformation and every day we may face options, which have multiple choices attached to each. Sometimes your controlling-ego doesn't want you succeeding as well on your own. It may create doubt or feed you hesitation to get you purposely go off track, to create a different outcome. Then, you will chastise yourself for being weak and creating this sabotage. To fully appreciate each opportunity that arises, you must be aware of the potential of each situation and be fully open to anything, without judgments or attachments. Don't hesitate to ask for guidance, if you question any negative thoughts.

We all know that 'chance' meetings can change the course of someone's life, you just may not believe that it can be your life. Most of you know in the depths of your hearts, the truth of your journey is not about the next bigger pay check, or a new car, or even a promotion for your career move, or the illusion of another person to make you happy. It is first knowing, that you have achieved compassion within your own heart to allow another to just

BE Who They Are! Then the opportunity at hand is to release the idea of judgment in what others do, or how they present themselves in any myriad ways of life. We are all human, which means that none of us are perfect, nor expected to be. And, that is the simple truth of the gift given to each of you - just be yourself, and that is *more than* good enough! You then learn to rise above the everyday frustrations, with patience, respect and acceptance of Self and others.

Compassion will be flowing through your heart, as well as the flow of the love within it. Accepting and realizing that, there cannot be judgment. Trust that you can learn to do this, one little step at a time. Do not let doubt creep in when you slip, or fear of failure take you over. Let it go, forgive yourself and move on so you do not let yourself be vulnerable to judgment, criticism or ridicule - either coming from inside or outside. Remember, when you focus on any kind of fear it is amplified into negative energy. Always keep yourself filled, as well as protected with positive energy.

**Exercise II:** Another important point to remember about judgment, is that it can set off a runaway digression into prejudice, discrimination and even harassment. This is where your insecurities can turn you into a bully, not wanting to acknowledge your own mistakes. Humanity starts with understanding we are ALL human, therefore not error-proof. People will forgive and think more highly of you when you can admit and accept any mistake you have made in the Past. Move on without blame - which is directly related to judgment. You don't have to be fragile or frail to have a misstep - just human.

\* \* \* \* \* \*

I know I can share the world with others without sharing the same world-view.

Too often critics create a premise and look for evidence to support it, to give themselves authenticity.

It is not always about how many 'points' that you scored that matters most, but how often you assisted others in their attempts.

Resilience in the face of adversity is perhaps your most valuable asset … though stopped in your tracks, you have not been derailed. Lynn Sheer

# *Creative Life ~ Part #19*

You may have heard it said that Life is no dress rehearsal … well, it doesn't even have a script. You simply need to deal with the cards dealt, or exchange them for some new ones, since your are the dealer. It is all about keeping in the flow or being washed to the side, perpetually drowning in stagnate water. You either take control of your life or let go of whatever is not working, for you to move forward. It's basic, it's logical. It's what adults living in the present do, so they can move forward. Why struggle along, when it's a smooth move in the flow? If your doors and windows are sealed shut, you are not a vessel for the Universe to bring the energy through you. It's real simple to just open up and go with the flow of unbounded, unlimited Positive energy - Love! Don't stay stuck in the fast-lane behind a slow driver.

You make your life on Earth more or less worthy, by what you give and what you create. It is your choice. Everyone is given some sort of gift or talent. To not use that creative energy is to refuse to fulfill your Divine Destiny. Some people are better students and some better teachers. Still, we all have something to learn from time to time, so the position changes either from life to life, or in the same lifetime. As you learn more, you can become the better teacher. It is a legacy you can give to others for them to learn also. Enjoy each unfolding moment - explore your curiosity, even if it is only reading or seeing what others have done and appreciating them. Sometimes, you have to be a voyeur or a participant from the stands, before you feel secure enough to try something on your own. Few of us were born as child prodigies - where those experiences or talents have been transformed directly into this life. Perhaps in the last life they were not given a real chance to pursue them, or get acknowledgment of the talent, so the gift is given again in this life.

**Exercise:** The Key to it all is that you must Consciously have an Awareness of these potential possibilities, so you grow and learn to access these gifts, as your own personal attributes. Go into your deep breathing - What is your Spiritual Vision or Mission? Think about it and then write it from your heart, not your head. This is yours, not something to impress or satisfy others. What do you really, really want for you to make your life happier and joyful? Envision this perfect world you can create with your dreams, visualizations, affirmations, and listening to, then following your intuition. This is not airy-fairy stuff, this is taking action to manifest your visions. Everyone - Yes, absolutely everyone has a talent, or creative bent that just comes so easy to them. No matter what anyone told you in your Past, *you are creative.* Remember to always be an example to others by projecting love and harmony, so they know that they can do it, too.

No energy ever dies, it is merely transformed and, Love is the strongest. Just as time is an illusion that is a boundary set, by a belief system in which you are living. You can learn to stretch it, find new possibilities, as perception creates reality. The Past may be negative and the future positive, but it is only the present that is the reality you have now. Fears can be in the future, only if you allow them to be created. When you put yourself completely in the now, you are creating all that is happening. It all starts from the Love within that you are sending out. You are not here by accident, as you do have a specific purpose. Empower each other rather than compete. Get rid of the game plan as you create your reality every day without a time frame. Love of Self is first, so you can accept the Oneness of us All. We are co-creators of ourSelves.

Thoughts create the positive frequencies around us - but only if they are Positive, especially statements of the "I AM ..." thoughts and verbalizations are the empowerment of peace, joy and love. Visualize and create what you want now. Listen to your intuition, nudging from Spirit - put it into action - make it happen, do make your Big Dreams come true. You must take responsibility to make it happen; Co-create it into reality. You are much wiser beings, as you accept involvement more in the Spiritual Energy, which is Love. See any obstacles from a different angle to flow through them. You are the receptacles of the energy - "I AM that I Am." Be that beautiful being that is within you.

The energy will fill you, so others see you in a special light, your glowing aura. You are the Divine in your creativity, so accept this gift that is given to you. Be very specific in what you want for your highest good, claim your empowerment. Listen with compassion and look with empathy, so you see it is a time of miracles. Build your vision for what you can create is beyond your wildest imagination - grace and love comes to you boundlessly, accept it for your highest good. Engulf yourself in a Positive vibration.

Remember, you attract back whatever you give out in thought and deed - positive to positive and negative to negative. This also includes your personal feelings - happy, grumpy, etc. So keep your vibrating energy clean and positive, then no one sends back anything negative to you in response. Send out the praise and appreciation along with the no-strings giving. If you want the good stuff to come to you - put out the positive, passionate desire for those things or opportunities. They may not be on a silver platter, but a door may be offered for you. Keep your awarenesses up and open. *God helps those that help themselves*, so it may not be the doorbell ringing, but being out and about to see the sign or signal for you to follow. Always be courageous enough to follow your dreams, no matter how wild or crazy they may seem to others.

Do your planning, do your research, so when it's plopped into your lap you're not going to run screaming, "Oh, my God, what have I done? I can't do this or have this, or whatever." Part of you is bringing to you what you deserve and your preparation 'as if, it is on a delivery schedule' helps it be fulfilled. You're expecting it on Friday, so now you need to do the following, so it will all flow smoothly. And, if it doesn't come on Friday, then you know it was not time. See what else comes along that needed to be included, or gave you info to change your plans somehow. Don't be one those people who gets caught with their pants down and others say, "Be careful what you ask for!"

It is your imperfections that make you *uniquely* who you are. So, why would you listen to someone who tries to "fix" who you are? It is your job to fix or tweak any creative characteristics or flaws as part of your journey in Self-discovery, of becoming who you are meant to be. Part of your change is this empowerment of choice, so it would be detrimental to allow someone else to choose for you. Realize too, that any brokenness, or the broken places in you, are beautiful also. They are part of who you are, your story and can thus contribute to your creativity. Honor your individual journey, your experiences with an understanding that there is nothing 'wrong' with you. These are ways to gain awareness, allowing you to learn your lessons and successes by what you create. Finally, there is a knowing that nothing is more important than the unconditional love that is always God-given to you, just for being you.

\* \* \* \* \* \*

Open your eyes so you are living in the moment. Take life for the moment.

"If you do not know where you are going, every road will get you nowhere."

Sometimes the biggest risk is not taking one at all.

Sometimes people are not even aware that they are afraid of change. They are just so comfortable in their current life, and sure that it will go on forever.

# *Listen ~ Part #20*

Listening is such a key element in the growth process. We ignore powerful signals - from our bodies, sometimes coming directly from our ears. A ringing or other sounds that can be both annoying and painful, because you didn't pay attention to prior signs your body was sending to get your attention. Whether you are pushing yourself to the point of exhaustion, or simply doing things that may be harmful to you - food, other addictions or too much *doing,* or the wrong exercise. You need to listen to your body as it signal you - *pay attention* - have some awareness of the need for inner and outer balance. If in the Past you have had people of authority yell, scream, nag or just being belligerent in critical or demeaning terms - you probably have shut down much of your hearing and listening ability. To clarify - Hearing would be more the actual physical capability of sound coming into you, whereas *Listening* has more to do with comprehension, or understanding and processing the meaning of the sounds or words.

**Exercise:** Talk to your body, let it know you are now listening to what all it may want to say to you - breathe deeply and it will soon respond to you. Depending on how much you have tuned-out people from the outside, it will correspond to how long it takes for you to truly trust even what comes from the inside. Do not give up, practice assuring your inner-Self that you do want to know, and you diligently promise that you will respond with changes. Once you understand what is needed - alignment, cleansing, change of diet or ingestion of certain things, then work to do it. Admit that this is "for your highest good" and agree to follow through. The only limitations on your health, well being and longevity is what you put on yourself. You may even want to ask about how much sound, music or silence your inner-Self really wants. What kind of atmosphere do you work in, live in or go and do in your free time? Do an emotional "sound check," and see what kind of reaction you get regarding all of these choices. I mute out all commercials on TV and generally listen more to CDs than radio - except in the car, because of the redundant commercials. I also like my quiet in the morning, so never listen-watch any morning magazine-talk shows. Because speaking and interacting with a lot people is a major part of my life, I like to limit as much of the sounds or noise that I do have control of, on my own time. I like to choose my conversations.

If the whole sound/listening process is more from your Past, an emotional or psychological problem, then go back to basic steps. Start letting go through deep breathing to find the connection to your pain. Often, it is your family dynamics. Perhaps you were not allowed to speak, or no one listened to you. Families with a lot of yelling can leave you affected many different ways. Once you have found it, then follow - Acknowledge - Acceptance - Appreciation - Gratitude - Forgiveness - Positiveness - Unconditional Love - Joyfulness - Peacefulness - Worthiness - Wholeness. Going through each of the basic steps seals in where the needed positive change is.

Remember to replace the negative thought with a positive, so you don't have a void that you can fall into again. Always be sure to 'Thank' your body for speaking to you and keeping you informed of what errors or situations may be cropping up. If you find that this is Karma related, Self-knowledge and forgiveness usually reduces it. Know you are responsible for every event you attract that happens in your life, through the choices you make daily. Never rationalize to yourself or others. It's ALL your choice, whether you accept it or not.

Any pain or illness can be avoided by listening and having an awareness of what is happening to your body, mind and soul. Visualize and affirm your perfection in all areas, cleansing yourself, your DNA and cells that contain the memories of all of your Past life negatives. Your body may then feel strong enough to take on opening-up that Pandora's Box. So, while you may not have a clear memory of some pain or problem, relating to what you heard or were told, your body does. Deep breathe and it will be revealed to you, or it may even come in a dream, so it can be released and healed for you to move on more whole and harmonious. I've had some amazing, very, real dreams regarding my past lives that have been scary, as well quite fascinating.

There are Archangels who are messengers of Father/Mother God and the Universe, who are here and available to assist you when you ask. How you listen, affects how you speak, but most importantly, what and how you say it. Source can help you develop whatever areas you feel you need work on, whether its your power, intuition, creativity or nurturing of others. Do not allow yourself to repeat a cycle from your Past to others. There is a love-force which ignites from the attitude of gratitude, that comes from and focuses on your highest good. You can learn to solve a problem from a higher level with the assistance. Breathe in the Light and out the Love to others. It all comes from having a purpose and basically living your new found truth. You are Source-Energy in physical bodies, as you develop your higher intuitive sense by listening and being open to have information communicated - Divine Will and Power.

Do NOT listen to negative people - even family who are telling you ". . . no, for your own good, because they 'love' you." Listen to your inside answers, which come as thoughts, feelings, or visions because they contain helpful-nuggets of healing truth. There is no point in arguing with those people, rather center yourself in that higher part of you that sees the bigger picture, to maintain a sense of integrity with yourself. While you collect further information, look for clues in your surroundings, listening to the perspective of others and using empathy. You then decide what actions - words you will use to best honor your emotions, staying on course for who you want to be, while moving through your life-purpose with your integrity in tact.

**Exercise II:** You need to think about Mindfulness, being Fully-Present from minute to minute, allowing every thought, word, and deed that proceeds from you to be positive, or erase it. Ask for Divine Assistance on this, as it takes Awareness and practice to learn, as every emotion that builds within you, keeps you in Your Truth about Who You Are. Take the moment you need to stop and breathe, as you catch yourself and ask, "Is this what I choose to think?" You do this by listening to each word, *as you are speaking it,* and asking yourself, "Is this what I choose to say?" Once you have learned how to have a running dialogue with your Higher-Self, regarding the whys and wherefores of your choices of what to think, say and do - trust will be built. You will know what you are creating and experiencing, so your responses are almost instantaneous. These empowerments are real accomplishments and will have you dancing along your Journey, instead of just walking. This amazing step enhances both your emotional and physical pleasures beyond belief, turning your past ordinary life into an extraordinary New Life experience.

Listening, it is so much more than you ever thought and so capable of totally changing your life forever. Your heart and soul are speaking to you - listen to them.

\* \* \* \* \* \*

Ask for your eyes to be opened. Thy Will Be Done - Trust the process.

When you bring Spirit fully into the body, it brings in confidence with it.

Your only obligation in any lifetime is to be true to yourself. Being true to anyone else or anything else is not only impossible, but the mark of a fake. Richard Bach

Keep your fears to yourself, but share your inspiration with others. Robert L. Stevenson

# Ask & Receive ~ Part #21

**Exercise:** As you become a more intrinsic part of the viable positive energy of the Universe, you may want to ask for the White Light to guide you in the best direction with Divine Right Order in your life for your Best and Highest good. There will then be no more hesitation or second guessing, as you learn to trust your intuition that has been fed by this positive energy. Any clearing of negative thoughts or ideas will be done when you ASK to have them removed - key word *Ask*. Your Guardian Angels have been there waiting for you to ask, to acknowledge them for their help, in whatever way you need on your path. It will take practice, but you will learn how to recognize their responses and suggestions. For me, their responses have been a very repetitive thought, which if ignored became more persistent-annoying.

**Caveat!** Freewill and choice are still always yours by Divine Right, your Guardians merely guide you and direct you.

As your inner child heals, surrounded by Love and Forgiveness of your Past Life/Lives, you will become a magical-child capable now of making Miracles happen in your life. You are developing into a Divine Consciousness, where you are now believing and accepting that anything, anything at all is possible. It is a gift that you have been given - actually it has been waiting for you to ask and accept all your Divine Consciousness, so you can put it all into action. As the Spirit within you shows you, your dreams can be manifested into reality. It is all from having actualized the positive energy and knowing you can do it. "Leap … and the net will appear!"

Even people who cannot see auras, will see that you are no longer the same person before your transition from the ego-controlled negative life. You walk lighter, as the light emanates from you, with your eyes almost glowing. Your speech will sound different, as your words are learning to be constantly-Positive, and you will have much to say about what you've learned. If asked, you say that it is available to others, if they choose to make the journey of getting Past their Past - of letting go of the conditioned-responses, and negative-controls so ego-driven. Many will respond, but they will be looking for the quick fix, the instant release, the immediate gratification. They may not want to go through all of their steps - as everyone has a different number to deal with, depending on how long their dogma has been so concreted over to protect it from any changes.

As soon as many people hit any bumps or even pain from the realizations of letting go of ego, they give up. Ego-protected is the easier road. No one ever said it would be easy, to look clearly at who we are and have been. Some may even return to try the process again later in this life, others will choose to wait until another lifetime. As always, it is their choice, as it was yours. Because you have now moved into a Divine Intelligence and Realization, you know that you can not rescue them, it is their journey. While you can guide or direct, it is not helpful to allow them to suck too much energy from you. It is as if an update of the old adage of giving a man a fish, rather than you teaching him how to fish. A teacher you can be, but the homework - personal work - is theirs to do, just as exercise or diet. One only can be guided, but they have to do the work themselves every step of the way.

Reassure yourself that many people, maybe even yourself, once you hit a certain point on the path, there is really no going back. You may slip, detour, backtrack or whatever you want to call it, when you need a break from processing, but you can never fully go back to where you were. It is as if, the Past has become this atavistic thing, as if you were thrown back to the Dark Ages, a cave or something. You may lapse and have to repeat steps, but the thought of actually going back is no longer acceptable within your being. Your soul has been given room to grow in your heart and it does not want to shrink back. The heart and mind's opening up cannot undo what it has seen, learned and experienced. As painful as getting Past your Past may be for some, they learn, and fully realize this *too* shall pass. and It will be a new, better day on the other side, with living in the moment.

You may feel bruised when a blockage is linked with your Past experiences you are holding onto - like fear of the unknown, or even fear of doing all that you can do. Awareness and acknowledgment has been a big step in resolving this, as well as deep breathing into where you feel the pain or blockage is. Do not hesitate to ask for help from Source, your Higher Self or Guardians. So, you will also need to take the time and go into that space where you can work with the idea of fear - fear of being more than you think you can be. This fear of results is not unusual, as most of us don't really fear failure - we fear success. No matter who told you what - you are a success.

**Exercise II:** If success has not been your usual way, then the fear says, "What do we do when we are successful, we've never been there before?" So it is also a fear of the unknown, or that bigger fear - *staying successful.* This is why you move in steps, for that sensation of small accomplishments, savor them, accept it and then you want more. Tell yourself, as you deep breathe that this is OK, and you will see this block will be released. Then take an opportunity to work with a bigger flow of positive energy into that space. Whether it's seeing it, feeling it, perceiving it; sometimes just moving your hands rapidly from your groin to your head and saying, "Open, open, open!!!" repeatedly will work on enhancing the flow of energy into all of your chakras. Doing these couple of different things, will usually resolve/release the fear.

Remember to check yourself for integrity in all situations - are you honestly wanting and accepting of all given to you? And, instruct others by the example of your life, not by idle words. Motive is good, to unveil your Past so that you can then move on past it. Think of old clothes that don't fit you any longer, clothes you no longer even want to wear, leave them behind - give yourself permission to release and let go. Consider that, just as you can put fresh clothes on your body, you can put fresh thoughts in your mind. You can try them on - then accept or discard them. As you exhale to be able to inhale, you can learn to release automatically. Your mind can move forward positively.

Divine Destiny is *your chosen dreams fulfilled*, whether you have been brave enough to dream them yet or not. Your reach should exceed your grasp, as you should always want more, especially from yourself. Know who you are today, not yesterday or even an hour ago. Now is where you are starting from. You are no longer the maid, you are Cinderella, the Princess, or no longer the frog before being-kissed into the Prince. It doesn't matter who you were, just who you are Now. Don't wallow in the Past, even for nostalgia. Be the Star of your own life that you were meant to be. Ask, it's yours! You deserve it. Believe!

\* \* \* \* \* \*

Never doubt that a small group of thoughtful, concerned citizens can change the world. Indeed it is the only thing that ever has. Margaret Mead

When you have a foundation you can get centered - Lifting life on purpose is the goal.

You can have brilliant ideas, but if you can't get them across, your ideas won't get you anywhere. Lee Iacocca

Example is not the main thing in influencing others, it is the only thing. Albert Schweitzer

It's Safe to Let Your Light Shine! A Gabriel Message - an affirmation to be used at any time, to bring you a sense of Grace or Protection.

Discovered what it is like, when you allowed yourself to reveal and express your most authentic-loving nature. You'll become happier than ever before.

# Vibrational Energy - Part #22

You are now ready for a science lesson. This was never my strong suit in college, so all I have learned has been from reading, lectures and questions to those who understand all of this a lot more than I do. Yet, as part of the process of growth, change and letting go, I've also learned through my own physical sense of the different levels of energy and vibrations going on in and through my body. I no longer feel physically comfortable around certain people or things. I also no longer subject myself to any kind of verbal-negatives, especially if it is directed at me-about me. Though I let go of a lot that doesn't directly affect me, that I would have argued with someone before, simply on fact or principle. At the same time, when necessary I will apologize when not needed, as it usually stops most people in their tracks. It is sometimes the quickest way to get them away from me, as it fulfills their ego. It is a realization I learned in Japan. Most people have no idea that they are being controlled *by an apology.*

I now have a much stronger sense of who I am and, how I want to be treated - respected by others. It didn't just happen one day, it was an unfolding of sensory-reactions that simply became stronger. It was more important for me to follow my physical-response, as to being around a situation or not. The big point came, when I began reacting to those positive or negative vibes and feelings - I either enjoyed staying, or I left with whatever excuse I needed. Sometimes people were not surprised, or tried to get me to stay, or didn't really believe I would walk out - I did, without looking back. More than once, I would call someone on what negative they had said, simply by asking them to clarify what they meant. If I was wrong, I admit it immediately, which will also take the steam-out of their ego or self-righteousness. I may add a profuse apology to top it off, so if they continue, they are then beating a dead-horse and look foolish. I was using my heart fed-words to counter derogatory comments without arguing, then removing myself from all of the negative energy. This was purely my Intuition.

**Exercise:** The key is listening and paying attention to your emotion-intuition, as it tells you either slightly or succinctly when you /yourself are in alignment with the New You. And, if vibrationally are connected to Source, as to fulfilling the real you. Accomplishment of all this is quite easy and simple: always, no matter what anyone else says or thinks of you, or whatever you might have done or not done, you love and appreciate yourself as you are, *unconditionally - warts and all*. It is a sensitivity that you become in-tune with through your practice of acknowledging your true emotions and feelings. Take your emotional-temperature - how do you feel generally, or about this or that? Are you off kilter? Are you feeling negative about something? Do you feel off-balance, not quite 100% about something?

All of these things have and can affect your clarity, vitality or sense of wellness - physically or mentally. Bottom line would be - Are you full of Joy, that which you are promised as a child of God/Source? If you answered "No, or not sure" to this important question, then you better get yourself adjusted *Bunkie!* You MUST balance what you believe with what you want, or your vibrational energy will not match, and your *desires will not happen*. You can pray, affirm, ask etc., but if *you don't truly believe you deserve it* - it ain't gonna happen!

Things are finally beginning to take distinct direction, with the assistance of your powerful, newly-arriving energies. These energies may sometimes feel intense and for good reason, to give you a good thrust forward to enable you into your rightful positions. You may have hesitations, or even may feel otherwise ready for where your path has taken you. While the energy may be strongly moving, you may still be getting acquainted with your New-Self, and at times feel as though chaos has ensued, as if not a lot is making sense anymore. Take those well-practiced deep breaths, then release any strong feelings of everything having gone haywire or out of control. You may become emotional, have your breath taken away or even feel like crying, but don't panic. Sometimes being in control, feeling confident and totally speaking up for yourself, are all things that most certainly will become second nature to you - be assured.

I assure you, it is always the negative people and situations that give you those uncomfortable feelings, when you are in their lower vibrating energies of your old, Past world. Bless them, let them go, for they do not yet realize your God/Source connection. They, themselves are not very aware of anything much around them outside their own routines. Lower vibrating energies can throw you off balance, out of sync, or can make you feel vulnerable, until you use your deep breaths to bring you back to who you now are. As you let go, you allow your alignment back to the higher vibrational energy, trusting your Source connection for your new, higher reality, that is now unfolding along your journey. It is a vibration of Love and Oneness, as we are All One.

Thank God and the Universe for all that has been given to you, as well as, all you want to have given. Part of this whole, higher level vibrational energy is that you have become comfortable in speaking and acting "as if" you already have the things you desire, and are grateful for them. Claiming your power and freedom from the Past is not easy - if it was everyone would be doing it, like popping a pill! You still may stray off into that old mind-field, as the confrontations with yourself and others can be explosive at times. Success on your path can be either a dream or a reality from the vision. Key word is *enough*. You have to want it enough to shift your energy, to remove the blocks, take action to continually move forward. It is a balancing act of your vibrational alignment, who you've become to keep it in-sync.

Try to visualize that your thoughts are electric and emotions are magnetic with a domino, rollover-connection: Your beliefs color your thoughts and experiences, which affect your emotions. This determines how you react to situations. Always with the Law of Attraction - Cause and Effect - what you put out is what you get back. Which is always reflecting your vibration, which is all about the way you feel. So, what you believe, think and feel, the Law brings to you. Therefore, if you don't like what you've been attracting, then change that thought or emotion within you. It is all about keeping that new vibrational energy positive.

It is the kind of simplicity that I want to shout from the rooftops: Changing how you feel changes everything. If you choose to think higher-thoughts and feel lighter-emotions, you will raise your vibration significantly. As a results you will not find yourself gravitating back into old repetitive Past behaviors and thoughts of "I'm not okay." Yes, I know, it is not truly that simple or easy. But with practice, your total entity - mind, body and soul - can become a harmonic symphony containing all of your vibrational energy frequencies, as notes played in a complex composition of every octave of every major and minor scale. There are energetic lines here that cross and spin rapture that expands you. It is also capable of revealing *that* within you, which does not harmonize.

Listen closely and you will hear the notes within your present consciousness that require tuning and refinement, or indeed some that require elimination.

Perhaps a new creative composition in order to rise into a higher vibration. Actively choose to raise your vibrational fields in relationship to all of your environments, but focus your real awareness to be creative. Trust what emerges from your true core-self. *Unlimit* yourself, release any negative ideas you may have about your purpose and remove any conditions or beliefs that would limit your ability to do this. Feel the vibrational energy going though you, around you and within you, as you move into the vibration of unconditional love, peace and joy. You are Source, we are all One.

\* \* \* \* \* \*

Go with the Flow. The Universe can't bring in love when you harbor fear.

As we express our gratitude, we must never forget that the highest appreciation is not to utter words, but to live by them. John F. Kennedy

# New Friendships - Part #23

**Exercise:** You are ready for positive friendships when you have enough Self-confidence and Self-esteem to only associate with people who are good for you and to you. You have had your fill of toxic associations and are ready to sort through your address book and email contacts to come up with a list of people that you know have your best interests at heart. While you may have done this before, it is sometimes an ongoing process, as you continually change and you realize others don't or won't - bless them and let them go. You may have already attracted several new people that may or may not stay, or be who you need in your changing life right now. With discernment, you will eliminate anyone - even related to you - who does not fulfill a supportive, understanding or accepting role, as you know it is for your highest good, as for ease and grace in all that you do. No one wants confrontation that will hurt people. Relationships *without expectations* are key; simply sharing and allowing the other person, as well as yourself, to just be who you are.

While being compassionate and wanting to help others, you need to be sure you reward and take care of yourself. Never slip over into stoicism, as you will empty yourself out and have nothing but a shell or facade left. There will be resentment if you say, "Look what I did for others, and they did nothing for me" - as if it really was you and not the Universe bestowing it all on you. We are all humans here, which means imperfect with foibles and other short-comings. It is that constant flow of positive give and receive for us, as well as others. It's like they say on the airplane's safety talk, "Put your oxygen mask on first, and then help children or others around you." If you're not able to breathe or live happy, how can you continue to help others around you? A Good Samaritan is a wonderful thing, if they know what they're doing - how many people trying to rescue a drowning person was pulled under themselves? Even doctors rescuing a stranger get sued by the ungrateful or those looking to benefit wrongly.

When you focus on your growing strengths - have that list of what they are that people notice, or that you want them to notice - and your insecurities will dissolve away, or at least be hardly noticeable. These are some of the things that you can practice on your own, so when you're ready to slowly present the New You out there, you will be ready. And, if you flub up or a 'friend' questions your words or actions - just remind them we all have the right to make a few mistakes as we change - "I am a work in progress and laugh." And, imperfections also remind people that you're human and vulnerable. This is where bringing new people into your life is such a good thing, as they will not question the New You with all of this focused, positive energy. Too often, the old baggage of your Past is what people judge you on, or want to keep to define you. The key to people accepting this New You, is that what you say and do must be genuine. You are only limited by your own dimensions, not those others want to put on you.

**Exercise II:** Don't say you like or are interested in something that you're not, just to please others. Simply say you're not familiar or you're just learning, so you won't come off as pretentious. But they will never forgive you or trust you if they feel you have been phony, or worse, lied to them. Sincerity is key in your listening and trusting your own inner voice. You don't have to be with an "in crowd" that isn't you, just because you're trying to change to a New You. Trying or experimenting is one thing, but meditate, deep breathe and listen to your intuition. Also, if you feel any negative vibes of jealousy or whatever, be sure to return it with focused love to flow through and surround the other person - the Golden Light and White Light. That person will either change in front of you, or walk away because they won't accept your positive energy of love. Their Choice! I would often use the Lights before going into difficult meetings and it would be so amazing the rapport that would rise up in the room, as the egos began to dissipate. Again it starts with loving yourself unconditionally, with "warts and all."

The moment a critical mass of your energy is aligned with Self-Esteem and Love, you will magnetize positive relationships into your life. As with anyone we love, we want them happy, so do those things for yourself to make you happy. That love always emits itself for others to see, feel and respond to. It is all about having Positive Belief Systems, so anything can happen and does. It has never ceased to amaze me how many people do look for the negative, rather than the positive - both are so very easy to find. I often wonder how much criticism they must have endured in their Past, to continue to do that to themselves. It hurts to see friends who are masochists. Many of us are lucky enough to find good teachers or mentors along the way, who are patient with us, yet never run to rescue if we fall. They sometimes do know when it is time for you to move on before you do, as clinging to coat-strings will never allow you to stand fully on your own. Learning that balance when so many things are so new, it is not easy to let go of the hand that guides you. Yet you need to remember the path is your choice, and whatever directions you take on it are part of the whole process of your learning.

Just as the overprotective parents never allow the child to fully bloom into their capabilities and talents, those friends who can only see you in one scenario are not healthy for your growth. One of the biggest lessons I learned was not how long someone is a friend, but how mutually supportive that friendship was. For me, a variety of friends with whom I do very different things has usually worked best. I don't expect all my friends to enjoy all the diverse things that I do, and some I definitely enjoy doing by myself. When I share some similar situations with them, it amazes me the wide-range of responses that I get in return. This is particularly interesting if I'm trying to make a challenging decision. On the other hand, there are some feelings or pursuits that I would not share, but with one or two of them. For me this works, but what is so funny is that in the past when I've brought many of these friends together, how surprised I was that they didn't like each other. We see in people what we want to see and sometimes what we need to have in them, as they resonate merely for us. They all color my world, and hopefully I do so for them also. I am accepting that when they move on, it is best for us both.

I have never overlooked those people who for an evening, or some other short time may have brought enjoyment, education or humbleness to me. More than once, I have been the muse to someone - surprised them by being more interesting to talk to than they expected. Those 'synchronicities' of people crossing our paths, can give us much more wisdom than we would have guessed - life's blessings/teachings.

\* \* \* \* \* \*

Whatever you choose, however many roads you travel, I hope that you choose not to be a lady. I hope you will find some way to break the rules and make a little trouble out there. And, I also hope that you will choose to make some of that trouble on behalf of women. Nora Ephron

Some leaders are born women. Susan B. Anthony

Nothing in this world can take the place of persistence. Talent will not; nothing is more common than unsuccessful people with talent. Genius will not; unrewarded genius is almost a proverb. Education will not; the world is full of educated derelicts. Persistence and determination alone are omnipotent. The slogan 'press on' has solved and always will solve the problems of the human race. Calvin Coolidge

# *Doubt & Guilt ~ Part #24*

Doubt and/or Guilt may have been part of what brought you to the path to begin with, that real call from within to transform your life. Indeed, until you learned to accept your own feelings, you may have been a scream of frustration, or arrived quietly, a feeling of confusion, questioning, or uncertainty no longer being satisfied with your life, just wanting changes. Most of us were born and raised in cultures that readily exuded guilt and doubt as a method to control you, then spread from one to another to keep you from aspiring to any height at all in your life. But changing doesn't immediately or automatically remove that lack of confidence and conviction, if you still believe or hesitate at all, that you have made wrong choices or decisions. Unless you have faith that you can be empowered or even powerful, and really capable of creating what you want, you will be at the mercy of other people, your Past or any other shortcomings *you think* or told you have.

Particularly, women were indoctrinated to feel guilty every time they couldn't please someone, then doubt that they ever would. You have also been encouraged to feel guilty when you did something for yourself, knowing others - somewhere in the world- were in need. It was insane. Challenge yourself to see how guilt/doubt infiltrated your daily consciousness is and polluted your experiences in life that could have been so much happier. You'll really be shocked how deeply those unkind-tentacles reached into your reality.

You need to start to systematically eliminate the 'guilt/doubt habit' from your consciousness. When you do, notice how Magically people will treat you more kindly. Because you'll believe you deserve more, abundance will flow with greater ease, as you feel more free and joyous. Doubt/Guilt are poisons to the soul. As you grow deeper into self-love, you'll be even stronger in your ability to be authentic. Just be yourself, perfect in your imperfection the way you are and even as you expand into greater awareness. This is a process, small, steps even taken hesitantly are better than none at all. As always, you are the only one who can change the situation by changing your thoughts, words, attitudes and beliefs of being able to transform yourself. Sometimes *getting sane* feels quite similar to being crazy, if you are constantly flowing-over with pain from doubting, and uncertainties of guilt from within your mind's vision.The ego tells you that you are flawed and therefore not really loved, as the ego wants only perfection. Thus, you feel deep down that you are rejected, or not fully accepted by others, or even God. With ego and chastising at the helm, your world is perceived through fear and feeling unprotected. You put up barriers which limit and restrict the love that is trying to come into you. Layers of these walls were put up in times of stress, or when love felt unfulfilled and painful. This could have been from childhood trauma regarding your parents - divorce or fighting - or your own budding romantic encounters all rejected. While you may have pushed the initial pain away for your own survival, your ego replayed the scenario to build up fear of continued threats of pain.

Doubt says you have no legs to stand on your own. So, you may have put on that mask of coping, or involved yourself in other detailed things to forget those memories thrown back at you. Then, whenever you might want to reach out again, or someone reaches out to you, the ego promises you survival, but only from behind a wall. Self-doubt can quickly turn into Self-Sabotage unless stopped.

When you negatively question yourself, it is Not different than being negative. To clarify, awareness is about erasing true ignorance of your real life. Either doubt or guilt is a distorted view of who you are, and influenced by fear. When they come in, it restricts your flow of positive energy. Besides eating away at your edges, they also separate weaker parts of you. Those things that you have insecurities about pop up. Before this all becomes permanent or walled up again, you have to grab that doubt or guilt by the horns and demand that it is not true or needed. Once you realize that all boundaries are created by the ego, and recognize that when they are let go of everything is Love, becoming flexible and fluid.

Go back to your core beliefs from God/Source, expressing the Truth about you being the perfect child of God/Source, really loved unconditionally. Then you can affirm to yourself: "I no longer have any ego-distorted images of me. I am loved just as I am. I am more than *Good Enough*. I am more than *Perfect Enough* with all of my imperfections. I am more than Smart Enough to be valued just as I AM and Whatever I do. I am Deeply Loved for who I AM."

**Exercise:** This is where you will have to express your true beliefs about yourself to other people, so it may sink in that it is a real belief for you as well. You need to take some risks, granted maybe a little controlled, as to speaking to people who have noted the changes in you. So besides making very strong declarations of your worth of yourself, talk to people about how your changes have helped you. You will be amazed at how energized you will feel. Deep breaths - Love in and Doubt out - Love in and Guilt out. Seek out those insecurities about you, then counter them with your God perfection image and worthiness. Don't forget to send healing Love and positive Light energy to any parts within you, that may not feel "worthy or good enough" to the outside world and yourself. Remove the "what ifs" and "buts" from your vocabulary.

There is only the 'here and now' as you fulfill your Divine Destiny - "I AM Worthy." Live your life as it is meant to be and that is without any Doubts or Guilts for it! As you visually remove whatever doubt-guilt you feel within, be sure to replace it with absolute and positive trust. Also, always conclude with your affirmation by asking: Father/Mother God, all the Powers of the Universe, Guardian Angels and Source, I'm asking for and receiving Divine Right Order in my life for my best and highest good and the highest good of All! So it is.

If you are really feeling that you are spinning out of control, you might consider the power of surrendering to Grace. If still your Doubting or Guilt brings you any jaw-tightening, or pain in various areas of your body, it can be squelched by the infinite power of Grace, received simply by surrendering to Divine Will. It takes courage, may be repeated, to break through any real log-jams for moving forward. Nothing puts you faster, into the positive energy-flow than letting go of your own controlling ego. By invoking the presence of Grace to surround you, protect you and guide you past it all. Then, there can be no doubt, guilt or fear, as Grace is represented by inner-positive energy powered by knowing you're loved. It is inner-freedom and unlimited energy for the accomplishment of whatever you feel a need to do.

Grace is like magic, in that you now question why you ever even had any doubt or guilt in loving yourself. As it grows within you by accumulation, it gives strength to those little steps that build up the inner energy, readying it for any big push of courage. The ego has lost its control of keeping you and God separate. Grace is the real Now-presence of God within you, as you are within God. Just remember, whoever told you that you were not good enough, they lied!

Appreciation is another important part to understand, as it is true love with the absence of doubt, guilt or fear, or self-denial, or hatred of others. Accepting that you are part of the whole All - we are One - gives you a foundation that would never allow doubt/guilt to come in, as there would be no reason for it. So also, Appreciation is for everything that has been given to you in life and as your life in the big picture of us All being One of Source. You can either cynically sit on the bench, or take authentic, creative-risks. The Universe has gifted us with creativity - no matter how small you think it is - and your gift *back* is to use it. Without doubt, you can reach the top of the mountain, and manage to not fall off that mountain, because of any fears.

You have no need to ask yourself if you are going to succeed and realize your desire without any guilt at last. When you no longer doubt yourself or have guilt, it is a given they're replaced with love and respect for yourself. And with that, you treat others with respect as well, for you choose not to join in the competition to prove who is better. You know, in the center of your secure and peaceful heart, that there is no one better or worse. Own your successes, as they are from gifts given, with Love, Grace and Appreciation to Source for all through you, as a member of the whole One. So, doubt/guilt are no longer a part of who you are.

\* \* \* \* \* \*

Success is in the effort, in what you learned and who you become.

I AM worthy of ALL that the Universe brings to me to fulfill my Divine Destiny.

Difficult things take a long time, impossible things a little longer.

Vision is the art of seeing what is invisible to others. Jonathan Swift

# *Side Affects ~ Part #25*

With time, work and practice of keeping yourself open to growth along your path, you may feel the changes in yourself regarding how sensitive you may have become to other people's actions or inactions. As you've taken in more and more positive energy and releasing - letting go of more negative energy in this progression of growth, this sensitivity guides you to selecting or choosing to be around others like yourself. They are not only like-minded people, but their energy levels and vibrational frequencies are resonating at similar pulses that you can definitely feel. This is often referred to as your growth movement from ordinary, third-dimensional frequencies to real awareness- fifth-dimensional. Where you are on the scale is not as important as how you feel interacting, associating or being involved with what is lower-vibrating energies, or people.

You may be told, as I have, that you've lost your sense of humor, or that you've become 'so serious' in how you look at things. I no longer find funny any humor that makes fun of anyone, not that I was a big fan of it prior. But now, I find myself deleting a lot of what my wide- variety of friends and acquaintances have emailed me, that has anything at all negative about its contents. I am well aware of the ugly-side of life, so I do not feel it is avoidance, as much as it is my realization that any energy that I feed to the negative, only makes it grow. Intolerant people are rampant enough in some media, and seats of government, unfortunately. I don't need any in my personal life. Especially, if that energy is anger oriented, I do not want to get upset or angry with those who sent it to me, in their own lack of awareness.

So, I wanted to bring it to your attention and awareness, that as your energy or vibrational frequency becomes higher, you may lose your tolerance for what was once acceptable behavior by your friends and associates. You may get upset with them several times before you actually realize just how much you and your positive energy have changed. You may chastise them for what is now to you completely unacceptable speech and/or behavior. Likewise you may chastise yourself, as you cannot believe that you ever tolerated the acceptance of this behavior in yourself, or the other person. You quickly need to stop yourself and grab hold of your reaction and remember it is you that has changed, not them. Also, you never, ever beat yourself up for who you were before. Remind yourself that it is always all about the journey and you are looking into your own eyes when you meet another along the way. Acceptance and tolerance of those we have known from our various pasts need to be loved, as they currently are.

This judgment of yourself or others, who may be in your Soul- Group, is a mistake. Those Soul-Group people may have been through many prior life times with you, but that doesn't mean they chose to take a similar journey of positive change, or be a Lightworker, that you may be aspiring to become. It was your sole path, you chose for your soul, the group didn't sign on for it, nor could they have, as it is/was your path. Granted some people from this Soul-Group or other ones, may have directed or guided you. But, it is always those people who are different from ourselves that we continually learn our lessons from to grow. You need to be grateful to these people, not judging or criticizing them. They may have done considerable work, contributed to situations on your behalf that you responded to, that helped move you to your new vibrational level.

They need your compassion and blessings that they may one day in this life or another, choose also to make changes for a positive life. Listen and observe more before you speak or react, as you are at a more precarious position at your higher vibrational level. You can now see people more in their fear, confusion, doubt or lack of love. Your compassion-understanding may be something that will help them get past their insecurities. So they may recapture their belief in their own source of power is within themselves, and not in their egos, or others who may control them. If you remember, you may have once been where they are and you were able to transform your energies to the positive side. Don't let disappointment of this realization upset you, everyone is on their own path, be happy that you can accept them as they truly are, no matter what their energetic vibration. Of course, if it is really uncomfortable and they make you feel out of sync with your energetic vibration, you may need to limit, or even remove yourself from them. It is part of the letting go process for transformation and your focus is first to your path, for joy, peace of mind and heart in creating your heaven on Earth.

Don't forget, if you have shared information regarding your growth changes and they have not attempted any steps on their own, when they reach out to you, they may not really wish to be saved by you. They may be ones that want to bring you back down with them, into the mess that you had prior lived, or existed in with them. There are many times as Lightworkers, that we reach out a hand to others, truly believing that they want to change, but they just want more help. Unfortunately, many of these people simply want to suck your positive energy, until you can no longer give it, though it is a basis of who you are. You will then find, that those who took your offered hand, had no intention to extend it to others around them. It is all for them, as their egos are too big and controlling of them. As long as you will listen and give to them, they tell you of their struggles, with all of the details in their rationalizations, (yes, but …) so you will continue to give and show them more and more compassion.

There is a safety-limit and while you may need to make that distinction on your own, you need to know what a disservice it is to continue to *rescue* someone. Rather than describe how they need to take responsibility, they need to at least take some small steps forward. There is a point where it is neither healthy for you or them, for you to continue to be their counselor or crutch. There are organizations and groups that have professional people whose job that is. You need to simply acknowledge that, while you may have extended a hand and some verbal support, they may not be ready to change, or adopt any steps or principles for their journey of change. These souls now have every opportunity to change that you had, and still they choose not to do what has been offered freely. Perhaps, they know that they will have to work hard at it and that is not for them. So many will return to keep taking from others until there is no one, or nothing left for them to take. Bless them and let them go, knowing that no one did your path for you, and no one can do it for them.

On the other hand, do not become so independent in your journey that you do not accept gifts that are offered to you. You know the joy that fills your heart when you give something to someone, do not keep another from receiving those same blessing by not accepting. Being a Lightworker means, that you graciously receive all that is given to you *freely* from others. Especially, if the person giving is not surrounded in abundance. Their act of kindness in giving to you, will give them the realization of positive flow in that the more they give, the more they will receive. Of course, it is important that they don't just give in the expectation of receiving. All giving must be done from the heart, with no strings attached or response expected. Your gifts received from them may also help to increase their feelings of positive worth. You need to create a balance in your life, regarding your own giving of yourself and receiving of what others have offered. These lessons are endless of what you shall find, as you journey along your path of Self-discovery and growth.

**Exercise:** Even if you feel that you are at a higher vibrational level, if you are having an 'off' day or being bombarded by negative people, you become victim to old negative thoughts that stuck in your mind, like old, soap residue on a bathtub. The best way to clean them out is by writing them down and then to honestly question yourself as to where they came from. Once you understand their origin, you can comprehend why now they have popped up, or what helped them stay hidden so long.

Do your deep breathing exercises of Love-in and Fear-out, several times until you feel that relief sensation of release. Now, verbal command that, "All Past negative thoughts are to go from your mind, they are released to the ether, as you no longer have need of them for any lessons. Thank you for whatever lessons you brought me, but I have learned those lessons, so you are released. I forgive you for any and all pain, fear or problems that you brought to me. Thank you for your work, and I release you with love and blessings." Now, just to make sure, visualize a soapy, sudsy cleaning brush running through your mind and cleaning out little black spots, like mold to represent these negative thoughts. If you feel they persists, then put a name representing the thought on each one and scrub it until it dissolves. No matter how long you have been on your path, we all still have little pebbles that we trip over, so don't judge or criticize yourself as if you did wrong. We do not trip over the mountains we climb, we trip over the pebbles getting there. Remember, it is never about perfection, it about positive growth from lessons learned.

* * * * * *

Skeptics never fail, because they're afraid to try. Winners Risk!

Life is a Game - Participate, don't just sit in the grandstand!

Unless you choose to do great things with it, it makes no difference how much you are rewarded, or how much power you have. Oprah Winfrey

# *Ego~Drama ~ Part #26*

You can learn to experience and process your sad emotions for the rich information that they teach you, then once you have released them, the learning begins. You need to do whatever is healthiest for you to do - scream or pound into a pillow, let yourself cry. Depending on what the situation is, I give myself anywhere from 24 - 72 hours to totally wallow in my disappointment, sadness, or feeling of failure. While I may exploit comfort food, I do try to not indulge in liquor, unless I'm home alone and best if only one bottle of wine in the house. Friends at this time may be useless, as you're not going to believe or even listen to their sympathy-empathy, yet you may want to inform them, so they understand your solitude need or curt responses. Some things you truly do need to process on your own, so you can be within your own truth, as to *how you contributed to it.* This reaction can be a telling truth as to how far you have come on your journey, in that who or what you may want to blame for what has happened to you. Breathe deeply repeatedly, to be sure that you have released all of those pent-up emotions. Rid yourself thoroughly of any and all vile resentments, rationalizations, angers or fears.

If you resist this experience by pushing it down or burying it, sooner or later it will manifest in your outside-world affecting your health, energy, emotional feelings or ability to focus/think. If you hold it, it is a poison that can not be avoided, as it is contracting your heart, tightening it like a fearful, defensive fist shaking at the world. With repeated situations, it cannot open to give or receive love. The ego-drama, or emotional-explosions are like mini-volcanoes erupting when you least expect, from the fear and pain that can no longer be at all contained. When this happens, remind yourself that your feelings are like mini-earthquakes, i.e. heart attacks, that keep the Big One from happening. They are there to inform you, that it is time to identify these buried emotions and breathe some true acknowledgment and cleansing into them.

There is a part of some people who love the drama of it all, the living on the edge and almost losing everything, simply for the open attention, or expecting to be rescued. They are very Self-sabotaging or worse, Self-destructive-masochists. It is a cheap thrill that has become addictive and as with most addicts, based on excuses - rationalizations, so not to move forward. This avoidance is an incredible waste of time and energy. Choose to change and say: "I am assuming responsibility for my life now!" The ego can actually create drama, or take a simple situation and blow it out of proportion, to regain some of its control over your energy. Sometimes this can be rather bizarre, but as your positive energy keeps you moving forward, with the higher vibrations around you, the ego is desperate for its existence in your life. Yes, like all energy it has "life" so to speak, and ego is a master of disguise - fear, anger, manipulation, etc.

Things are not just put on you - they are choices you have made. Once you accept and take the responsibility for those choices you have made in the Past, then you can make new choices to change your life. It is, and always has been, your choice in how your life is right now. You have been making numerous excuses and avoiding the responsibility for your life. So, your work before you is to break-free of the perception that anything outside of you can affect you in any way at all. You need to work at living each moment accepting this. The ego-mind traps you back into the belief, that things outside of yourself can bring you good or bring you harm. The truth is they are nothing but consciousness - your consciousness, created by you - good or harm, your choice.

**Exercise:** Fear is sometimes carried from one lifetime to another, waiting for you to be ready to shine the releasing light on your perceived failures of the Past. With your focused-breathing into them, these fears can be healed and released. If they are also of some perceived losses or betrayals, forgiveness of both yourself or others may be involved. Even if you do not remember the acts or situation, they need to be blessed, or the lesson forgiven to move on. This Karma can make you feel powerless because of the emotions attached to it. The fear gets your attention so that you will heal it, so it can be released. Surround yourself with the Golden Light of Divine Healing, Forgiveness and Unconditional Love. Now, take a deep breath and detach from all of your Fear! Love -in and Fear-out. Deep breathe and send the Love - Light to where it hurts most. These are steps that need to be repeated as often as necessary!

My Divine Destiny is infinitely more powerful than disease, failure, dysfunctional relationships, hatred, greed, corruption, war or any other human-created maladies appearing on the screen of Life! When you stay Focused on the Light Energy from God and the our Universe, nothing can stop you. Never give up! No matter who tells you that you can't do something. When you truly believe with Love-Light energy, that Intent creates the reality when you hold your thought for seven or more seconds. "Father/Mother God, all the Powers of the Universe, Source and all of my Guardian Angels … I AM asking for Divine Assistance, so that the Success of my Divine Destiny is Assured Now, for my Best and Highest good, and the Highest good of All! So it is. Thank you, Thank you, Thank you."

It is not that all of your dreams must come true, but who would you be without them. Take your successes in life no matter how large or small - if you truly desired it and got it - that is Success! Always Appreciating the small things brings you more. It is all about the joy it brings to you! The joy is yours, it does not have to make any one else joyful and no one can deny your right to be joyful. If a thing or person brings you joy, that is all that matters. You decide and don't let anyone, their ideas or rules tell you, or keep you from your choice of joy! You do not need approval from the outside, as to what makes you happy or gives you joy. Showing someone they are lovable, helps make them be more open to loving themselves - the first big step on their journey.

Recognizing and handling ego-drama shows your growth- awareness, especially if it was a habit that you previously practiced. Drama people are sometimes influenced by others vying for attention when their insecurities surface. Just like children who can't get some positive attention, they go for the negative by doing something that they know will result in punishment. No matter how sabotaging or masochistic, it gave them the sorely-needed attention that their ego was dying to have. So, to avoid being pulled into creating drama or acting it out, you might not want to be surrounded by other people's drama. As the new positive energies rush through your body, visualize them scraping off, ridding you of any accumulated muck from Past drama, see it literally flowing-out from you. When you feel afraid, ashamed, angry, etc. visualize the Golden Light surrounding you and feeling protected, loved and filled with joy. Feel it within and let it flow-through you from head to toe, giving you all of the positive attention and love that you could possibly need.

\* \* \* \* \* \*

There are no Black & White rules, there are only Choices. Make the right ones!

There is no 'try,' there is only 'do.' Yoda, *Star Wars*

The older I get the less I listen to what people say and the more I look at what they do. Andrew Carnegie

Channel emotions and energy into the pursuit of your goal.

# *LOVE ~ Energy ~ Part #27*

Nothing, absolutely Nothing is more powerful than the Energy of Love. It is the ultimate blessing of the journey to rediscovering who you are and were always meant to be. Love can overcome anything, especially in believing in Unconditional Love that you learn to have for yourself, because it is given to you abundantly, endlessly from God/Source. It is a power that creates absolute bliss in who you are, and what you do. Creating a new reality with every step you take, lets negatives flow through your brain, and not be affected by any of them. Choose only the positive things and people to hold on to, as Love is the base energy of All positive Light Energy.

Do Not get attached to any negative relationships, as far as changing or rescuing them. Be connected to the positive person and yourself. To have unconditional love is to have no expectations. To love as if, there is no tomorrow is the bravest, yet wisest thing anyone can do. When you love yourself, you can release all attachments to another when they are not of the same positive love-energy and thus negative for you. This is not about perfection, but about acceptance of yourself and who you are. If you give yourself up, then you let others control you. There is no reason to have others control you - God has given you Freewill - now give it to yourself!

When you fuse love into your body and soul, you accept who you are in choosing life as it is, no longer needing to test it or push it to the limits to feel alive. As you accept your life, it flows with more than enough energy and vibration, so there is no need to live on the edge to feel fulfilled. Acceptance of Self is a wonderful part of love. Being present in every moment of your life by freely lifting it up, not analyzing or questioning it as it is. Just live and love every moment in the present. Rise above the fray, as other people make their choices in the course of their lives. Those filled with love choose to not be a sad victim within it or from it. Love removes self-judgment and criticism.

The world and everyone in it reacts to each other, if you are putting out love that makes it a better place. What footprints are you leaving behind? If you don't have to prove anything to any one, think how freeing it would be. Do not give your power to the Past over you. It doesn't matter who or what you were yesterday, it is now, only the present that counts. Be free each day. This is it - Stillness. Knowing presence - awareness tells you, you do not need to suffer when you are filled with love. Evolvement usually comes from no longer suffering from what your thoughts created. Nothing you ever did was a sin - no such thing exists any more. You made mistakes and hopefully learned your lessons from them - period, end of discussion.

A new version on an old adage: "It is better to have loved and lost, than to never have loved at all." How long a great relationship lasts is not important, the intensity or joy you receive from it, as long as it is mutual, is what is important. Just as is said to let go of someone or something that is not working, is for your best and highest good. So too, a relationship that you felt you brought into creation that has now served its purpose. Do not judge the ending of a relationship, as any failure, but basically having fulfilled your time together. Think of it simply as an experience - some good, some bad - that you can recall as learned-from for your growth experience. With anything in your life, seize it and passionately enjoy what is good for you for however long, and then let it go, so someone or something new can flow into your life. Don't compare yourself, or feel a lack of success to others who boast long-term this or that. Just because something lasted a long time doesn't mean it was a wonderful or joyous experience most of the time. "Twenty minutes of wonderful is still better than twenty years of ordinary." What works for some doesn't work for others.

Don't be addicted to sympathy - there is always someone out there with a sadder, sappier story they are stuck in. Get over yourself and searching for sympathy. Move on, pretend to be happy until you are. When you lose or question your trust or faith, it is all about ego wanting control, which once again is fear. When you go beyond any reasons, you discern *a truth* with your heart and intuitive knowing. It takes place in the moments when you let go and simply allow yourself to see what was there all along. How quickly any person evolves is directly related to the level of willingness to change; new openness to seeing things differently, or questioning one's self. Self-love is Key.

**Exercise:** Again: Whether you laugh, cry, scream or shout, it is the awareness that is the first step, for it tells you either that you love who you are, or you definitely need to change. If it is change that you want, then you next need to truly learn how to laugh out loud and love yourself. It is that Love-Energy that will be the foundation that will get you on the path and return you to it, no matter what detours take you off it. Affirmations to help: "I am One, and complete, and whole. I am that I am. I am completely aligned to All that is. I am truth, integrity and Oneness. I am love and peace, and clarity; I am courage, knowing I am fully aligned in my soul's deepest intuition. I am healing and getting over the rejection of those who could not now accept my passion for what I believe in. I am allowing all abundance to come to me with great appreciation. Thank you God/Source for all You have brought to me. It is amazing how surrounded I am by Love. I am in true, Vibrational alignment of who I have become."

**Exercise II:** Appreciation is true love-energy - it is absence of doubt, guilt or fear, or Self-denial - or hatred of others. In-sync of the whole - looking at All through eyes of Source - State of Godliness - Bliss - Hope. Make a running list of all positive things in your life, add to it once a day or at least once a week. Look for things to love and appreciate in your life as you are open, willing and allowing, for more that Source wants to bring to you, with great Love and Appreciation.

When your love-energy is strong you can reach out and build bridges of love, as even insignificant moments of compassion still will have an affect on the world. It is reflective of who you are with you so loving yourself just as you are, in a deep embrace that has no limits - boundaries, no conditions, no beginning and no end. And, this deep love for yourself and valuing of yourself is the foundation for every thing in your life. When you love and respect yourself deeply, you treat others with respect as well, for you choose not to join in their competition to show who is better. You know, in the center of your secure and peaceful heart, that there is no one better or worse. And, that all of this striving for recognition/reward is simply a display of ego Self-doubt. You no longer define your life by how you have been hurt, instead you define yourself by how you have grown.

Love truly conquers all, as it is the answer in every situation. Where you act out of love and integrity, then those true energies of love open up and flow through your heart, to glow and share with all others you meet on your path. Now, you are stronger, wiser, much clearer with more understanding. Allow these energies to flow through and release any shame, hurt or fears that lie behind human suffering. Let the love flow, letting go, for there is nothing more beautiful on this Earth than to let go Love. Just let go, just feel what it's like to be free, as with this Love-

Energy you are free. Embrace and feel the freedom of what your next action is to be. Truly feel what you really want to do with your life and then do it. Just do it from love for yourself.

\* \* \* \* \* \*

You can give without loving, but you cannot love without giving. Seneca

Appreciation is true love, of being yourself with the absence of doubt or fear, or self-denial - or hatred of others.

Disappointment to a noble soul is what cold water is to burning metal; it strengthens, tempers, intensifies, but never destroys. Eliza Tabor

Argue for your limitations, and they are yours. Richard Bach

# *Talk About It - Part #28*

We all have our stories. By that I mean, either those we were told about ourselves when really young, or those we told regarding ourselves from times that we did remember. How much, or even if any of these stories may be true or not, we may rarely question ourselves, unless they are challenged. Then one day a small voice in a far corner of your mind asks: "How long are you going to keep telling that old story? You know very little of it is true any more." Kind of like a fish tale that has become part of your fabric, your make-up of who you *are,* but now, more like who you *were.*

Part of the journey is letting go of all the rationalizations, or facade or dare-say - lies about how you *managed* to become who you are, despite all those things you overcame - or did you? The problem with stories is that the more they are told, the more *real* they become to you, your ego and definitely your subconscious. How could you possibly accomplish nearly what you could have, when you had so much to work through, or had going against you? What you need to ask is, "Are you ready to let go of that crutch, and stand on your own two feet with responsibility for your Past?"

Some pain from the Past - a loss, mistake/missteps or just whatever, does need to be talked about - no matter how painful. Though inappropriate rehashing can not only make old pain very new, but can also turn into a competition or one-up man-ship, as to who had the worst childhood. If it is your truth, it is only healthy when dealt in truth. As I've said before, no one was raised in Disneyland, but that doesn't mean that you are forever stuck on Fantasy Island. If you're not ready to talk - write about it. There is something very cathartic of the release that the words onto paper can do - almost like automatic writing in its honesty. I've been teaching Memoir Writing for almost ten years, it changes people like they never expected. Honesty can do that, but written down makes it even more powerful and good.

Releasing the pain is a necessary step along the path, otherwise it turns into scar-tissue that will only get worse over time and 'infect' other stuff or people connected to it, as well as you. Separate the 'chaff from the wheat,' so the process will be effective and get it out of you one way or another. The fabrications may have been to cover up the severity of the pain. Either way, you don't have to suffer with it all pushed down inside, eating you up, creating disease or wasting energy for the avoidance. Emotions have nothing to do with intellect or talent, if they did I wouldn't be writing this! For most of us, painful emotions take us right back to that child who made mistakes, or wasn't good enough to some significant adult.

I had a friend who had been molested by her father in her preteens. We were in our twenties before she ever told me, though we had known each other since kindergarten. When I tried to get her to talk about it, she insisted that she had put it all in an iron-clad, steel layered box, concreted over and it would never, ever be opened. She then told me she wanted me to forget what she had said and never bring it up again. She was fierce in her words and her stern face was actually scary, I will never forget it. She never saw that her scars were still festering, as they prevented her from having or choosing the right men, relationships or marriages. While she never drank, because her father had, she was a true, raving shopaholic, as with the driving-need to collect things, as her sole possession. Her obsessiveness with it eventually destroyed not only her health, financial stability, but also her relationship with friends, as well her children. I won't even go into the whole non-forgiveness thing she refused.

We all know people who continue to stuff the dirt under the lumpy rug, rather than take it out to deal with forgiving themselves or any other person involved. Just as anger is a secondary emotion - no one simply just gets angry - there is something that caused it, even when that something has been buried for twenty-plus years. So we could say that anger is also a tremendous waste of time and effort, or energy. How many people do you know that continually bring up things that happened from their Past over and over again - the old 'beating a dead horse syndrome?' They don't really do anything about it, they just talk about it, sometimes it's set off by a similar situation, or totally out of the blue. It may all be a 'woe is me' or 'poor me' syndrome, or just the need for attention. I've often wondered if their attachment to the negative was part of them not liking themselves, or basic to their excuse for not being their best. Or unfortunately, them feeling that they did not deserve to have any, or a lot of good, positive things in their lives - sad, very, very sad.

Every time I overheard my parents having an argument, if it was serious enough, my mother would dredge up the same old things that my father had done at least twenty years before. Do we want to be around these people? - No! Would it help if we said to them to let it go? Probably not. These kinds of ego-driven patterns are what some people think work for them. To others, they may feel some satisfaction of trumping the other person. But obviously there was no happiness, joy, or even love involved. So these people stay in their ruts and we move on. I can't imagine, as being in the space of who I have now become, that I would remain more than a few minutes, even on the sidelines of such a negative confrontation. To me, it would be a very tremendous lack of respect for myself to do so. Those people who say that they like a good argument, are usually looking to show how smart they are, or simply that they can be louder, if not as clever. It is pure insecurity on their part.

I used to believe I was being helpful by correcting people - in whatever context of their mistaken statement. I don't do that anymore, unless it's something that would send them off in the wrong direction or trouble. Confrontation is no longer part of what I want in my life, or the exhaustion of energy on it. I constantly button my lips, reminding myself that everything is a choice, and while I may have concern for friends that I feel are doing what is negative, or not in their best good, I may state something once, and then remain silent - hopefully.

Many people are quite content in their ignorance and really don't want your opinion, even if their facts are entirely wrong. We truly all do see things with different eyes and hear with different ears. How often I've been amazed when watching the same movie, lecture or whatever and others with me came away with very, varying results, feelings or ideas. While there is no way to convince some people, even with the facts clearly stated in black and white, as they say.

**Exercise:** With and within yourself you need to acknowledge what of your stories are truthful, or only repeated to heal from them. Sometimes it is good to make those lists again - who inspired you? Who criticized you - blew you off? Do Not settle for less than you are. What others think negatively of you is *not your concern* any more. The process of life unfolds one step at a time - try to make as many steps as possible - happy steps, even joyous. You can choose to make the process a happy journey, even thinking of the bumps as a roller coaster that gave you a good learning experience, if not a happy one. Everyone loves a good story, just make it funny or show your sense of humor in how you learned from it.

\* \* \* \* \* \*

As *A Course in Miracles* says, "Mistakes require correction, not punishment." Seneca

The Light of God is infinitely more powerful than any errors we may have created.

A solved problem looks trivial when moments before it seemed insurmountable.

Channel emotions and energy into the pursuit of your goal.

# *Perceptions ~ Part #29*

Be a Lightworker and Guide of new consciousness. Feelings are not to be confused with emotions. A feeling is sensory awareness, and not always definable or measurable. Not only do they vary from person to person, but within yourself they vary from extremes, as to where you are - mentally and physically - and, of course, emotionally. The senses, or your sensory awareness, can be opened up or closed down rather quickly, depending on your emotions. These feelings can be used both ways to either heal yourself or make you sick - truly your choice, though heavily influenced by the situation you are in. Moving your mental control to the side, you can allow your intuition or your feelings, to lead and guide you in the right direction and choices. Think about it. And then, wake up every day with anticipation of the positive, to create your own positive reality. It truly is what you make it out to be, as you are the co-creator of Your life.

Your personal experience is what colors your feelings and interpretations of *all* that comes into your life. Even siblings or a twin, would have had a different 'personal' experience or perspective of their life. It would be like watching the same *life*-play performed by a different set of actors. While you know the basic premise, one group is definitely different from another, as in their interpretation. How often do you speak of your childhood or family scenario? Can you look at them from a more forgiving/loving perspective, now that you have grown and changed so much?

Understand that perception is not a fact or reality. It is a thought, belief, intuition or interpretation from your own personal perspective. This is one reason why "eye witnesses" are so often wrong or contradictory of each other, even when viewing the situation from the exact same spot. Can anyone really look at an action-scenario especially a crime scene and *not* have judgmental - prejudicial filters adjust what they have seen? Subconscious or unconscious, these life-restrictors have been there and proven time after time in psychological research experiments with average people.

**Exercise:** Think of some basic key words and your interpretation of them related to people in your Past, Present and well known people of varying backgrounds: Peace, Judgmental, Strict, Love, Grace, Control, Power, Critical, Honest, Wisdom, Weak, Joy, Happiness, Strong, Reliable, etc. Now put those same words out to your friends for an interesting-honest discussion with open-acceptance of each other's views of them related to those famous or mutually known people (remember acceptance is not agreement). Think what these words meant to you some time in your Past.

Did you even ever think about their meaning before, or when you were throwing them out as descriptions of people - even people you never personally met? Choose some other words that evoke strong feelings - examine them, talk about them. Now, take it a few steps further by adding emotional tag-lines such as Jealousy, Fear, Pain, Anger, Insecurity, or others that would put the person doing the judging in a particular frame of mind or emotional state. Get to know your feelings and how they've changed - hopefully for the better. Most people, especially parents, do the best they can with the tools/understanding that they have/know. How much education did they have in the field of parenting, or even psychology?

How Flexible Are you? How Adaptable are you? Your perception is what your beliefs - feelings and emotions - make of any situation you may be in out of choice, or default by some person or group. Everything about your life you create, whether by planning or spur of the moment. Any actions, any day is as you perceive it to become. You have had many daily actions that were similar, yet some you perceived positive and others negative. Since your perception comes from your thoughts and creates your actions - be careful what you think! Heard that one before?!? Ask for what you want as you go to sleep and then listen for answers in your dreams, or as your morning unfolds, see what messages you receive.

Shortly after finishing Graduate classes - Bilingual/Bicultural Studies with a concentration on Business Management - I had applied to jobs in China, South Korea and Japan. Many things considered, I accepted the position in Japan and they wanted me to come as soon as possible. There was much confusion in what needed to be done, and most unrecognized on my part was my husband at the time being totally pissed, because he had expected an overseas job offer *before me*. We had agreed that whomever got a job first, the other would go with as soon as able. I had also gotten an ESL (English as a Second Language) Certificate, so if his engineering job came, I would have no problem working wherever he was. My knowledge of Japan was very limited to what I had learned from one of my professors, who had taught there years before, but little else than general media exposure. With Japan's Bubble economy burgeoning them onto the world market as the biggest player, it was a frenzied place. I had never heard of, nor knew where the city of Nagoya was until I found it in a world atlas.

Many delays in transportation, communication and information, my frustrations along with jet-lag and lack of sleep lead me to a burst of tears when we finally talked on the phone. My husband immediately insisted that I come home, as he had rarely heard me cry or break down in any way. We were almost broke, as grad school had been expensive and I had to cut back on my work to do well. I had also only bought a fixed, cheap round trip ticket, so I would have to wait at least until that time. I had perceived something almost smug in his demand for my return, which gave a strength in my backbone I had not felt in a long time - usually before in dealing with my mother. I stayed seven years and was enormously successful - my husband could only hack a little over two years, and was shocked when I chose Japan over him. My constant use of intuitive perception, rather than judgmental feelings about a people that I had much to learn about, was the foundation of my success in Japan. It was the most pivotal experience in my life and the benchmark for my growth in who I was to become. You may not be aware of when perception is fully working, but its *affect* to your life can be unmeasurable - I know.

The more open you are, the more awareness you may have regarding things that you perceived in a different way, at another time - recently or long ago Past. With expanded information, your new perception of something or someone may drastically change. Think of how many times someone's misperception caused problems, or even danger for someone. It may be a moment of truth where your new perception is proven totally wrong. Think about how you perceive the world and how much truth you put into that on your unproven facts. So life is what you make it, as it all comes from your perception - right or wrong, positive or negative. The more open you are to information, the more options to have a more, real understanding of it all. How attached are you to your perception - that is the question? Hopefully, it is wisdom that comes from those learned experiences and further knowledge, not just hearsay or assumptions from others speculating.

I can easily count the many times I did not listen to my intuition, but followed the perception of others and the mistakes that happened. I have now learned that true intuition comes from my Higher Self - Source, whereas perception can be influenced by the ego and other outside negative forces, including fear. Be aware.

\* \* \* \* \* \*

I would rather regret the things I have done than the things I have not. Lucille Ball

Life shrinks or expands in proportion to one's courage. Anais Nin

The right man-*woman* is the one who seizes the moment. Johann Wolfgang von Goethe

Good judgment comes from experience; Experience comes from bad judgment.

# *Worthiness ~ Part #30*

God and the Universe know you are capable of creating great things, no matter what happened in your Past. Let your Past go and move on to doing and being all those things you are more than worthy of doing and being. So, do not base your sense of worthiness on what-ever someone said or told you in the Past. You live in the present, and your true worthiness is today and as it brings tomorrow. Other people's opinions or statements do Not make you who you are or will be - only you can do that. As said before, God and the Universe have long ago forgiven whatever you knowingly or unknowingly did in your Past. If you have any sense of unworthiness, obviously you still have not forgiven yourself. Remember the truth is of today and that truth is, you are worthy of all that the Universe wants to give you, so just be open to accept those gifts.

**Exercise:** People respect those who admit their mistakes and go on to do better things. You are worthy, so don't ask Why - you are God's child - loved unconditionally, warts from the Past and all. Take as many deep breaths as possible, or as needed to forgive yourself, then say clearly: "I AM worthy of all that God/Source and the Universe gives me. I am open and ready to fulfill my Divine Destiny for my best and highest good." You are never given only one chance in life for anything. The Universe has abundance in all things, including opportunities. As you grow and change, so do your interests, passions and talents. The Universe is constantly offering choices. No matter who put that wet blanket over your feelings of Self-worth in the past, you can take it off - Now.

How do you feel? 'OK' is a very ambiguous word. It is acceptable for passing conversation, but not what you should say to yourself, or write in your journal. Honesty with yourself, or a friend who sincerely cares, is so very important. Think about how much you use the word OK - Are you? Is it? While placating is sometimes necessary, denial of your feelings is Not OK. Your sense or feeling of worth starts and ends with you, not with others, no matter what their status. How can you Not be worthy when you have God within you, part of you, loving you? You do not need to be famous, a hero, or rich beyond compare to be worthy. Your smile to a child, a "Thank you" to someone assisting you, or any random kind gesture makes you more than a worthy person. How we interact and treat others speaks much more about us than our good looks, nice clothes or expensive material possessions. It is always who you are on the inside, yet those are the things that many people looking for the obvious-outside don't see.

Your worthiness is also defined by how well you accept and give compliments. If you discount or deny compliments, no matter how large or small, you are also denying your worthiness of it to be acknowledged. Likewise, if you have questions of your own Self-worth, you may hesitate to give compliments to others. Patronizing or false praise is not honest and often disdained, but true recognition of another's action or dress, simply lets them know that they are noticed, recognized and appreciated. Getting those good positive vibes as well praise from the outside, boosts anyone's feelings. When a good leader or boss gives honest praise and appreciation, the employee is not only willing to work harder, but has more loyalty to do well, than any large paycheck can replace. Within a family, these same principles work as everyone wants to know that their participation, no matter how small is recognized. With children, time spent with them is more valuable than money spent on them. Many parents learn too late that children want a part of you, not just the things you can give them. It truly does make them feel worthy of being your child.

As you move along your growth path, you are being realigned, not just in your general thinking, but your values and priorities. Little by little other people's definitions or expectations of you will lose their influence. Even if never before, you will be more assertive. You are becoming more of your own person, more of your true-Self. While you still may not have chosen a definite destination, you are certainly moving ahead. You are both the conduit and the creator of what you express. Hopefully, eventually, you will be the sole-creator of your soul's desires, as you completely understand your Divine Destiny. As you learn to tap into all of those ideas that are just below your great consciousness to get into the flow, you have to let go of your barriers or restrictions. Listen for the positive, inner-voice to speak, then your eyes to have a clearer vision of seeing all possibilities. Those small leaps of faith will grow as you learn to trust your intuition. Trust your choices, also as they speak as to your level of Self-worth - it is clearly saying "I believe in me!"

We may feel guilty asking the question 'what is best for me,' when others appear to have greater needs. But, remember airplane safety - put your oxygen mask on first, then help children and others. If you lose consciousness, what further help will you be? There will always be someone who needs your time and energy. If you let others continually drain your energy, what will you have for yourself? Make yourself a worthy-priority with each decision asking: 'What is best for me?' before helping someone else. Also, you are to help others without doing their work for them - don't feed their 'built-in helplessness.' In other words, someone or some group/agency has always come along to rescue them, possibly from childhood. Perhaps they never got a chance at learning responsibility or accountability, or even respect for themselves and others. Those things are all basics for Self-worth. It is their path, they need to experience it. And, that is the lesson of having priorities, allowing others to do their own healing work. You are being a shining light or teacher-by-example, but they need to feed their own inner-flame.

As you listen carefully and trust, the Universe will respond synchronistically to bring you those things you need and want, as your beliefs fall into alignment of you being worthy to receive. Don't let the ego-directed perfectionism get you out of the flow, to keep you from receiving what you deserve. It is once again fear, that we are *not good enough* to receive all that is offered and given. Wrong! You are good enough and if someone should point out or suggest an improvement, you say, "Thank you," if it is so and move on. You don't beat yourself up. And, if it doesn't fit what you visioned, you say, "No, that's not what I had in mine." As the saying goes, critics exist because they didn't have the creativity or talent to do the work in the first place. Don't get drawn into the 'perfectionist game' - trust yourself, your intuition and your abilities. An original is just that, it didn't come out of a cookie-cutter. Perfectionism also sucks the passion out of you, as your energy is wasted on tweaking details, which can cause 'death' to your creativity. Enjoy the results, as it flows from you letting it go, as creativity is just that. Remember, *Winners risk* and still are exhilarated even when they don't win first prize. Worthiness comes from the true satisfaction of a job well done and fulfilling your own Self-sense of accomplishment. Thank you very much!

* * * * * *

We are all worthy of one another. Edward P. Jones

In every aspect of our lives, we are always asking ourselves, "How am I of value? What is my worth?" Yet, I believe that worthiness is our birthright. Oprah Winfrey

Worthiness doesn't have prerequisites. Brené Brown

Your problem is you're... too busy holding onto your unworthiness. Ram Dass

# Situational Awareness ~ Part #31

I feel like I'm channeling a weird combination of Don Quixote and Joan of Arc. The Don Quixote is fighting for principles - people being taken advantage of in numerous, but basic everyday, or things we need to do for our well being. The Joan of Arc is, hopefully not really rescuing people, because that voids their power of choice, but bringing them awareness for what they may choose for themselves. While working at listening to my own Divine guidance, on the one hand, I'm standing my ground on the other. The magic of awareness here, is to know how long to continue one's efforts, if no actual real response or results is revealed. You can't make someone love you or themselves, or convince someone who is so delusional with ego to let go of their old Belief Systems. In other words, there are some cases that cannot be won, reasoned with, or worth the extensive energy use. Perhaps Karma will bring them to their knees, as some people simply need more "effective," painful lessons than others.

I and you often need to stop beating our heads against a wall and move on to others, who actually want to know how to change their lives in a more healing way. As I have said before, staying true to your Self as you walk the path is no 'Sunday walk in the Park.' While not constantly being pelted by trials, errors, conflicted-opportunities for experiences, those lessons will be there to trip you up, as you grow to experience so much more. When difficult or conflicting moments do happen and they will, as we still have lessons to learn, you don't need to let them get to you. You don't need to replay them, as if on some recorded loop to relive it, exam it, edit it - Stop! Let it go.

Take the lesson from it, so you don't put yourself, or allow yourself in that position again. Discard it, do not hold on to it, as it is a moment, even an elongated moment, from the Past. We have no time machine here, except our own memory of the Past. You can not change it, you can only learn from it, then let it go. A lot of deep breathing helps! My new mantra is "Look for the positive and you'll find it; as well the negative, if looking." I don't get it when some people insist on looking for the negative in everything, then belabor it all in detail once they've found it! Do they just not want any joy in their lives? I know life is not perfect, that doesn't mean I can't try to enjoy it as it is.

Eventually, you will learn to remove yourself from all these situations, as your awareness kicks in that this is not a good place for me to be, or these are not the best people for me to be around. Learn Awareness, like listening, is a skill that can be learned, honed and finely tuned to keep us from repeating those moments, or situations that we no longer want to, or need to put ourSelves through. Yes, the negative will continue to come into your life, none of us lives in a bubble, or alone on top of a mountain. What an awareness allows is for you to keep the positive energy flowing through your life, so none of the negative can stick to, or affect you. Don't even give negativity a thought from your mind - if you notice it, let it flow on - unattached.

You don't need the trauma or the drama. Stay in the positive flow. Remember when the lessons stop, the game is over, as you've learned everything in this life and can move to the next. Trust in your intuition always, as you take risks and chances to fulfill your purpose, not dampened by others and their negativity. Yes, you can make a big difference, but pounding 'the old, square peg in a round hole,' just doesn't work sometimes. People do change and even grow, so you can always come back and work with them in the future.

You never know what you can do until you try and even if you fail badly, it is a dream you no longer have to say, "If only I could …" Cross that one off the list, move to another. A friend broke his back skydiving at fifty. Luckily, he returned to his healthy-self and he still says it was one of the most fun, exciting days of his life, and he was no wallflower. Every day can be a new experience and sometimes what you couldn't accomplish before, you may have learned the skills to now complete it. You are not a quitter, when you have simply felt that the goal is no longer giving you the satisfaction you desired. I have a friend who is tech-savvy without the training, which gives her great satisfaction in the accomplishments. Unfortunately, she is sure that I can be also and gets upset at me for not trying, as she knows I'm smart enough. Smart has nothing to do with it. I don't want to be tech-savvy, I just like to use tech-things simply or basically, it truly exasperates me beyond that. Do not do things you don't enjoy doing, when there is no longer any enjoyment in it. *Who* are you proving *what* to? Your ego?

While talking about it may be one step, and doing another, being it or totally feeling yourself involved is what is key. You may have been fulfilling a parent's vicarious-satisfaction, not your own. Many people who have musical or other talent, learn that it is *not great enough* for them to sustain that dreamed of career. Yet, that does not mean that they have to throw away that instrument or dancing shoes or paint brushes. Their personal satisfaction in their talent should be enough for their *own* enjoyment. Perfection is not needed for Joy. A purpose of relaxation may be their reward. They are your dreams and goals, not carved in stone. Change them if you choose.

Jealousy is another thing driven by fear and the ego saying, "Why wasn't that me?" or "I could do that if I tried!" The ego usually jumps in and says that, but you *didn't do* that thing or you probably *didn't try* to accomplish it. Variety is not only said to be the spice of life, but a statement that *none of us* are great at everything. Choose what really makes your heart sing, and learn to do that thing very well - not necessarily perfect, but enough for a sense of accomplishment. Think of this frustrating-chastising kind of fear like having your whole body Botoxed and you can't move a muscle for months! Of course, then you have the perfect rationalization for Not doing something, thus Not failing.

It's easy to give up becoming the Winner, when you break your leg as the competition begins - there is always next time. Rarely is it something once-in-a-life-time, unless we choose it to be so. There are always options and opportunities if we are open to them, and fully risk participating - which means *not sabotaging* your success by breaking your leg sub-consciously! How many people practice to exhaustion, and then oversleep for the competition - figuratively or in actuality? How many times I've seen participants in my workshops go the full distance only to have some minor thing throw them off at the end. This is pure self-sabotage, that they truly need to get some awareness about in their lives. You can be your own worst enemy and the ego will help.

**Exercise:** As with all areas of fear they stem from our Past, especially the childhood part. Explore your different fears of success, jealousy, risk, perfectionism, etc. and see what may get an emotional reaction. What things have you desired or invested time and energy in, only to have dropped out or found some realization to not continue? Make a list of them and the reasons or excuses for your non-success. This is not about Not getting into

Juilliard, this is about quitting long before, because you *didn't believe* you would ever have an opportunity to even apply. Delve into it with your deep breathing and writing to forgive and let go.

Also, make a list of those people who told you not to bother with trying. How much of it was you and how much all the negative influence of others? My mother always said I shouldn't waste time on my writing, just be a secretary like my sister. I was a good secretary, but I still loved writing more. Are any of those people still in your life? Why? Even if they are related to you, you don't have to allow them to influence your life. You will be surprised what you have opened up - an unlimited vision of what you can do, even if you aren't perfect or the best there is. It is never too late to dream or to fulfill them. They are your creations. Strength is nothing more than knowingness and understanding who you can be. That knowledge and acceptance of it, of yourself, no 'being' can ever take that away from you – ever, any where, if You do Not Allow it to be taken.

\* \* \* \* \* \*

You'll never know what wonderful opportunities await you, unless you change to be open to them.

# *Soul Journey ~ Part #32*

Many say that we are on a Soul Journey - a Spiritual Being experiencing life within the human body. Others think we are only humans trying to recreate, or find our Spiritual-selves to become a Spiritual Being. Whichever you choose to believe, it is a process on a path that is a journey helping you to realize more of not only who you are, but who you were meant to be. Some of us know of our Divine Destiny almost from birth, others of us have it thrust upon us and still others fall into it, as if from revelation - aha! Once you know it, the Universe expects you to fulfill it, but you are not alone, ever. All will be given and shown to you, as you learn and ask. The answers can be discovered in the quiet moments, in the moment of deep breath, or in the moment of true acceptance of yourself. The Universe only gives suggestions for you to think about, consider and choose or not, as you discover your own inner-direction in your process on the path. Always know it is *you creating* your direction, so take ownership for yourself, and your journey.

With the Spiritual awakening process you question things that you've never questioned before - authority and structure. You even question why you're here on Earth? What is the meaning of life? - and Specifically, your life? What is it that you should be doing right now? You know there's more out there, but you can't seem to put your finger on it. You also think the answers are out there, eventually you will learn that they will come from inside you. Yet, you realize things just weren't running as smoothly for you, as before your journey quest. You know there's a better way, but you don't know if this path is it. Now, know you're going into a whole new level of experiencing life and understanding it, though you don't know how this journey will get you there. The rather convoluted awakening-process can be lonely, because it is about rediscovering who *you are* without having others tell you, or their belief systems shape and create your life.

You feel yourself withdrawing into you, not wanting so much external activity, or need of stimulation, or the drama that you've had in the Past. In your quiet moments, or frustration, you call out to God/Source - sometimes not sure if S/He is even listening or at least a Higher Being or Power is out there. You may also ask for help, or guidance, or having your question of 'is there something more to life, my life?' You know your old beliefs don't seem to be true anymore, or things the way you were in the Past. Even your Past dreams, goals and desires, you no longer know if they matter, or what truly does matter. It is tumultuous how you came to your path-change. You're here now.

It is important to take a simple, deep breath, as it opens the doorway for the Universe to love you, to remind you of your Angelic origins and compassionately show you the way. You are not alone, tens of thousands of humans are currently going through a sort of similar process of the awakening of Spirit. It may appear to be confusing, and you may feel you are lost, but what you are doing is very natural. You are allowing the old human façade and the illusion of who you thought you were to fade away. Know that all of the answers are within you, the Universe is only there to guide, the choices as always are yours.

**Exercise:** You can breathe through it All – anger, fear, pain or sadness – the pure energy of emotion. To move this energy, simply concentrate your breath on the specific thing bothering you. Keep your mind quiet by *Strongly* repeating, "I can do this, I can do this, I can do this. I can heal myself." And, in steps you are going to heal yourself. When you turn your emotional frequencies on, you breathe them through. This creates a space for you to listen to your intuition, as it will now speak to you. What's important is that you listen to it and do what it says, no matter what, you need to listen and completely trust your intuition. You brought the pain in, now you can remove it.

For the older Souls among us, they may not have had a clear purpose in their coming here, as they usually already had so many experiences. They just want to go with the flow of using their true intuition, or recognizIng Divine coincidences - synchronicities. The important thing is to let your Soul be the guide in your life now, and welcome the love It has for you. Allow your Soul to be the guiding light and force in your life now. It won't push you, but It can take you into expansion to fully embrace the certainty of Oneness between your Soul and God/Source. Feel the peace, comfort and ease that comes from knowing you don't have to do anything to attain this Greatness. It is Who You Are! Be one with your Self, with your Soul and one with God. You will then be confident knowing you are a child of God. So let this presence settle into your bones and allow your Soul the pure freedom to sing, dance, praise and love. Joy is there for each and every one of us. Honor your heart, listen to that voice, feel, get back into your body and feel yourself, feel the direction your Soul is guiding you in. You can not go wrong if you do this, I promise.

Every ascended master that you are familiar with has had to master the questioning you are now being presented with. None of them got to pass by this initiation, therefore it is a possibility that you can make inevitable, as the power is yours. Use it. Think of it as your magic wand, with your Soul's power to say the magic word. Spirit may be tangibly weaving its magic in your life, but it is doing it through your Soul's belief in you. Simply step out of your way from your fears and see what is flowing to support you every step on your path. You will be amazed at Spirit's presence in the depths of your heart, showing you the truth of your journey as you achieve more compassion for all from the love within. This pure intent-love on the journey leads one to manifest from that compassionate heart. It is the foundation of why you truly let go of old energy, and all old belief systems. Part of this is your karmic journey in search of redemption and resolution of the pain you caused others and/or they caused you, which only forgiveness ends. That is also receiving of unconditional forgiveness for yourself and to others to have peace.

As you continue the journey of rediscovering your Divine nature, you are surrounded with love and blessings from God/Source and the Universe. It is going to be a long and arduous trip down the paths that you choose, rarely straight, but eventually up and forward. As said before, there are side trips, detours, even stops or backtracks when the going gets too tough. It is easy to slide or return to your bad habits, since they are well known, worn and so comfortable to fall back into. Yet, as you have glimpses of who you can be, you will find your way back to that path of growth.

Keeping your sense of humor may be difficult, as will be the refraining from criticism, judgment or basic chastisement of yourself and others. Was it because of your doubts and fears? Here we go with sabotaging your succeeding again! Allow yourself to take guidance from your magical-child within to receive the unconditional love, honoring and respect for the Soul Journey that you have been on, to heal whatever needed emotional vibrations. You are soon open for the higher level energies, that come easily with acceptance in all things and freedom from fear.

\* \* \* \* \* \*

Reach high, for stars lie hidden in your soul. Dream deep, for every dream precedes the goal. Pamela Vaull Starr

You have to count on living every single day in a way you believe will make you feel good about your life - so that if it were over tomorrow, you'd be content with yourself. Jane Seymour

You cannot have real change if you hang onto old behavior - it just doesn't work.

Fear doesn't drive change -- but it does perpetuate mediocrity.

# Over Analyzing ~ Part #33

Too often, you think too much and think of all kinds of reasons why to do, or not to do something. Your over analyzing shackles you. Looking for a 'sure thing' can only immobilize you. Life does not come with any guarantees, and no sure things - except that God loves you unconditionally and you die when it's your time. Life is meant to be lived more spontaneously, so more joy is known. Don't be reckless, but don't inhibit yourself either. And, don't pressure yourself to hit that home run, or be the best the first time, or the last time. Make being 'in the game' the thrill that it is. You do your best and that is the reward, and experience you take from it.

Remember, you can only have control of making You happy. It is a choice for everyone, you have no control over what others think or want for you, or from you. Once again, ego and fear are trying to limit your life, don't let them. You may have a sense or awareness of all the energies, as you are transitioning and you are in your mental body, or in your analytical trying to 'figure things out.' It would be better for you to just feel the energies, feel the experience and feel what is now happening around you. As you feel who you are, you will find that the alignment with the vibrations around you will fall into place.

So, if you allow your analytical to shift into that new higher vibration through feeling it, that feeling, being aware and sense of presence is what will allow you to feel more comfortable as the New You. You have in your conscious and subconscious the generational beliefs, as to who and what you are/were. These have been handed down to you from not only your parents, but numerous generations, and from your peers with embodied, cultural beliefs in which you have been raised. These beliefs are reinforced subliminally, then attract true evidence of your perceptions. And so, we often have the challenges in life, because we are looking for them, expecting them, because we've been told *subliminally,* many times what our life *has to be like*.

Therefore, your past lives put together a puzzle representing things you have not yet accomplished, that then actually becomes your life lesson. For generations, you have had a reality of life that was very defined for you - you are this, or you are that, think this way, think that way. *Never let anyone define you again.* Let your new independence and freedom be reflected in your thinking and what you do with others be instead, your life's lesson.

Become your own best-coach to try new things, explore new thoughts and think of life as exciting. So, you take on challenges to go a different way to stir things up a bit in your life. Then Old grooves, or Old patterns and Old ways are effortlessly released.You can excitedly explore *the New,* just for the sake of deliciously seeing and doing it from another perspective. Get up and out to find new inspirations in new ways for new experiences. If simultaneously, counter-arguments arise - cognitive dissonance - do look at both, but also approach this new experience with a 'can-do' attitude. Self-mastery is changing the external through internal change.

As Gandhi said, "Be the change you want to see in the world." Life is about finding out and you find out by daring to make choices to see where they lead. In life, choices constantly exist, so you have to make them. But, they don't have to be irrevocable and yet, some of the choices once taken, you cannot retract easily. So, *those* you count-up as life experience and count the choice as right, then be glad for the experience it gave you. Consider perhaps, every choice you make is the right choice, even when it doesn't look like it. The good thing is you made a choice. Indecision, or no choice is avoidance of life, or giving it up to ego, which rarely makes a good choice for change.

A new understanding may be that *no decision*, is still a decision. Whether than you making your own choice - misguided or not - you have allowed yourself to be controlled by ego-circumstance. Don't be surprised if there's an awakening here. You are the only thing that you have total control over - why would you give that up? You can always make another decision to change the prior one, when new information informs you! Think of each day like a wave from the ocean - while each one is different and sometimes unique, when it is gone, it is gone. While you may have some things to remember about it, like a great surfer, you look to the next one to carry you once again for an experience of life. Each wave may teach you something new, unknown - balance, survival, when to let go of it, joy, exhilaration, accomplishment. But, you also know as you come ashore, or into the shallows, that tomorrow there will be another for you to learn from.

What to think of also is that we are like the waves, gone and replaced by another. Some of us will be remembered more than others. For some of us, who may have given back more to the ocean, Mother Earth and other waves, we are remembered. But basically, we all then eventually fold back into the oceans to return again and again. A surfer does not say, "I want that great wave that carried me so magnificently back again." They just look for another one, that may do the same, or even better. So we let go of that day, that wave experience and look for another. That's the way it works. How many past lives do you think you have had? You intuitively know, don't you?

Along the way, you've learned what you know now, as in your DNA there is Spiritual knowledge learned for eons. You've picked up the pieces and parts of Spiritual purpose and learning. You also have made all the mistakes you needed to make and it fills up the wisdom in you this time around. So, are you going to make all those mistakes again? Should you choose to speak to your Higher-Self with intent of learning that Spiritual Wisdom and it will come to you as shamanic energy! You will be so much wiser in so many ways for doing that.

**Exercise:** Perhaps you've come into this life with the same fear you had in some prior life. Rather than analyze this, or even say you're cursed with something of some sort, get above it. Don't let any negative energy that you brought in affect your life lesson. Do your deep breathing and talk directly to your Higher-Self to get rid of it by replacing it with some positive DNA from a better, prior life. You can! Ask your Higher-Self to reach right there into those energized layers of all of those lifetimes and pick out the DNA that had the hero, self-assured, courageous, loving, peaceful, healthy, empowered or who -whatever you want to claim for you now. If you can open up enough to relate to the expansion of consciousness, to the joy of release, to the idea that anything is possible, it is. Your Higher-Self can search into your own Akashic Record to find the purest DNA that was ever yours, pick it up and place it upon the attributes of the current you.

It's easy or it's difficult, depending upon how much you believe in this. You're going to have to start expanding your consciousness to include the things that are unseen. This healing doesn't happen all at once, but if you sit down in a quiet moment with a pure heart and say to Spirit, "I would like these things and I give permission to activate my past-positive DNA energies (whatever specifics you want) that are needed in my life to accomplish the purposes I came for with joy, for I deserve it and I've earned it." You have already created them in your own Past life - they are yours to enjoy again!

\* \* \* \* \* \*

Let go of whatever belief system or thought that doesn't work for you anymore.

It all starts with self-reflection. Then you can know and empathize more profoundly with someone else. Shirley MacLaine

The risk of a wrong decision is preferable to the terror of indecision. Maimonides 1135 - 1204 AD

# *Being More Aware ~ Part #34*

Awareness, as previously mentioned, is the first step on your moving past your Past. As I've said, it may come out of the blue, or simply no longer wanting a life continually filled with pain or drama, or the repetitive existing rather than living. There are other ways to acquire awareness; some people do it with meditation. It may take months, or even years before they get the idle-mind chatter down, so they can realize the stillness. They then, finally hear their own inner voice, though they may not even realize it is their voice at first. Once they've learned to plug into the stillness and have learned to listen to that inner voice of intuition, 'suddenly' they become aware of a whole other world that was actually there, but not 'seen' because they lacked awareness. It can be simple things like colors, sensitivity to touch, or honest feelings about something they didn't have before, or seeing themselves or those around them clearly in the mirror.

**Exercise:** We can start making changes in our life without awareness, but it would be like living haphazardly or Rube Goldberg-style where all is simply thrown together, and any part may break at any moment's notice. Not exactly having a solid foundation, or any knowing what might befall oneself from one moment to the next - perhaps it's not the best choice. Yet, one might choose to purposely put awareness into practice by slowing down and doing more real observing. This will only take a day or two, or if you are brave, give it a week. Absolutely, everything - every single habit or basic thing you do - you do differently with awareness of what and how you are doing it. From the time you get up in the morning, make it the other side of the bed. If your bed is against the wall or your partner sleeps on 'their' side, just change for one night to see the difference. How does that feel? What thoughts come in? What do you do first - shower, brush your teeth, etc.? Try to reverse or change the order of what you do and how you do it - brush your teeth first, or start your shower with your feet instead of your face or arms. Pretend you have a broken arm or leg, how would you *Have to do it* all differently? Does the weather affect you? How? I had very little experience with fog before living in San Francisco, I learned to love it and now in Dallas I sorely miss it!

How do you choose your clothes, put them on? Change it. When do you have breakfast or eat for breakfast? Change the order and change your menus for lunch and dinner also. Change your whole process for going to work, or your usual daily routine. If you drive, go a different direction, as much as you can. Try public transportation - now for some people, especially those who live in the suburbs and in their vehicles, this can be an eye-opener of a whole other world. Yes, you will have to plan in a lot of extra time for this whole experiment, but I guarantee it will be worth it in the long run. How often do you walk around your neighborhood?

While living in San Francisco for twelve years and about three-quarters up a high hill the last seven, I worked at walking everyday. The hills, and my destinations, did contribute to which way I went. Yet, when I was just out walking, I did make the effort to go off down different streets to let my feet and exploring take me to the destination. It never ceased to amaze me how often I'd see a new building being built - which there, with the limited space - meant something had to be torn down first. I often stood staring, searching my mind to remember when was the last time I was by that area and exactly what *was there* prior. Sometimes, I truly had no clue as I hadn't looked. If speeding by in a car - especially an expressway - what do you really see?

This whole process should bring you to eye-opening awareness as to how much you don't notice, on a daily basis. It may be something small like a package or item left on a side table in your office, or a new painting hung in the lobby, or flowers or a new hairstyle or color of someone that you see daily. Those things that you did not even notice before, with changing your routine, you begin to notice, to be aware of what is around you - the good, the bad or simply the new or different. So, the advantage of all of this? With awareness comes some discernment, and with discernment comes the realization that life and everything in it really is a choice. Those things that you choose that make you happy, those that you feel you must do. Or, those that you rationalize, as it is easier to do than create a wave, or confrontation, or even havoc. Have you adapted or just settled?

Awareness also brings to mind what you might do differently because you are responsible, accountable, respective of others, or the environment or simply life. In other words, awareness can open a true Pandora's Box, which means you can't go back, you have to deal with it. Again, it is about change. Is this the way I want to live my life, or what I know is finite in this body with a limited warranty of existence? Do you need to have someone special die to make you see it all? This is unfortunately one of the biggest shockers for change.

So, you see how powerful awareness is, no matter what path you take to it, the results are the same - change. Your path may spiral around, or your journey may have many detours or tangents that you explore, or adventure-off for some experience. But once you are ready, you will come to understand your Divine Destiny, that was chosen by you before you were even born into this life, which you also chose. It will again be, your awareness of your acceptance of all that you need to do to fulfill that Destiny, whatever it may be that leads you to make the right choices. By this time, you will have learned to follow the voice of intuition. Once you are in the flow, the Universe brings all the things to you that you need to make sure that your life is harmonious. Now in a joyous bliss, you know who you are and why you are here. Amazing thing that awareness - it is all about living in the now - being in touch with yourself and others.

Technology can not replace the pure, personal human contact experience. Too many people are hooked on the internet or simulation games. Many young people, or those wanting to be up-to-date, take pride in techno-gadget skills. Others, believing in the energy of true interpersonal skills, think it is actually the need for attention, the ego disguising itself as faux-social connections. It is limiting their life by receiving one's communication second hand, yet almost beguiling - tempting people that they are *needed*. An attachment-separation has been created as to being in control of others. This kind of ego flaunting is indulging oneself into an 'imitation of life' and if the person is put into a live-action situation, they may not hold their own so well or the real responsibility to what they've said or done.

Granted, through diversity - looks, talent, interests, etc. - you find new ways of connecting with one another, that you could not have found, but are they real? Being individuals, with different thoughts and beliefs, is what makes us who we are. When experienced-actively life is individually shared, we then learn to interpret our experiences with others on the path, who need direction or support - "understanding can release fear." Synchronicity, the capacity to manifest things, people and unknown circumstances into your life, is collaborated with you believing things show up because of your thoughts. There is no true coincidence in this world, just conditions/causes coming together with infinite God/Source intelligence guiding these happenings. Every thought is connected, as each of us are. Make it real.

* * * * * *

Exploring yourself can be as important and interesting as exploring everything else. It should also come first.

No pessimist ever discovered the secrets of the stars, or sailed to an uncharted land, or opened a new heaven to the human spirit. Helen Keller

Start by listening to that voice inside, the one that tells you something doesn't feel right. Don't ignore it, as it is your inner-core truth. Even if you haven't heard it or listened to it for a very long time, give it a chance to be heard.

# *Preferences ~ Part #35*

Perhaps as a child you did the "Connect the Dots" game. At the beginning the shapes were very simple and finished them correctly guessing the right item, to the praise of your parents or teachers. As you progressed, your confidence would be such that as soon as you connected dots of four legs you would guess "a horse," and then would be disappointed that it was a cow, as you actually liked horses better than cows. Or, you may have guessed a dog and it turned out to be a pig, because again you preferred dogs. Still, your subconscious mind learned to 'connect the dots' for lots of things and actually doing deductive reasoning, you were right more often than wrong. You were learning - growing from these preferences practiced - influences of yourself, your parents, teachers, and friends. Also, athletes were good people, even heroes as they saved the team by some great feat; an actor or performer won an award because of a great talent; or someone won a contest because of their beauty; bosses made a lot money on the job because they were smart. These were logical conclusions from the cultural influences and even more so, subliminal programming of it.

Eventually you developed 'sensors,' those things that resonated within you subconsciously, as being what you wanted, or what was good to have, again influenced by those around you. These varied from what food to eat - often from television, clothes to wear - friends, activities to do, classes - schools to attend, jobs to seek, people to date, etc. on and on. At the same time, what those people around you said, or thought of your selections also influenced, or often changed your sensors. We all developed preferences and believed that they were what was best for us, as they would make us happy, fulfilled, or even eventually successful, etc. In your youth or early adult years, still connecting-the-dots may have been easy. No surprises here. How you judge something is related to your personal context - the framework of how you look at it, or relate to it. You're constantly collecting various information from even greater sources offering to influence you.

But those influenced decisions were affecting more of your future life than you may have been aware of at the time. Something "taken out of context" means the whole picture or the circumstances involved that created the situation, is not included. Context is what shapes our life and is the decisive direction of what we do. Therefore more than experience makes the quality of what we do - if you've been taught incorrectly or inadequately, for instance, *affects* the source of the effectiveness. But satisfaction from that process doesn't always play out the way expected, as choice can be a wild card - "Why not?"

Skip ahead to a mature adult and perhaps a job or relationship that didn't work out the way you expected. It was more disappointing, it just wasn't supposed to be that way. It had seemed that everything had been perfect, or even resonated with us at the beginning. Sure you may have had to adapt, or do things you didn't like, or be treated how you would have liked, that's life, you were told. Most of your sensors were still being fulfilled, but maybe some new sensors you had chosen totally on your own had now been added. The happiness was gone, but you didn't want it to end that way at all. Fear may pop-up, as you still wonder where will your happiness/success come from now? Some people may have even questioned, why you were naive enough to add *happiness* to the quotient. Were you trying to live a fairy tale, or what? Who did you think you were? You seriously expected happiness?

I think most of us accept by now that certain people and things are brought into our lives for a particular purpose/learning experience for us, and when it is complete you move on, or they do. Yet, some of you cannot accept the ending, even if it has been an obvious drifting-apart for the good of you both. The problem here is sometimes the person or thing has keyed into, too many of your Past 'sensors,' those things that for so long you believed and deeply knew, or others told you were best for you to be happy. You don't just leave a good job, or good marriage/relationship because you aren't happy all the time, do you? If it was good, is happy overrated or necessary or do your adult responsibilities trump being happy?

Let's take the long, 'happily' married couple: when you first met and were together, it reflected to you so much of what you sought to have in this life and in a relationship. This person *fit* all of your preferences, they clicked all of your sensors at that time. Then, you grew in different directions from different stimulus, which created new sensors. This is especially true when the relationship started young, or lasted many years, or one person had more upheavals than the other. It may be difficult to accept reality, that you are on different paths now. Resisting change, you make rationalizations of what you thought it could or should be. You mentally-created it to be something that it was not meant to be - what you wanted in the long term. There were many tremendous benefits for the short term, but eventually your paths were diverged to go separate ways for peace of mind, that delved happiness.

If you cannot accept this scenario, it turns into the 'square peg in a round hole' syndrome. You are trying to keep something that no longer fits, simply because it once triggered some sensors within you. The fantasy is sometimes continued by anger or emotional outbursts-

tantrums, as reality of the situation becomes more obvious and now impossible to accept. While you are not your emotions, you do allow them to control you sometimes. Just as both the cow and horse have four legs, there is *now* only a small part of this person or thing that originally triggered the sensor that is real to you any more. The rest is unfortunately, not what you want, or most importantly need at all now.

**Exercise:** Space and time are needed to step back and be more objective in order to let go and detach from the situation, relationship, job, etc. Once the clarity is brought in, you can see the lessons which this whole thing has been for you and that those doors of new growth opportunity are swung wide open. Yet, you need to accept that you had to go through the experience, whatever it was, to reach those the doors with the opportunities. Those people you knew, job you had, or even children you created, had purpose in your life and you in them. So, the old adage of 'something good always comes out of something bad,' is not often realized until later down the road with clarity and acceptance of what it was.

We sometimes only want to remember the good stuff, yet it is usually the difficult times that are the best teachers, they bring the new learning opportunities you needed. This is why the Universe reminds you that there really are no mistakes, all of your experiences have a purpose and reason for you to learn, if you are willing to do so, even if painful. Sometimes those people or things from your Past will again cross your paths, or you may even be able to continue an untangled-relationship/friendship - depending on how debilitating your ending may have been. If you cannot verbalize it, try writing it and you may want to think of the gratitude of the lessons of growth that were given to you. The main thing is that you have changed, whether they have or not, and you are on your own path becoming the person you were so meant to be. And, you know your New preferences as you forge ahead.

* * * * * *

You may be disappointed if you fail, but you are doomed if you don't try. Beverly Sills

It is never too late to be what you might have been. George Eliot

Are you just putting in time, thinking it will all be better when you die?

Greatness is when people with power treat people without power well.

# *Freedom - Independence - Part #36*

A recent extensive survey of numerous countries found that "freedom of choice is not only a universal aspiration, but the single most important basic of human happiness." But, as with many things, there are strings attached, or priorities that need to be dealt with before one can be thinking about what 'choices' do I have today. As the basic, classic Maslow's Hierarchy of Needs has stated for many years, the whole area of "Biological/Physical" and "Safety needs" must first be met on a regular basis before a person can ponder the "Belongingness and Love needs of family, affection, relationships, work groups, etc." Most psychologists would probably say that it is actually the 4th and 5th Steps, or rungs on the Maslow pyramid of "Esteem" and "Self-Actualization" needs that real Freedom, Choice and Independence kicks in. And, most definitely this is a sad thing, as accepted research states that over 90% of the world's population, or more surprisingly, almost 80% of those in the USA *never reach* those final Maslow steps.

What is the point of this? Well, for one thing it says a lot about people who are on their path of finding themselves, whether it's for Spiritual purposes, or simply knowing themselves - Maslow's Self-Actualization. A side note would be, that Spirituality usually evolves as one knows oneself, which involves truth - which then branches to forgiveness, love, respect, higher power, etc. So, once again we can look at this as a connect-the-dots: Freedom - Independence (Self-Actualization) requires: responsibility, accountability, respect - first to oneself, as you can't respect others until you respect yourself. There is love of self - same reason as respect, life satisfaction from being self-sustainable - you're supporting yourself and contributing back to the community in what you do.

Now, we get into the more nebulous areas, of which Your freedom of choice means that you also give and respect it for Others, as well. In other words, 'social-tolerance' in how you believe/accept others to be able to do as they choose. I always say, if God can give us Freewill in what we choose to do, why can't we all do the same with others? So that respect is for All peoples and Everything sentient - like the environment - not being wasteful of anything, while also sharing what you have in abundance. This is the Basis of Buddhism - "Do no harm to anyone or anything." Legally this is *freedom without license*, meaning not being licentiousness - doing what you want only, without regard to what affects it would have on others.

Personally, I do believe in the "Gratitude-Attitude" - whatever I ask for and it is given to me, I say 'thank you.' This can be even something as basic as waking up to a new day and all of the great possibilities it may have. Then again, at the end of a day and being thankful of all the basics of food, shelter, with all of my friends, along with being able to do what I wanted to do that day. Sometimes just recognizing and acknowledging that, I've had happiness that day, which most of it came from my expected Freedom and Independence. I may not be happy with some things in life, but my happiness was of my own making, as Maslow says of your self-esteem coming from accomplishments, which usually stem from expanding and doing new or creative things.

Most people are on their path because they were not happy with how their life was going and knew it needed a change. Or, most specifically knew what was their purpose in life, or why they are here. Part of me cannot imagine living in a country where I had so little choices on a daily basis, yet I saw it when I lived in Japan and other countries I also traveled to. I can understand that some would prefer death, than to continue under such restrictions. So many of us, take so much in what we have for granted, as in the simple act of choosing when to eat, what to wear, where to live or what job to do. How many other people who complain about the lack of choices in these things could never ever comprehend not having to make those decisions?

**Exercise:** Most people rarely feel that they are complainers or negative, or lack appreciation for what we all do have. So, if you are brave and honest enough, start keeping a scratch tally sheet for just one week of every complaint, negative thought or feeling of you not getting what you or other people wanted. This includes the little, trivial, petty things that you allow to pop into your mind: driving, someone pulls in front of you - they're a jerk, right?; or the customer service was not attentive enough; or someone that you think took your spot or whatever on purpose; or angers you for not saying thanks, and so forth. Notice how long it takes you to start catching yourself, or even if you do - I would hope so! What this exercise reveals is that we may not be doing horrible, negative things like stealing from people or on your job, but you are often knit-picking others, or even yourselves to death, with what is really trivial pettiness. Will the world truly end without your favorite donut?

As the saying goes, "You never know what you've got, until you lose it." Garbage or public transportation strikes really bring that home. Most people are dong the best they can, and if you truly have a legitimate complaint, take it to the Manager, don't keep bitching and complaining to your friends, like some drama queen playing poor me! Once you complete this exercise, acknowledge that you are not always controlling your thoughts or feelings, or even might be setting yourself up, by *allowing* these things to happen. Don't go to *that* store with bad customer service, or change your schedule to not be involved in some heavy traffic. The next step is changing your own bad habits, or even putting yourself into negative situations.

Take control of your thoughts and deeds by deliberately self-programing yourself into constructive acting and thinking. Then the stronger you will be and the more natural the positive response will be. Soon, your pattern of thinking and acting will automatically be more positive instead of negative, as you've established a new constructive habit. Think about what you *can control* to change it, and what you can't - for now - how can you best adapt to it, until change is possible? Just stating appreciation makes it better, as you are now surrounded by positive energy. The old fake it 'till you make it' syndrome works.

I remind myself that Thomas Edison tried over ten thousand different filaments before he got that light bulb to stay lit. So, we step out and we try new things, then learn to laugh at ourselves when we fail. Self-confidence grows just in the act of trying - experimenting with new things. Maslow said, "Self-actualization … finding what you were born to do. A musician must make music, an artist must paint and a poet must write." He did not say that you had to become rich and famous doing it, to have become 'self-actualized.' It is in the 'Doing' that many people find their 'Being.' It may not be your career, but it can be your passion, for that brings happiness. Just as finding the right mate may bring you happiness, it is still your choice to personally be happy and not *their* responsibility to make it happen. You cannot look to others when you 'feel' inferior, weak, helpless or worthless - those are all feelings that *you create* inside of you. And, Maslow's Self-fulfilling Prophecy is absolute truth: *Whatever* you believe you are or you can do, you will - be it negative or positive.

\* \* \* \* \* \*

Controlling is not the same as Leading. Leaders lead by inspiration, not by bossing people to only do it their way.

Remember … authentic trust is earned … not commanded!

Your mind is a garden. Your thoughts are the seeds - you can grow flowers or you can grow weeds.

# Sabotaged Decisions ~ Part #37

Many of us on the path tend to sabotage ourselves in ways that have kept us comfortably 'less than' who we are, or can be. Basically it comes from the ego-minded limitations that needle us almost daily. You get to the very edge of success and if there is any little doubt or fear, you feed it like a weed taking the nutrients from our soul. You believe from the ego-chatter that you are lacking somehow, but how can that be when there is no lack in the Universe? Ask yourself also, if you are a child of God, how can you be lacking, for God is absolute abundance in all things? Trust yourself that the seeds of your idea or dream were generated by your Soul. From this level, there is pure love which is your truth, so keep your faith to never give up on your seeds coming into fruition.

If you can create it, you can make the intangible, tangible. It is that Self-fulfilling Prophecy of believing "I can do this!" This moment will set you free from your Past, as well as any fear or doubt you have, and propel you forward on your Divine path. Choose your intentions, your behaviors and your words to be based on Love, coming from your heart/soul center, with a deeper understanding of yourself. These feelings are connected to your intuition, so they usually are a good base for making positive decisions.

**Exercise:** Good decisions cannot be made when you are upset, angry or emotional about something or someone - that's just basic, or common sense. The whole scenario of taking a deep breath - counting to ten is widely accepted to somewhat get enough of a grip to make a decision, if one is needed. Once you understand what emotion(s) that you're involved with and where they *came* from, then you can usually dissipate or release them according to whose responsibility it is for the emotion.

Remember, Anger is a secondary emotion - it doesn't just happen, something else inside or outside caused it to be reactive. This sounds very adult in handling of the emotion, as that is what you must be with your "Self," in order for the emotion to be released. Then the important thing is *not* to bury the emotion - examine it so it can be resolved and released. Buried emotions only fester and come back up over and again. It's as if they've grown or developed a whole larger scenario, than what set them off in the first place to sabotage you. When you understand where they came from, you can heal them.

Research has shown that these buried emotions are the basic cause of diseases, stress, headaches, etc. Fear or anger may have been added to the repressed emotions and soon you will feel the drain of all of this turbulent negative energy. Once again, go back through your step process of deep breathing to see understanding of it, and the responsibility of it - yours or the other person - to then let it go. Don't forget to apply forgiveness to yourself and anyone else involved. Still, you are only concentrating on yourself here - if the other person does choose to hold onto their anger, etc. bless them, let it go as you then physically move away from them. Ask yourself, where did this old emotion come from in your Past? Understand it, breathe it, bless it and release it. Now, what needs to be changed? If you do not process these emotions you will continue to sabotage yourself - in new and creative ways all the time with your ego helping it along.

Take "emotional out-bursts or situations" to be opportunities for change, or do you want to keep repeating these scenarios to greater or lesser degrees? Holding on to your emotional pain *will* hold you back from advancing on your path, because you will always have that distraction that limits your clarity for trust and unconditional love. You need to take these things as *lessons:* the person or thing that pushes your buttons does so, because that is their *subconscious* role in your life, until we learn the lesson they are helping us with. Through your awareness you can learn how to respond differently and let that Karma go, once and for all! It truly represents that old adage of having a real 'monkey on your back, or dragging around old baggage' from your Past. Learn the lesson and let it go! These are niggling things that pop up for us all, even when we thought we had learned the lesson.

I recently went through this at a meeting of volunteers, and while I was proud of myself for not losing it with another person, it took numerous verbal/written exchanges before I saw that I needed to leave this group. With sheer frustration over the other person's petty uncooperativeness, I finally saw the group had truly served its purpose for me. As well, this other person had no intention of changing and would always consider me a threat to his position, though I had no interest in it. Part of me felt bad, as the people that were to benefit from my participation in the group would no longer do so. I can only believe, that my leaving would simply be another lesson on their own path. I had to do what was best for me to continue forward on my own journey, for staying with the group no longer worked for me. For many people this can be similar for a job, relationship or friendship. You may still care for someone, but no longer want to be involved with them regarding their behavior or actions.

When you can accept people as they are or choose to be, there will be little resistance in your life. While you may present your own opinion, it is just that. Remember it always takes at least two to argue and if you don't argue, there can be no argument. It has taken me a very long time to now get to the point of simply stating what I want to say, and if others choose not to believe or accept it, that is their choice. We agree to disagree. I am also learning to keep my opinion to myself when I have not been asked, or have simply just overheard another's statement. Unless it involves something life-threatening, I simply let them go on in their ignorance, rather than correcting them, as most people resent your opinion anyway.

It requires discipline and a willingness to disengage from old patterns of behavior, which create more Karma for us. When all flows easily in your life, you know it is coming from your heart and never negatively controlled by that mind-directed ego. Trying to fix someone else's life is not your job and they will eventually resent you for your efforts. If someone wants to talk, fine - listen. It doesn't mean that you have to fix things for them, or tell them how you would handle it all. And, if they don't want to talk, then you accept that also, without any attachment to their actions or decisions - it is their life. Some people only want a wall to bounce, or echo their problems off of, it may help them to see solutions for themselves. No one really wants a band-aid, unless they are truly bleeding.

While sometimes the gut-action is necessary, for peace of mind a well thought-out and informed plan is best followed. It is also good to, for some things, have a Plan B to fall back on if needed. And I have sometimes felt like most of my life has been lived from Plan B, as being open to change does that to you. Even with the best information, mistakes do happen and you are still accountable for them. Always admit any mistakes immediately, as people will support and respect you taking the necessary action to correct them, rather than blaming others or denying it. With all the cameras these days, even politicians are learning. If you can't live a day without some rationalization, then you may want to question why you are on the path to begin with.

\* \* \* \* \* \*

I was raised to sense what someone wanted me to be and be that kind of person. It took me a long time not to judge myself through someone else's eyes. Sally Field

I didn't belong as a kid, and that always bothered me. If only I'd known that one day my *differentness* would be an asset, then my early life would have been much easier. Bette Midler

If it is a common fact of life when you lie to others, it is a sad truth when you lie to yourself.

The real task is to do what is right, the slacker or con man does what is easy.

# *Again, Self-Sabotage - Part #38*

Self-Sabotage actually means not wanting to change - it's wanting to stay with what is familiar, comfortable or your status quo. One could say that getting to know their subconscious is not a priority. Why mess with those beliefs that have been incurred since childhood? It has nothing to do with being smart or stupid, or even if the routine is bad for us. Most humans have a fear of the unknown, which usually kicks-in the instinct for survival, or what is life-known to them. This means, unless that desire to change/grow/succeed comes with a 100% life-time guarantee, they're not going to go for it. It may all be tied to one's negative childhood life, bad examples of others, or perceived/real failures. Or, that old time favorite - 'not good enough' for the 'big time.' And, the only way out is for someone to express encouragement, praise or appreciation for the work or efforts that one does. Having a mentor has saved more than one life from self-destruction.

Is not that Chatty-Cathy inside-voice, just a cover-up for a desperate vulnerability? Slowly, with small steps, can some people begin to believe that they can do more, and that they are worth more. As one's Self-worth and belief in Self begins to increase, you will become empowered, then usually more successful. Yet, it can be a rather fragile thing, with inside/outside negative words or criticism shattering all that had been accomplished. So, one needs to create a belief in Self-love and worthiness, as well as one's ability to do a job or create a project successfully. It is only after many little successes, that most people have built up enough confidence to really withstand rejection, and accept the integrity of what they've done. We humans need to have our worthiness applauded, from the inside from ourselves and the outside, those that matter so to us. As you increase our self-esteem, you'll have acceptance to once again take another step up.

One can give peace and forgiveness to oneself, with the peeling open of our psyches. If you succumb to the opinions of others and lose belief in your worthiness, you will sink right back to that *comfortable* bottom rung, easy and all too familiar. Few people ever forget where they came from and fewer started at the top of the ladder. It is at this point, that many people often want desensitizing of those feelings of unworthiness, by settling into some form of addiction or escape. Self-sabotage then has a *compadre*, or *cohort* in this to fight off the demons of being declared unworthy. Fear, as said, truly is *False Emotions Appearing Real,* which can quickly turn into a black hole sucking all body, mind and soul down into it. Too often, then you've convinced yourself that success is not your destiny and why did you so foolishly think that you could be? In truth, it is not failure that you have a fear of, but that whole *totality of success*, when you believe you are, of course, so unworthy of it. Then too, the fear may be that once successful, you must repeat that success over and over again. *As if* you will never be allowed to fail, or succeed less than you did before.

But why would you sabotage your desires when you've learned that beliefs are not truths? Who do you think you are? Better than your family and friends? Often you are afraid of losing the love, friendship or just acceptance of others, who have not changed and grown as you have, or even want to change. If good stuff is happening to you faster - even if you worked hard for it - than to your family or friends, then you often cannot handle it. They may not have even said anything to you, yet your guilt will react to what you believe or feel that they are thinking, or resenting about your success. Self-sabotage is one of the most destructive ways *you* stop *your* own progress. You can even get rather creative in how you do it, so consciously, most of the time you don't even know what you've done until it's too late. Those *accidents* or *illnesses* just before or even during something special, is nothing more than self-sabotage. It is better to have an *acceptable excuse* than fail. And, it is still self-sabotage when you allow or accept - knowingly or unknowingly - others to sabotage you.

While both men and women of all races sabotage themselves, even in the twenty-first century, it is more common for it to be women or people of color. What is this really all about? It is about "power." The Power that you may think of is defined by a *White Patriarchal Society*. Real power is that sense within each of us - raised or taught. A deeper understanding that is so grounded in who you are and what you stand for at the same time. What kind of fear stops you from facing your own power? It is not fear-based power exerting your will over someone, as that is usually short-lived in a free society, or possibly what you experienced in your childhood. The kind of power that can come from inside you, honoring your intuitive-Self is the only way to find true peace. How worthy do you think you are? No one can give you this kind of power. You just need to accept that you already have it and accept the responsibility that goes with it. Go back to your deep breathing and the source where this lack-feeling came from. So, if you know who you really are, no one can take your power away. You really are independent of what others think of you, because you know truly in your own heart *who you are* and can be. It is the most important gift you give yourself, as all else springs from that knowledge.

Beyond your self-sabotage for feeling your insecurities or your lack of power, you need to acknowledge other reasons you may not feel you don't deserve something. Anger quickly follows next in your self-sabotage and is often directed at yourself in a self-destructive way. You may have felt years of suppression, in that you were told that you were incapable of earning more than your father or *white men*, so you never dared to do so. Finding your power takes a commitment to you, yourself, as it means loving yourself unconditionally - 'warts and all,' I say. That means every morning really look into that mirror and say, "I love you." And then, every other mirror that you pass to get a chance to reiterate it, even if it is silently. Most people can't do it to begin with, but as they repeat it - the old 'fake it till you make it' - they slowly do develop their Self-love, Self-esteem and Self-worth. If it helps to have an end benefit, the more you love yourself, the more you have to give and love others - unconditionally. You must come first, or what you think you feel or give to others will not last past the lust, or momentary happiness. You can project whatever images onto your mind screen; it's your movie, anything goes. Play the positive new role, and don't be an extra in your own movie.

**Exercise:** When you love yourself more, you take more time for yourself, as your awareness of how you spend your time grows. It is amazing how that inner-child grows happy doing what it wants to do, surrounded only by those people that it enjoys. You may begin to rethink your job, some of your friends and even your contact with some of your relatives. One of the biggest steps, that I've talked about before was keeping a journal, especially writing in the morning when all of your feelings are fresh and more freely released. Eventually, as you share some of your changing thoughts, because some people will notice and ask you, these may be people you want to talk to about what you're experiencing. They may also be on their path and while each path is unique, they may even share some insights.

There are also many groups, classes and seminars that you may want to visit, or check out to see if they resonate with your intuitive-Self, as your intuition will be speaking up more often, now that you're listening - you are listening to your inner-Self aren't you? This new, positive intuition will keep you from slipping back into the negative voice, that always said 'No, or You can't,' etc. There are always many numerous books, if you prefer doing your experimenting-exploring of self on your own. Again, search various bookstores, including some metaphysical and used bookstores - a lot good stuff out there is older and out of print. Give yourself plenty of time and see what grabs your attention or resonates deep inside, once you pick it up and glance through, reading here and there. The more outside sources and input, the better you will be at what works best for your growth and changes.

\* \* \* \* \* \*

Nothing in life is to be feared. It is only to be understood. Marie Curie
Nobody can make you feel inferior without your consent. Eleanor Roosevelt

# A True You ~ Part #39

It has been said by more astute minds, that "Showing-up" is the first step of changing your life. In this way, I believe that 'Showing-Up' is not only a metaphor for acknowledging and deciding to change, but actually doing it. It does not mean that you have to go off and join a 12-Step program, not that there is one specifically for letting go of your Past, though they all deal with it indirectly. But, Showing-Up would state the difference between someone "phoning-it-in" - lacking sincerity. Or, having said *you'd do it,* so many times before without conviction - that it all has no meaning, whatsoever. Showing-Up puts a face to it - yours. And, hopefully, that means real determination and sincerity about changing - letting go of the Past. All of these are the peripheral things, entangled with making your journey, or your return down the path. In other words, not an exercise in futility.

As you become more honest with yourself - in a loving way, no negativity here - you are also truthful with others about how you feel, your opinions, and most importantly said with love, not revenge or anger. You are learning to give yourself permission to be who you really are - a capable, responsible, accountable person who now has something to give - and supportive of others. As we all have our ups and downs, a valuable network of people is one of the smartest, most productive things you can do for yourself. Most people stay inside a comfort zone - rarely rise above it or falling below it - because it's consistent with their concept, or image they hold of themselves.

Any time you try to make a change in your life, whether it's losing fat or earning more money, it will stir up resistance inside you, because you're attempting to move beyond the safe, familiar comfort zone. So, you consciously need to choose new people carefully, in that you're comfortable with what say, yet they are may be people who can raise the bar in challenging you to do more or be more. Any new group should also be alive and growing or changing as you change, so are supporting of you in your growth/development. Remember that some people are only meant to be in your life for a short period of time. You need to understand that letting them go, or them letting you go does not mean that what you learned from each other was not significant. Blessings in disguise are those *who first saw* something special in you.

**Exercise:** The real key to changes in personality and behavior is the mental Self-image. When the self-image is "reconstructed," the person changes. You are more than just a body - you have a mind and a spirit also. You will always act or behave like the type of person you SEE - visualize yourself to be in your mind. The real secret is not just trying to force new behaviors, but *changing the visual-mental, Self-image* which controls the behavior. Put your energy in a New mental picture and the New vision will create New behaviors. Best of all, the new actions that spring from a positive new visual Self-image will not come without as much effort or willpower, because they're hard-wired into every cell of your body. The "unseen forces" are now working for you instead of against you.

To change the Past's deeply embedded negative images in your mind from years of conditioning, takes simple steps of choosing and then visualizing - in detail - what do you want that new image of you to be? All the negative images or pictures of yourself must be released - even bless them and say, *'Thank you, I don't need that, as I AM no longer that person.'* Remember you cannot have a vacuum - so any removed behavior must be replaced by the better designed, visualized one. These changes may not happen overnight, for some patterns *will not* go quietly off into the dawn. The deep breathing and processing to release them may have to be repeated. Be patient, positive and kind to yourself as the visualization process proceeds. I have post-it notes, I have written affirmations and full visualizations also written down to keep me on track and I'm positive until they come into fruition.

Granted, for most people compassion comes with age, as they have lived through enough of their own indignities, embarrassments and sufferings. Certainly, they have learned some awareness from all those experiences. The point is that you accept that, while as an individual, you are not really as unique as your parents may have told you. We are flawed in one thing or another, which makes us usually rather vulnerable - and actually quite human. Once you accept or resign yourself to your humanness, you are more capable to extend it to your fellow human-beings - thus compassion. This means in as you want to change, there were obviously some imperfections. To take it another step forward - and hopefully it doesn't take a leap - you begin to acknowledge that we are also, all One. Again, there being only one race, the human race.

This tolerance and acceptance does not mean that you will be walked over or accept ineptness, or in any way put up with fools-lightly who play on your feelings. Yet, few of us if any, will reach into those twilight-years without having lived through and usually become enlightened by, some trauma in your life - your own person or family. A crisis that takes you to the brink, or beyond what you ever thought you could tolerate, but does make you stronger. And yes, life with all of its foibles becomes sweeter with those simple things - the sunsets/sunrises - having more meaning. No one says you have to erase those Past memories that were such good lessons, that taught you such an incredible appreciation for life.

I have donated blood for over twenty years, except for the seven years that I was in Japan, as they didn't want a foreigner's blood unless specifically donated for another foreigner (long story). When I had more time available, I did what is called platelet-donation. It takes about two hours to do the aphaeresis, as they take out plasma or other components of my blood they need and return all the rest back to me. These various platelets have a greater value, as they're not restricted to blood type, so they can be used for more transfusions. The point of this that I was thinking, while being drained one day, was how many lives I might have saved that I would never know. While this may be a real act of life to prevent death, what about all the sad people who are dying a slow death, because they are still trapped in their Past. Some may not know, or believe that they can change their lives for the better. Things don't have to be done the same way, just because they always have been. Wouldn't it be nice, also easy, if a transfusion was all that was needed. But, no it doesn't work that way. Letting go of your Past pain is not easy or nice. Better yet, the life you save *is your own.*

Yes, every day in every way, I am better and better. Yes, I do slip and slide-off track and remind myself, that it is one day at a time. I lose count of how many times I do catch myself from doing or saying something negative. It used to be daily now it's weekly - so am getting better. Which doesn't mean that I don't do negative things, but they are so much less with the New me. I make a point to look for all positive things when I am in a not so good a situation and I find them, and it helps. I am not really a Pollyanna, but it certainly is nicer and less of an energy-wasting than perpetuating anger, or any other long list of things that me and so many others are capable of doing.

\* \* \* \* \* \*

Truly a paradox, that only in growth and change, do we become the people we are meant to be.

Take on each new challenge as a new adventure, and find the help you need inside of you.

Never make someone or something a priority, when the response or reward is neither equal nor worthy of you.

It is better to under-promise and over-deliver, than to disappoint and rationalize.

# *Fear and Pain - Part #40*

The loss of a love relationship - even when the ending was best for both - can create a pain experience so strong, that celibacy or even loneliness are preferred to going through it again, because failure that might ensue. There had to have been moments of love and happiness, even joy that brought you together to begin with, but when the pain is fresh, those moments may not be accessible to your cognizant feelings. That realized, with time or at least deep breathing, it can be brought into awareness and how can I learn from this loss? Also to be sort of considered, is how can I hold on to the positive of the relationship, or learn what to do to not repeat a negative partnering. Examining your own contributions to its failure is preeminent, though not immediately.

These negatives include you being an enabler, or allowed the other person to continue their negative behavior despite consequences. Rationalizing is not just about oneself. We often cover up behavior of those we think we love, even when their actions preclude that it is not love, but abuse. As you all know, the circumstances of your own pains in childhood reflect your adult relationships. The childhood built on helplessness, or trying to please may have been survival tactics, but are a sure prescription for an unbalanced, adult equality or happiness.

To most people, if you reveal all, you're usually afraid that the other person won't love you, as you must be badly-flawed, since prior relationships ended. The truth - though while you need not reveal 'all' upon first meeting someone - is a basic part of the foundation of a new relationship built on trust. It is kind of like the fisherman telling about the fish he caught which 'grows' with each telling. If you do have the center of attention, are you not going to embellish, especially if no one is around who can or will challenge it? So, it is not just telling the truth about yourself to others, but even accepting the truth to yourself. Tell yourself, truthfully, is it worse to lie to oneself, especially when it is done repeatedly? But if you are not open and honest in revealing who you are from the beginning of love, how long will you keep your past foibles or secrets hidden away? Do you not want that other-someone to love you unconditionally - 'warts and all' I say? No one is perfect and you may miss out on a great opportunity for love, because of fear.

**Exercise:** Follow your own path and do not fear being different from those around you. Make a list (or update it) of all those people who would be upset or angry if you changed. Once that is complete, and hopefully it is not a long list, what do you fear most about their disapproval? If one or both of your parents are on that list, and they are actually still alive and viable - what will they do to you regarding your changes? Throw you out of the house? Disown you, or remove you from their will? Scold you, spank you, say how you've embarrassed them and what will the neighbors say? Maybe it is your boss - will he fire you for standing up to him, or for working regular hours instead of the slave-time you've given to the company? Or, likewise your coworkers - you won't be the brunt of jokes or cover for them, or do their work? Why would you fear people getting angry with you, when you're changing for the better - maybe because they're not better or changing?

Now that you've dealt with the people, now make a list of the things you fear (or update it). Take them one by one to examine them closely and how much control you have over them. Any weather items - earthquakes, tornadoes, hurricanes, etc. you have absolutely no real control over - other than watching the news and planning ahead or moving to someplace that has no dangers - good luck. These things you fear are only negative thoughts, which you/someone have put in your head. The more you think, or talk, or write about them, you are *asking for them to be brought to you*. Self-fulfilling prophecy, OK?

Any fear-based thing - maybe not instantly - can be changed in your mind into a positive, if you will only look at it from the positive, rather than the negative. Are you fearing that you are going to lose a job that you don't even like? First, you must accept that change is a good thing, as it helps you to discover the illusion of limitations that you have built around yourself. The trials and tests in your life are not punishment, but *opportunities* to find your true freedom of expression and creation in your life.

Yes, losing things or people can be difficult, yet with time and awareness you may understand and accept how those experiences have helped you to grow on your path. Love is not only the answer, but the first step of conquering fear and pain when you start with loving your-Self. The awareness includes listening to those thoughts that are going on in your mind and make sure that they are ALL positive thoughts. When the negative ones keep coming back, just say to yourself or even out loud if you can, "No, I'm not going to think that. No, that is not me, that is not what I want in my life." It helps to have a good photo or visualize a real happy time or place. Then fill your mind with positive affirmations, especially "I am ..." statements of your love for your- Self, your worthiness, happy, joy and include that you are the Perfect Child of God with all of your imperfections.

Again, fear and pain can be conquered by forgiveness - first of Self and then anyone else connected to these feelings. This means that you can no longer be critical of yourself or others. A loving - forgiving person isn't critical - catch yourself if you do and stop it. It is amazing what doors are opened and opportunities come calling, as forgiveness cleanses all of it out. Don't forget, forgiveness doesn't mean that the person has to remain in your life, if they are negative. As you take full and total responsibility for your life, you are no longer blaming anyone - not even the parents - so forgiveness for everything in the Past must be done to release that pain. *Responsibility is empowerment*, as it puts you in charge of yourself, so you can release the negative, bless it, let it go. Now freed up, you can move on with your New life.

Finally, you then get to the gratitude, for what love started, as gratitude finishes, to make sure that the fear and pain cannot return to you. Even the negative experiences were often something you learned from - eventually, if not immediately - so gratitude for them makes you stronger. The memory of the pain fades, as you learn to laugh at the fear you once almost let yourself drown in. When you have learned to go with the flow, you can not drown, as that positive energy will carry you where you need to go. So most of all, you must be grateful for your bravery and true willingness to change, against probably a lot of many difficult odds. That willingness extended to letting go of old patterns of negative beliefs and replacing them with positive, fulfilling New thoughts, to keep the negative ones from returning. It is a long, continuous path - journey to make sure that fear and pain never return to your life. You can do this!

Remembering love and feeling physically surrounded by that love. You can learn to understand that the prior loss is not as important as the love once shared, that made life worthwhile. And, no one can take that from you, as it was always with you, as to the value of what matters and makes life worth living. Everything else can be taken, as it is temporary, but the world and anyone in it cannot take the love that you have felt, that you have given and known. In that you are also now very rich, fearless and pain-free.

* * * * * *

A baby only has two fears - falling and loud noise. All other fears are learned.

The greater part of our happiness or misery depends on our dispositions and not on our circumstances. Martha Washington

There are those who are lazy, and think that they are clever by lying, cheating and stealing, as if it is the only way they can get ahead. But the vast majority of people are worthwhile and do good, kind things because they are ready for a new world.

# *Emotions and Feelings ~ Part #41*

In the domain of Feelings, intuition or inner knowing speak to you of wisdom and compassion through quiet whispers. While most dramatics best describe the nature of Emotions, as they are more of reactionary, especially of misunderstandings - verbal or behavior of others. Often, unfortunately, they can be essentially explosions of what is perceived to be happening to you. A good example is Jealousy. It is a form of insecurity and represents ignorance, of thinking that one can *control, or own* another's feelings and/or emotions. Perception is a powerful influence on emotions, since what we believe is not always true, yet we don't want to be *distracted* by the truth. It is a basic real insecurity of wanting to be right, in that you were wronged.

This dark-side is at least occasionally common in most of us, and may or may not necessarily go back to recognized Past lifetimes, or simply your family environment of this life. You can become more aware of it by paying attention to yourself in your day-to-day life. Ask, Where is the energy coming from, when you exert your power or hurt others - verbally or physically? Was it something they said or did, or didn't say or do? At that instant, you may not even know where all that negative emotion came from. You may even have sensed that you were the helpless victim of some outside circumstance - sort of a de' ja vu reaction. There is often a karmic-tie between offender and victim; both roles reflecting aspects of yourself - again from previous or current life. It is more than a person 'wearing their feelings on their sleeves,' some are simply looking for any excuse to bark or show their believed perceived power. Truly, the bully is just showing his insecurities.

**Exercise:** With repetitive awareness of your negative actions or statements, comes the realization of another opportunity to change. It may only be, the observance of others doing things that you have done. Then, with the acceptance of the need for and power of change, so you can look at your own inner wounds in a different way. Yes, again, as these things are continuously revealed, you start to forgive yourself and others with an understanding that may come slowly, in steps. While the anger may flare up, sometimes even uncontrolled, it can be dissolved, as you can get in touch with the layers of sometimes unknown emotions beneath. With the repeated deep breathing - love in; anger out - into each and every recalled pain, you release it. Often these emotional pains are directly connected to specific spots of your body. So, one at a time they must be visualized and loved, forgiveness and purity needs to be sent to the physical areas in the body itself. There may be sadness, grief or even fear that is physically and also emotionally there on many levels. Don't forget to refill yourself with protective Golden Light energy and White Light for guidance.

With regard to sexuality, it is very important for women and men to acknowledge the offender aspect where hatred and anger are realized or felt. You need to release any identity with the role of a victim, as it robs you of your freedom - not just with sex or a loving relationship, but joyous living. Hate is such a waste of energy and a primary result of fear. The release of this sexual-arena is a major karmic game, as being played out from one lifetime to another in which you have fulfilled both roles, the victim and the power-monger. Remember, it is never really about sex, but power and control.

Once you can reach that place of forgiveness – first forgiving yourself and whomever else - the negative mantle is lifted so freedom imbued. Acts of violence, repression or sexual violence may be more painful, but there may be Karma or lessons involved. These may take many lifetimes to release the sexual blockages, or work through sad emotions. Loving, sexual passion is a gift from God/Source for each of us to enjoy and express your sensual feelings. Do not keep any of the negative emotions, fears or anger buried, they keep you from the joy.

On the other hand, male or female sexual blockages may occur on the level of the heart, or the head as a fear of surrendering, giving up your power, or fear of deep emotional intimacy. Again, this fear may be from numerous prior lives, or this current environment in which you were raised. It relates to who in the family was the stronger, more powerful or cruelly dominant - the woman or man - either what you saw or made a participant of. The game of sexual attraction, that initially was innocent and spontaneous, became threatening, as the man or woman learned it was dangerous to openly show their true emotions, or open their heart to their partner. Their love made them vulnerable-victims, or subjugated to mistreatment, physical and/or emotional pain, which of course, built the deep-seated fears about them surrendering to their emotional/feeling side.

For survival, they may have learned to participate in the physical act of sex, while keeping their feelings separate. Much like prostitution, where the man or woman may be sexually-present at the physical level, while their feeling-nature is rather absent. Also, it is not done just for money or an addiction. The emotions are locked away because of their fear to open up, or become vulnerable to rejection and pain once again. There may be remembrances of being abandoned and emotionally scarred also by feelings of inadequacy, ineptness or also unworthiness. These are all things that may require professional aid in overcoming and working through to release.

The fear of real intimacy is not just a trendy topic for some women's magazine in male bashing, as many women have the same fear-based problem. While we all may strongly desire a fulfilling relationship, most of us will be lucky to have short bursts, or actually only moments, of what is often referred to as the ideal emotionally and sexually gratifying relationship. But true intimacy, frightens most of us, as it means we are asked to take off *all our masks*. You never know how many inhibitions arise, that you were not aware of prior. This is then the moment of truth, what we talked about before - the trust that you will not be judged by your love one, or by yourself. Many men and women would rather not be involved in the sex act, than do so inadequately, because of perceived fears of performance. No one is totally free of all sexual blockages. You must learn to be comfortable talking about all sex-related fears. It does take time to conquer them.

But deep revealing counseling and a loving partner won't prevent you from experiencing your sexual energy, balancing what is comfortable. Being in the flow with loving awareness in a relationship treated with care, respect, patience and love are vital. Along the road to discovery of a full and joyful experience of sexuality, your love and compassion will grow for yourself and your partner. Your part in this is actually helping to heal an ancient history of the struggle between men and women. These energies want to come together again and join in a dance of joy and creativity. Anything that you contribute to this at an individual level, has a positive influence on the collective-soul of men and women. At the forefront, as always, is your Self-love making the energies of patience and love available for others. Look for the positive in others and if they respond, then love passionately, as if there is no tomorrow, for we never know.

\* \* \* \* \* \*

Love yourself first and everything else falls into line. You really have to love yourself to get anything done in this world. Lucille Ball

The ultimate lesson all of us have to learn is unconditional love, which includes not only others but ourselves as well. Elisabeth Kubler-Ross

Have the courage to say no. Have the courage to face the truth. Do the right thing because it is right. These are the magic keys to living your life with integrity. W. Clement Stone

True love and strong emotional feelings should be for people and the glories of nature surrounding us, not for material things that have price tags.

# Awakening ~ Part #42

Sometimes because of the way you were raised - this and prior lives - the pure energy of love is not clear or evident, as experienced in confusing ways. Sadly, many parents may not have always been very participatory in raising you, or even oblivious with little concern of your presence. Unconditional love was not there, though you may have received admiration for some of your talents, or skills in school or sports, etc. Gifts or toys may have taken the place of time they spent with you, if money was more readily available. This lone environment challenged your notions, in which you learned the so-called definition of love. If this was what you were shown love was. Logically then, all this affects your relationships - with yourself and others - making you search for that elusive, sought-after unconditional love that you have heard of, but do not know.

It sometimes starts during puberty, that an awareness of it grows and that others have different opinions of what feels good, happy or natural to them, and what does not. With age and more Self-awareness, you question your parents' outlook on things, as you search for your own sense of identity. Unless, of course, if you are a totally adaptable child, then you may never question, simply accept and repeat your parents' beliefs. Some children do realize - around 8 or 9 - that 'this is all there is' from their parents and replace the longed-for attention/affection from other mentors or teachers to learn love.

Yet nowadays, with so much New Age or Spirituality coming from so many sources, most adults research, or at least check out the "Dr. Phil" (no negative intended) psychological growth process, as any change, or questioning is better than none. Simply said, now most of us want more love and are learning one step may be the transition from ego-based consciousness to heart-based consciousness. It may take a while for people to learn and more importantly accept, that ego puts controls and restrictions on love, whereas, unconditional love is just that - no strings. I love you 'warts and all' love. Something some children may have never even longed for, as we don't miss what we never had. Yet, if they received any from a grandparent or other kind caretaker, they know there is more than the limited-love their parents gave - "We'll love you if ..." The truth of this experience once realized may cause pain and even a sense of abandonment. Or more sadly, that something must have been massively wrong with you, that your own parents could not love you in the way, you had seen others loved.

You may bury these painful emotions, until as an adult thrown into such a state of feelings for another, your vulnerability-blindfolds you, or creates illusionary images of love. Emotional survival in this confused condition, may encourage you to accept a conditional love, when unsure of exactly what unconditional love is, or even available. Any love seems better than none. Experience has the advantage over age, as some people never learn to expect more from love than what is offered. This, unfortunately, may include only non-participatory sex or patronized attention by controlling strings. There is always the chance that you may learn from others experiences, so you don't have to get emotionally beaten up in the romantic fray of so-called limited-love.

This may be processed through friends, reading, TV, movies, etc. Yet, the naiveté of most would be that others' mistakes would never happen to you. Truthfully, you must completely know and understand what unconditional love is, to be willing to hold-out for it. That truth comes from having that same unconditional love for you -yourself first, before you can give or get it from another. For some, sadly *the thought* of totally loving-oneself from your head to toe and everything in between would be absurd. How could you, when no one else did/does? You may even consider it rather egotistical to love you -yourself, when little worth has been given to you. So wrong for you.

**Exercise:** This, for the child in all of us, is huge. It means examining and letting go of ALL, absolutely ALL of those conditions that non-loving parents. They did the best they could, so forgiveness here is important - as well as everyone else who had an opinion of you - expressed or otherwise regarding your worth. This means it is no longer the status quo of: "You are loved IF ..." - fill in the blank - of those people who put restrictions on you being *good enough* to love. This is the awakening - You are worthy of love just as you are - 'warts and all.' No need to confuse love with a parent's pride in your certain achievements, or being rewarded for living up to external standards of whomever - for whatever. It is now about what you want to achieve in this lifetime for yourself, knowing that achievements do not equal real love. Then you have no need for guilt if you fall-short or didn't win a prize. There is no need to achieve all the time, or make it an addiction.

It is also important to understand that your new *independence is unconditional love for yourself*, no longer confused with emotional dependency on your parents, or being needed by your parents as an object to taut about. There is a difference in assisting your parents and being used as a substitute parent by them, to them. It is not unusual for parents, who did little for their children, still expect the children to take care of them in old age, simply because they were your parents.

It is common for the child to want to please their parents and get the love, so sorely needed. But when carried into adulthood, or the parents happiness and acceptance is put before yourself or partner, or your family, that is not love, given or received. These are destructive and dangerous entanglements of energies called love, but don't even come close to any true definition of it. Sadly, many parents lacked any experience of unconditional love in their own childhood, so all they knew was control, putting guilt or fear onto the child/adult. When perpetuated, love and need become convoluted into justifying them into equals, which they are not. This can quickly escalate into a parent believing that they actually *own* their child.

This child/adult may then feel that they are only loved and appreciated by how much they give of themselves to the parent - stop giving, the returned love stops also. Thus, it is a common that we often choose our partners in which we have a symbiotic-emotional see-saw dependency, even jealousy and possessiveness, as a form of love. The true energies of unconditional love are diametrically opposed to any of this. So, your association or need of love, as you mature, meet people or be in certain situations, challenges you to discover who You are and how You want to be loved. Skewed or unconditional? This alone is why so many people are ready for change in their lives - real love.

**Key thought** - Spiritual realization is that your soul chose to be born with your parents and families for the lessons that you chose to learn in this life, as also in all prior ones. You wanted to change these stuck and rigid 'love' energy patterns of this family soul-group. You came in with a certain Spiritual sense or awareness, that made you different from the rest of the family's expectations or ambitions, that challenged the family's basic assumptions about life. You may have been looked upon as the odd-one-out, or even as the black sheep (I was). It may have taken a while for your confidence to grow and find your way out. But you did, because you were Spiritually more aware, being an older soul than your parents. At a young age, you may have been aware something wasn't quite right about the love in your family environment. Once you found the way out, you attracted like-minded people into your life, who now reflect your awakened state of being.

**Exercise II:** The real awakening work comes, as you let go of all those bits of ego-based fear and illusions absorbed in childhood. Acknowledging that many of these imprints contributed to creating your personality, you only release those that no longer belong to you. This is an intricate, on-going process. It is about reinventing yourself, picking and choosing what works for the New You, even if changing your mind several times. This is all about You, so You cannot be so concerned about what your birth-family thinks or says.

Remember, it is not your job to save your parents or family from their fears and illusions. If they choose to find the path to change, that will be their souls' sole journey. You can share information or your experiences, but you cannot do it for them, as no one is doing it for you. You may have family Karma, in that you've had previous lives with many of the same people, but this is only about You and Your past lives. It is about being focused on your own inner growth and expansion, the possibility of changing that karmic pattern over a family, so it will not be passed along to your children.

This awakening process is available to all, including your family, when they are ready to go through their own struggles on their journey. Your Spiritual family is of kindred-souls that often you've known from Past lives through friendship, love or a shared mission. You share an inner-likeness based on love and respect, which reflect your awakened divinity. Yes, You are an accumulation of all of your Pasts, but as you learn the awakening process, You alone choose who You are to be today - now, in the present of this life.

\* \* \* \* \* \*

There is no such thing as a problem without a gift for you in its hands. You seek problems because you need their gifts. Richard Bach

I have always grown from my problems and challenges, from the things that don't work out, that's when I've really learned. Carol Burnett

Most great success comes from having made some big mistakes or bad decisions. It is also the foundation of wisdom.

Things may come to those who wait, but only what's left behind by those that hustle. Abraham Lincoln

# *Rescuing Others - Part #43*

Eagles teach us that we have the ability to soar to great heights, if only we find the courage to do so. Hope opens up the door to all of your possibilities and you have tough choices to make during all your lifetimes. Sometimes this results in decisions that lead you to reinvent yourself totally. It is basically a Sole-journey of the Soul, as many of your personal and private issues from the Past arise. We All belong to the Human Race, that is what being One means. Yet, you are here to *only advise* and assist others along their path. To rescue them, or try to do it for them, would be counter-productive for them and their growth. It would be the same as the over-protective parent, who doesn't let the child learn from their accidents or mistakes. The only thing that would be justified, is the hand-grabbing to save a life, but still, do not take on the responsibility for others' choices. Help them only if they ask for it, speaking of your own experiences to give encouragement, your love and respect for them, if you feel that. You simply cannot be rescuing someone, as they will soon resent you and blame you for any problems or failures that beset them later.

What is most important is that they acknowledge and learn that everything - good, bad and in between comes from within them - their choices. There is no one to blame for their actions or beliefs, or their outside choices making them do something. They may have been spoon-fed things - from this life or prior ones - but, it was/is their own choice to keep those beliefs, believe them or let them go. While you may have empathy and sympathy for others, you can not be drawn into curing their pain for them. You make a difference in another person's life, as a positive support, when you know who you are and your belief in yourself. Your actions and behaviors exemplify who and what you are more than any words. Believing in or encouraging another person is not rescuing them from the experience they created, as they need to learn how to work their way out of it. A child grows strong and usually independent when they've learned to experiment in all they do in life.

**Exercise:** During any assistance, you may have tapped into the fear the other person has. And, while it felt outside of you, it was blending with what was your own. It may also have been the collective consciousness' aspect of fear amplified through you, so you were actually bringing in way more than what was your own. Even when you are in a good, solid space, fear can slip back in. If you can catch yourself, don't let yourself go there, don't tap into it. You simply must acknowledge it with detachment, as you take a deep love-breath in - breathing in compassion, and awareness. Let it all surround the fear, and then breathe it out to release-let it go. This is how you train your body, your mind, to make the permanent changes for you.

You must practice for your own self-assurance, just like a real fireman running into a burning building, if you are prepared, you can help someone without being pulled into their drama. Think of some Good Samaritan jumping into the raging current, only to be pulled under also, by the panicking, drowning person. What is accomplished if they are both lost? Practice your affirmations, knowing you can do what you have set out to do - "I Can do This!" With any doubt, then in comes fear and the battle ensues for you to keep yourself positive, as well as the one you are helping.

Having averted an entanglement that would drain you, there is no room for energetic exchanges, that would place an obstacle that keeps you from meeting your own goals. So, don't make promises or keep rescuing someone that takes you too far off your path. This may necessitate more character-building skills and challenges, until you fully understand what your personal, even evolutionary destiny is. At the same time, supportive assistance can be a well, learned lesson in proving your own strength in your new beliefs. When you reflect the beauty of others with encouragement, you see beauty where and what you never saw it in before. As you return to walk the path laid out in front of you, that assist of another can usually makes you even more determined, so now you continue without any resistance on your part.

So, there are positives for you in assisting, but not in rescuing.

You learn how much you know, by being a teacher. As you raise your vibration again, more of your old stuff comes up, then you find more truth on your path. Empowered, you dare to reevaluate what you have been taught and even what you believed. Like the Gordian Knot - an intractable-problem solved by a bold stroke - Alexander cut through the knot, with one solid swing of his swift sword. You learn that you don't need to follow-suit with *the way things have always been done before*, or by a distorted Belief System or ego fantasy.

You may think that *your intentions* are good for another, yet you may cling to the belief that your ideas or suggestions need to be followed. They don't, they are Yours and may not work well for the other person. Remember, it is about being supportive and assisting, compassion, not rescuing or a need to develop a follower or disciple. Everyone must find their own path, for their own experiences of learning their own lessons. Empowerment of oneSelf is the main reason you cannot rescue another. The key that sets them off is the acknowledging of their own contribution, or negligence as to who they are and, it is by no means effortless or painless. Yet, they do have to accept that they cannot continue to grow as they were, or become who they believe they were meant to be, *if* they don't correct their actions.

Even if others had abusive parents, that was their choice prior to birth, for their learning experiences. They must also accept that they *were not the only ones* to be abused, someone out there had more and they let it go to grow - change. There is a freedom in their personal transformation, as it is for themselves and a certain limited state of mind that they are conquering in the process - "I can do this!" They can only bloom and grow, when they take the risk to step out of their protected or hidden environment. It is all about releasing and letting go of who they were, when it is no longer working for being happy. You will be amazed always and sadly sometimes disappointed by those who simply refuse to change, because of the personal effort involved.

It is important for you and others to understand that they made a sacred contract with themselves long ago, to work passionately to fulfill what they came on Earth to do. These things are private and personal, though you may help or guide others by sharing yours. Make compassion contagious and you just might change the world! Or, you could suggest they open up to their Guardian Angels, or follow their intuition, which may all be quite new to them. Talk to them of the step process. Learning that All energies are infinite and shaped by their own consciousness is not an easy step to believe, so it may take a while for them to process. To accomplish it all, they and you need to continually release attachments to any negative experiences and restrictions, that you both may have put upon yourselves. Remind them that when they are in the flow, all is easy, as all is right for them. All things come when you want it, Ask for it and believe you deserve.

Any rescuing takes away from you and your path/journey, so get back to it as soon as you can. Success in transforming your life requires planning with objectives and goals, as to where you are going. Most people spend so much time worrying or dwelling on the things that *they don't want* in their lives, that they've not taken time to figure out what *they really do want*. What you think about and hold in your mind, brings attention with energy to draw it into your life. So, stop worrying about what you don't want and start focusing on what you do want. The Universe needs to know what you want and need. When things happen easily and naturally, you know you are on the right track and in the flow. Then, remind others of how it can be for them.

\* \* \* \* \* \*

It is best to learn as we go, not go as we have learned. Leslie Jeanne Sadler

That which does not kill us, makes us stronger. Nietzsche

It is in your moments of decision that your destiny is shaped.

Anything worth doing, is worth doing now! Ralph Stayer

# *Love As A Healer - Part #44*

You planned your lessons from the parents you chose, your other siblings, birth order, race, status, etc. Whether or not you had financial abundance may have been balanced by love. Some people have said, 'Love was in such abundance, we didn't notice we were poor.' Others may gripe and complain, not having known love, but that they were dirt poor and never knew when they'd eat or have to move, as their parents continually blamed one another for no responsibility of the family situation. How the children managed to move past all those things spoke of their own self-determination and love of Self. True wealth is so much more than money, it is a real abundance of all the senses being filled with love. We know that love cannot be bought, yet it can be freely given and shared for unlimited reasons to unlimited people, animals or any living thing that you choose. Love is a most amazing thing and nothing, not even fear is stronger.

**Exercise:** To your most inner depths, into each and every bone, you need to reach down and root out what parts of you that need to be loved, for it is also the great healer. Love erases pain, fear, doubt, insecurities, etc., as it releases you to freedom. You can learn to love all of yourself, even if you felt unloved as a child from those around you. Visualize yourself surrounded by the protective Golden Light, allow the abundant, unconditional love of God/Source to heal and to wrap around you in the most protective way. Once you have savored it, show your gratitude and then remember to process forgiveness of your Self and others. Let go of what you were *not* given in the Past. This is a visual that you should practice often, until you can truly feel its warmth and protection. I can now use my forefinger in vertical circles in front me and I instantly see - feel the protective

Golden Love Light around me and the guiding White Light in front me. Remember, cancer and other diseases come from unconscious, unresolved old bitterness, that previously existed in this life or Past ones. There is never a shortage of love and all you have to do is *ask for it*, then it pours over you from God/Source. Believe you do deserve love.

Much of your Karma is driven by the wounded-child of your Past, and those repeated negative-realities that it creates in your life now. Realizing how you are affected by it, you may want to choose to NOT be a victim within it or from it. Once acknowledged, your now destiny then is to choose in this life to learn, to work through and release that Karma. Rise above the fray, you can take control of your own life. Do not give away your power to your Past negative emotions to have control over you. Remind yourself that all these choices are Yours, You've chosen to make in the course of this life. Taking more responsibility for them, and accounting to others, may be another thing for you to acknowledge, if even aware when they are happening. Love can be your healer - emotionally and/or physically.

Stillness gives you a knowing-presence and awareness that you do not need to suffer. In the stillness, You learn that most of your own evolvement with suffering usually comes from Your thoughts You've created, and most of that is what is stored in your unconscious. By asking yourself where those negative thoughts came from, you learn those untruths about yourself, you can dissolve them, no matter who it was that said them. You are God's perfect child, loved unconditionally and gifted in every way. This may be a process, that can only be done in small steps because of the possible pain, but each session you will feel renewed and truly loved for who you are. When You know this and accept this deep in your heart, you finally can rise above those negative thoughts to forego any more suffering. To receive in Your pure love and acceptance requires that You empty out your vessel of all hurt and rejection, even if you are not aware of all that is in there.

Self-love - only unconditional love - is required to complete your process of transformation and rebirth. As very, small children, most of you loved yourselves because you felt love. You believed that you were deserving of all the love and abundance that this world had to offer. All too quickly, the majority of you were told that you were wrong and were bad, or not worthy or your intelligence or your beauty was no longer good enough. You were probably told that in order to survive this reality, you needed to fit in more like everyone else. You therefore shifted your innate positive beliefs or unlimited boundaries to adopt those of your families, societies and cultures. You then most likely, stopped loving and believing in yourselves, as you allowed others to influence your path.

The lucky ones of us eventually found someone who saw more in us and within time, slowly you began to once more emerge as the bright-star that you are. As belief - empowerment in yourself grows from the positive response of another, you become more trusting and knowing who you are, as well as who you are meant to be. Bravery, then creates independent experiments, which build confidence and sureness around you. If you don't have to prove anything to anyone, think how freeing it would be and suddenly it is. When you can give that love to yourselves, that you are craving from others. It is then that your need for others' approval and acceptance can no longer imprison you in a state of insecurity. It is as if by magic you realize that you are loved, and lovable, and loving to others.

The channels of communication with your Soul are reopened when you willing touch, old emotional hurts residing within you. And, these traumas are parts of you that have been isolated or unloved in your Past. Breathing love deep into those feelings or spots in yourself can reintegrate these fragments, so you feel whole again. Repeat as necessary, or whenever old, achy pain returns. The releasing makes sure that you've had no attachment or identifying yourself with them.

No longer then do any parts of yourself feel unwanted, unloved or not good enough. You have accepted them, just as they are, with your love transforming them into something better, as they are filled with love. Healing your Past restores your feelings without fear and improves your intuition and guidance from your Soul. Remember to embrace yourself, knowing you are not alone and that you are truly loved, safe, and secure. You love yourself as you are, without judgment, regrets or expectations about your Past, as no longer any barrier of suffering and loneliness. You are connected again by love and feel inspired.

You will learn that what you give to yourself, you can easily give to another. But what you deny to others, will be denied to you - not because you are being punished, but because your heart has closed. A closed heart, like a tightened fist, can neither give nor receive. This is where love again saves you to open your heart. Idea: You can give without loving, but you cannot love without giving. Again, that love starts with yourself and again, it must be unconditional, no exceptions. Stand in the mirror, looking from the top and work down telling you, yourself - not from the ego, but from the heart - how much you totally and completely love yourself. It is not easy and should be done daily, if not at least weekly, until you smile. If you know the joy and freedom of loving yourself unconditionally, then you will have no problem in doing that for others.

For too long, Universal Consciousness, or humanity has sat and licked their inner wounds of the Past. People hang onto their guilt, or stoicism and suffering, as if a 'badge of honor' rather than allowing the areas of hurt, distress, or maiming to be healed. Like a sick dog, they continually focus on them by licking day after day. They are starving their hungry souls, though they have a sense of a need to be filled. Some do this with food, others with alcohol, or emotional dampening drugs prescribed, so *lovingly* by their trusted physician, or maybe street-sellers. Some never come into the understanding that their soul is starving for what truly gives it joy and sustenance - real unconditional love. For some there will be an awakening to the true simplicity of love and forgiveness. Others will never accept that the solution can be that easy. They truly believe they need to suffer, as it's their toll for this life.

Anger - as said - is a secondary emotion - something/someone has to spark it - this comes from a key or button pushed from your Past. Anger comes from fear, which cannot occupy the same space as love. On the opposite end, your Smile is a healing essence to yourself and others. It is a life-force Spirit-energy directly connected to your whole body - every single cell. It also raises your vibration, which affects everyone as it helps you connect to them - they can feel and even see that positive aura. A smile comes from happiness, which is a natural by-product of love. All proven healers of the mind, body and soul, are people filled with joy that overflows in their smile.

Americans are 'smiling' people - we can be spotted when we are in other countries by our smile. It is a most common, positive thing that we are taught as children - smile for your photo, smile and wave at Granny or Auntie, smile when you're happy. When I lived in Japan, I was often asked about my smile and infectious laugh - I am a basic happy, positive person. Stoicism is a solid part of the Japanese cultural foundation and smiling is considered being not a serious person, or even foolish. Some of my trainees even felt that I needed to know not to smile so much, as people who didn't know me would think that I was foolish, even stupid.

While in my seven years there, I adapted and assimilated to many things Japanese, but not-smiling was not acceptable to me, as it truly was who I am. I once explained how Americans smiling was key to us, as we had even put the "Pursuit of Happiness" as part of our Declaration of Independence. What I did learn, was to combine the use of a big 'apology' - a really big Japanese cultural thing - with smiling, which no matter what country I was in, could stop anger in its tracks.

\* \* \* \* \* \*

When we live in gratitude, our giving becomes receiving.

Show appreciation for the moment and expect a miracle.

Beginning is half done.

Clear your mind of can't. Samuel Johnson

# *Positive Attraction ~ Part #45*

Whatever you are trying to attract into your life - a partner, new job, or living situation - you must believe yourself worthy, or equal to it in your heart, soul and mind. Your thoughts and feelings must be positive not only in your desire, but also must know you deserve it. You must love it enough to hold a true visualization of yourself within it and know truthfully that it will make you happy. And it must be healthy and joyful, as you live in or with it. In other words, not a partner who has negative habits, or does not respect you, or isn't equal to you, or a job that will cause you stress or again not even be respective of you and your talents.

Then, and only then, will the Universe allow it to come to you without struggle or strain. You shouldn't have to fight for it, if you are in the flow of it, as you are then one with it. Of course, if any negative requests are granted, it is for the lessons to be learned, even if repeated until you have learned them! It is more than 'be careful what you ask for,' you need to learn what is your truth? - what do you really want in your life? Of course, those answers will change with time, as will the requests. But this may clarify why God doesn't always respond.

Positive Attraction does not require a miracle or quantum leap, just your consciousness to be ripe and ready for your heart's desire. It will come naturally, when you are in the flow, as if the next logical step. You cannot feel any stress, frustration, or negative thoughts, as to you not being good enough for it. If you are matched to something you truly deserve and together you have unity with it, Universal law then brings it to you. And, while no one can interfere or be able to take it from you, in a relationship, your time together may have a preset-limit by Divine

Destiny. For example, the couple that falls in love, has a child and then one dies or leaves - it is perhaps the child for which you were brought together. That Divine Destiny of genes, or the limited time that both parents contributed to forming, raising or guiding the child. Part of this lesson is that no one dies before their time, yet why you must make the most of every moment together, for none of us knows when anything may end.

Also accept, that once the lesson or experience a person was brought into your life to give you has been satisfied, then they may be removed from you. Too, there is the being grateful for what was given to you - 'better to have loved and lost, than to never have loved at all.' It may be hard to fathom that there are those poor, lonely souls that have never known the rapturous, joyful bliss of unconditional giving-love, even for a moment. Again, the idea that "I would rather have twenty minutes of wonderful, than a lifetime of ordinary." Yet in reality, we all truly want more than twenty minutes, we all want a life more than ordinary, because how few among us would admit to being ordinary or mundane? Is it negative ego or positive pride that makes you think that you are above the crowds?

That is a question to ponder, while I do think it is a choice to feel you are worthy of more - whatever more means to you. Gratitude is an attitude that the Universe responds to - the more grateful you are, the more is given to you. Appreciate something for what it is, and it will grow and bloom into something wonderful; find fault or minor imperfections, then it withers and dies. I do believe we should grab for the brass ring and what's attached to it. Just don't get caught-up in the details and also it becomes an issue, when you try to put expectations on your attractions that involve other people. Understand, visualizing a creation in front of you, other things are created around you.

The Universe offers us so many glorious opportunities and gifts beyond the comprehension of many of the unawakened masses. How many men and women are still stuck in a common-ego "Fairy Tale?" A female who holds on to a modernized version of the belief that a knight in shining armor is going to gallop up on a white horse and save her from her personal misery. So, she spends all her time "miserable" believing the only salvation is meeting her "knight." For a man this might be a new car or job, or money that will bring to him women swooning, or respect from others. They both believe their misery will be solved by an external factor, rather than doing the Self-Inquiry and steps to heal - empower themselves in true understanding. If ego desires and needs are still being perpetuated. As the priority of your manifestation skills, there will always be a hidden glitch in what you receive. Material things have a finite satisfaction and never really fill that gaping-hole within your soul, as being loved for who you are.

**Exercise:** Thinking a relationship will fill the hole or gap, or needing someone from the outside who completes you, is a real false panacea. Mutual, or one sided, expectations of love need to be clearly examined, acknowledged and discussed. How much do you need to flaunt your material possessions or status? Can you list ten things that attract you about your loved-person that is not physical or material? And, vice-versa? How much have you shared and agree on regarding beliefs, ethics, family, politics, religion, etc? There is no real fine line between love and hate - for the opposite of love is not hate, but apathy. How much/many of your Pasts have been shared, acknowledged and let go of regarding behavior, etc.? Can you honestly say to each other that your love is unconditional? Do you have any "ifs" regarding your relationship or love? Is there trust, truth and no bad skeletons rattling? What details bonding and intimacy to you? Do they come with time or situations? What are the real reasons behind a pre-nuptial agreement?

You are being shown that none of this defines who you really are. It is all merely a framework which can be changed as you do. The ego of illusion causes us to falsely identify with whatever we thought we couldn't live without. On the path, most importantly is the true shattering of your illusions - who you thought you were, what you thought you needed and how you conducted your life. Much is gained back of what was lost in new and unique ways. Really more than a challenging process, it has been exhausting, frustrating, depleting and sorrowful. You faced so much fear, anxiety, sadness and regret. Now, look around and appreciate the love found and the joy in your little things. You are truly protected and loved, manifesting the grandest vision of what you want in your life, as you remain calm, peaceful and in harmony within the divine flow.

There is a freedom from the Past, as it is done and over with. Releasing has put the synchronization of flow in your life, as you surrendered to let your Past go. You are now into the present moment, listening to your intuition and allowing it to guide you. You are in the flow with your soul and your truth, which means it all must resonate deep within you, as it is what you set in place prior to this incarnation. Now, all you have to do is step out of the way, and be open for the Universe to flow it all to you. What is it going to take, for the love of your dreams to walk into your life and stay? What about real financial abundance to come into your life, to fulfill your Divine Destiny? Ask the Universe to show you how it gets better than this. All it takes is for you to Breathe deep and

Release the Past, the negative thoughts, the pain - yes, it's can be as easy as that, when you've done the work.

\* \* \* \* \* \*

Joy is a net of love by which you can catch souls. Mother Teresa

Acknowledge Each other - Give Praise and Appreciation

Don't be afraid to take a big step when one is indicated. You can't cross a chasm in two small steps. David Lloyd George

# *Being Present - Part #46*

"The past is history, the future is a mystery and this moment is a gift.
That is why this moment is called 'the present'."

As I've said before, the best way to shake your awareness into the present is to break your daily routines or habits to see how they change your perceptions. By simply trying something different - food, clothes, TV shows or an activity you've never done - your mindset alters and you may even gain a whole new way of looking at your new world. A few mistakes are good for a laugh or experience to entertain others, so don't be afraid to shake yourself up a bit - even go radical! Laughter opens up more possibilities.

Do Not Ask, "Why did I do That?" When you ask "why" it takes you back into a loop of your own failures, to all the times in the Past when you did something like that and the emotions or judgments that went with it. 'Why' brings up all the stuff that you believe makes you do/say stupid things, like those adults in authority from your lost youth or childhood who would question you so embarrassingly. This solidifies that limiting reality into your current experience or situation. Instead, ask *how* it came into your mind - was it your own thought or someone's suggestion? Was fun a point of its creation, or were you into challenging or testing yourself? 'Seemed like a good idea at the time.' We do want to eliminate the 'should have, would have, or could have' from becoming a part of our "future past."

**Exercise:** The small trivials, rituals, necessary duties of your everyday-life have piled themselves up to such an extent that you cannot see beyond them. The old 'can't see the forest for the trees' problem. We do forget who we really are, or want to be when we do forget to put ourselves, our dreams and heart desires in the forefront, or allow our soul destiny to be lost in the mundane. You need to free yourself, so you may continue on your path to fulfill your journey of self-discovery. It is time, if you haven't done it before, to make a list of the "Twenty things that I would like to do or accomplish in the next twenty years." Put a date on your list and title it as such.

These can be places, people or things and, of course, never any limitations. Write as much detail as you want, but no reason is at all necessary. Leave enough space so that, as you go over the list, you will begin to see ways of doing them that you may not have considered. Encourage close, like-minded friends to join you in their challenges, so you have a support group that can urge each other on, or giving ideas or connections for completion *without competition.* Keep this list to take satisfaction in those things you've crossed off, as joyously well done. There is rarely an astronaut, Olympic winner or other prized success that did not start off as a dream. Taking the highest point of perception is being positive and capable of handling whatever you need to change into a higher vibration. All is not chaos, but a balanced view - evolving like a moving target to set the intent of having a multi-dimensional life.

While Shakespeare said that "All the world's a stage and we all play our parts in it ...," many Spiritual philosophers believe that the big secret is that we created this game of life on Earth. We're making it all up! And, we continue to create it every day. Also, that we have the power to make it the way we truly wish. Most of us are way too serious about making money, collecting material goods and being 'king of the mountain,' instead of having fun and playing the game, *without a concern of success or failure.* None of us gets off this rock alive or with our toys, so why the big sweat? Being in the present also means enjoying each moment as it comes to you, not just letting it pass by, waiting for the next big thing. Sometimes, *this is as good as it gets,* for we may not be around for something that might be better.

There is also the realization that what is great to one is not so to another. We should not need multiple-choices to appreciate what we have. Yet, sometimes we do need to see what is out there, to have the gratitude for what has been given to us. It should not be our choice just because it has been someone else's choice. But, like the Sushi go-round - you wait too long to make your choice, it will be all gone. Indecision is like clutter in your life, the reason you hung on to it is never known, when you throw it away. Some things you get a second chance and some you don't.

If you can see it, hear it, feel it, taste it, touch it or smell it, in this moment, then it is of the present moment. You are not thinking or dreaming it into existence. It is actually here, now and so are you to experience it. Sometimes, an anticipation is an intertwining of your happiness and fear of the experience. When you begin to emerge from yourself into the present moment, your outside thoughts may stop and you may feel a deep silencing of peace filling your mind. As an inner door is opened, you are allowed to experience an infinite essence of your Being, your true nature. It gives you the opportunity of pure-real consciousness that is a dimension of you that exists in Oneness of who you are and to become. This is very powerful and as you learn to tap into this dimension, you will be given the information through your intuition, of the direction for fulfillment of your Destiny.

Once you have realized that if you keep playing the "re-runs" of the same old regrets over and over, you cannot possibly move on or forward. Holding on to decisions that you'd made when you were younger and less conscious are holding you back. These regrets were taking up room, that could be filled with happiness, light, and new fun situations that you want to bring into your life. Are you still marching to a different drummer, or has your music inside dried-up and died? You need to have focused on forgiving and releasing your Past *and* owning that all the decisions you've made have brought you to where you are *now*. You are the accumulation of it all, so even the missteps make you unique. You no longer create these same experiences again under the mistaken belief that you must do this in order to survive physically, emotionally, or economically. You are free to change.

Time and time again you have broken through old boundaries of thinking and feeling. Every time you felt suffocated in traditional structures and rules, knowing deep inside that your soul could not flourish in a fear-dominated environment or relationship. You have felt the necessity to break-free. It has been painful at times, to say goodbye and travel new roads alone. Yes, difficult and very heavy, but you had to stay true to your feeling that something wasn't right, that it did not make sense to you. You just knew it was not right for you to stay.

Adaptation is not an option when you know in your heart that something important is missing. While you could temporarily, or even partly adapt yourself to an environment that didn't truly resonate with you, at the level of outer behavior, it just doesn't work. You have to eventually cross the inner valleys of self-doubt and loneliness, before you open up a new horizon, where you truly fit. In other words, being in the present you cannot even fake it, for a bit anymore. Definitely, repressing or ignoring your problems is not possible if you are to remain in the present.

\* \* \* \* \* \*

Tough decisions - regarding people, places and things - have to be made to grow.

Awareness only takes a moment, of course, you must have your senses intact and open.

To be in the flow means that you have learned that the stream of life is constantly moving. Being in the current, you see how things change around you and with you. The stagnant pond never has any fresh input.

# *Choosing Drama ~ Part #47*

It may sound cold and perhaps heartless, but one reason that some people create drama is so they know they're truly alive, with the byproduct of attention from others. Like most processes, it is a Step System: a) Because they can't love themselves, b) they create an edgy drama that makes them feel alive, c) they suck in energy from people around them, who love them and d) give them attention, so they don't have to love themselves. This can be as basic as a toddler throwing a tantrum, a teen who does self-mutilation, to a grown person attempting suicide. Sadly, they scream and kick and suck whomever into it they can. You can make some choices about how much or long you choose to rescue someone. Understand, if they don't learn to love themselves, they will *never* believe that you love them. It comes down to truly believing they are worthy of love, so the drama is a test - "If you love me, you'll save me." The same confrontation we all have to make with ourselves if we want a different life, rather than one stuck in your Past, that said you weren't worthy of love.

**Exercise:** It really is easier with the toddler, as this is a wake- up call that they need more attention than that cookie, or toy they are insisting that they need right then in the middle of the store. Stop, get their attention and promise that you (if parent/caretaker) will play a game, or read a book, or give *something of your time* when you do get home. You must follow through with it, so that they will trust and then believe you. In many ways it is easier to nip this in the bud while they are smaller than you. Teenagers are a whole other category, for it seems that reaction-drama is what most of them are about with you. Acknowledgment, if only applauding them for creating such a scary-wonderful drama, works better than ignoring, or simply you saying, "because I said so." While at first, they are highly annoyed with you, it is important to clarify that their action stop, as you're not going to take part in their dramas anymore. Getting them to talk is always the hard part, but sticking to your guns and trying to find positive attention is what works for them. Also counseling helps, when they won't speak to you, if their actions become dangerous to themselves or others.

This actually also works on adults, since these dramas are coming from those lost-teen years when they needed so much more attention. Whether you are simply a friend, family member or parent, you need to understand that it's not going to go anywhere, other than more and more drama, repeated ad nauseam. Simply saying you love them will not help, you need the key words of worthy, creative, or anything that connects to something that they like to do. Some humans create events in their lives, as they desperately need attention and are champions into the blame game -'it's not really being their fault.' Even when things seem to be going quite well for them, they subconsciously or otherwise can't accept that they can be happy. The *worth of love* is missing here, so they either create a problem, or make some small infraction - their own or another's - into a big problem. Sometimes you just have to ask the person what do they want in their life, or if they want to learn how to create a different way of living their life?

If they say yes and only if it is a strong yes, you might share how you started waking up and becoming aware of creating positive events in your life. How much you know about their Past, can help you direct positive things for them to do in their life. You may also lose them, as soon as you mention that they have to take responsibility for themselves and their lives. At this point, you may want to look into your own life, as to why you're brought in, time and time again into other people's drama.

Are you a rescuer? Is it your job to take care of the world? Does being overly compassionate to others help you to avoid taking care of yourself? You may have gotten caught in these dramas before with other people, or you're naturally attracted to drama. You may even participate in it as your own way to find yourself. It's time to step back, take some deep breathes and maybe acknowledge to yourself what your involvement is. Are you only looking to be the hero, or has this person or others around like you more? Is it time to let go of those drama friends and that whole drama process?

Sometimes you have to agree with people to make them go away, as facts won't work with drama they will have a million excuses and rationalizations. Once you accept that they will not listen, don't waste your time trying to convince them otherwise. However, please remember your part in this participation. If you are rescuing, you are involved in ordering/controlling others' lives and you may have now chained your life to theirs. The prison guard is no more free than the one who is the prisoner, if they let themselves be overly involved. The teacher is as confined to the classroom, as are the students who sit in their seats, if the teaching is redundant. The writer is confined to the audience chosen, until they change their projection. I'll say it again, the one thing to be said for rescuing: "When you want more for the other person than they want for themselves, YOU will be frustrated."

**Two personal stories:** Many years ago, my future ex-husband's older cousin committed suicide. To me she looked like she should have been quite happy. I was perhaps nineteen or so and not even married yet, so what did I know? She had a nice house, three pretty good children - not to close in age - I think the oldest, a boy, was maybe nine or so and the two girls, maybe the youngest two or three. So they were spaced, and presumed planned. I can look at it all now from the perspective of what stresses mothers. I know she had a basically good husband who loved her, regarding those things in his providing for the family, though I don't remember what he did for a living. I don't think it was a white collar job. I do remember the last time I had seen her was Mother's Day, and she had a large, gorgeous orchid corsage. Something my father would never have frivolously spent money on for my mother - I was impressed. I learned later that to some women these kinds of things were important, tangible-signs of caring and smart men followed suit in delivering them.

Most importantly, I remember overhearing, don't think I was a close enough relative to be told directly, that they were sure that it was an accident, as the son or the husband had been due home and would have rescued her. It was then mentioned that she had tried several other times before - not sure if it was the same from carbon monoxide - sitting in the car or what. The point being several people, including her husband, knew she was not happy and obviously things like the corsage did not help. Therapy was not acceptable then, but who knows if she would have gone. Also, knowing her mother and some of the relatives, I'm not sure how sympathetic or supportive they may have been of her talking to a stranger about one's problems. It wasn't a real communicative family, which may have been part of the problem.

The other story was a close friend of mine, again many years ago when several of us were going through our divorces. It was not easy, since divorce was still a rather unacceptable and uncommon thing. Admittedly, the four of us didn't have really big or bad, ugly problems, we just weren't happy and not willing to put up with it, as was done then. We had grown considerably, since our early marriages and our husbands had not. A friend of my friend, who had actually been divorced a year or so sooner, had many emotional problems. She had felt she would do better leaving her son with the husband and finding her *Self* - a new term back then. Unfortunately, she did a lot of that searching with the aid of alcohol, drugs and indiscriminate sex - a lot more than the rest of us. In between all of that, she had numerous suicide attempts with my friend rescuing her over a dozen times. She had self-committed and also been formally institutionalized in various mental, drug and alcohol institutions, all to no avail.

I had only encountered her a few times - once my friend, who was living with me then - invited her over. She consumed two-half bottles of hard liquor by the time I came home from work. I was not pleased and also concerned as to the exposure my son may have had of her behavior. I assisted my friend in helping her fine jobs - which she rarely lasted at more than a few weeks, though she was intelligent and talented in many things. After several more attempts and causing more problems, with other friends who had tried to help, I wanted nothing more to do with her, and finally my friend eventually did the same. Many years later, on seeing my friend again, I thought to ask about the woman, but she had no idea. She wasn't sure if she had just left the area, as she had done that many times before, or if she had finally not been rescued from an attempt. It was sad, as such a waste of a human being, yet there is usually a point when self-preservation kicks in for the rescuer. You have to sometimes let people go on to their own devices. I do believe that no one dies before their time, or that lessons learned for this life may include suicide.

Today, of course, both women would have been put on some depression medications and perhaps, they would have helped or not. I currently have a couple of acquaintances that have been on them for years and neither seems that much happier. I must admit that, I also do not understand why they aren't happy, they both seem to have all of the trappings of what we usually consider the right formula. Though again, nothing is ever as it seems. Of course, neither of them has had any great epiphanies, or made any major changes in their lives in over twenty years. How they truly feel about their worth or being loved, I've never questioned and they've never shared. I do know that neither has let go of their difficult Pasts. They still both partake in dramas, though I have little participation any more in them. Perhaps for them the taking of a pill is easier than the confrontations of change, growth and letting go of the Past.

\* \* \* \* \* \*

You never find yourself until you face the truth. Pearl Bailey

The price of greatness is responsibility. Winston Churchill

Empowerment is the inner joy of knowing that external force is not necessary to be at harmony with oneself.

# Loss ~ Part #48

Over the years, several movies have dealt with helping a loved-one to die, rather than them continuing to suffer. As the saying goes, "There, but for the Grace of God, go I," in not having to live through such a thing, or accept the consequences of participating in such a thing. I do believe that one has the right to choose their own death, if they know they have an incurable, debilitating disease. But, euthanasia only truly helps the ill, not the living who love that person, though they may try to understand. I loss a mutual friend from her own subtle hand and I worked to accept it through my beliefs, while my other friend could not. She took it totally as a personal affront, that it was a 'greedy act' of our friend removing herself from our friendship. She was really, furiously angry at having the friend choose to leave her.

She did have other factors overwhelming her own incurable, debilitating, degenerative-disease, which she controlled the pain with extensive bio-feedback. Her grown son, a long-time alcoholic, had died the year before and she knew she would soon have to go into a wheelchair herself. It was all, too much for her and taking the pills would give her that fast departure she wanted. It was her decision alone, believing her family would have insisted on her becoming hopelessly-helpless. She had always been the one to take care of everyone else. Her one daughter felt some of it, was because she was so vain, still really looking so young for her age, but a failing body.

While my friend had a certain understanding of ultimate love, as she'd had many pets euthanized from suffering. I don't think she forgave our mutual friend for leaving her, before she, herself died. To me it truly was a brave act. I can't say how I'd feel about living in a wheelchair, since I also consider myself to be a very, independent woman, usually wanting to help others. I do have several friends, who have set-pacts with other trusted friends, to help if needed to euthanize themselves. I do know, I don't want to live off a machine.

**Exercise:** We all have had loss of one type or another. The key is *how long* we choose to punish ourselves, or if others involved, that controls our quality of life. If you can't talk about it, then perhaps writing may work to release and let it go. Since there are no accidents, and no one dies before their time, understanding the loss will only come with reviewing that other life to you. It helps to search for what positive things came out of the relationship - yes, we don't have an experience without a lesson. Of course, you've already been dwelling on the negative loss, so no need to rehash that again. A prison does not have to be four walls with bars, we've all created them on our own.

What did you learn from this person when alive? Your lessons-experiences with them? Methodically go over dates, situations, events or just anything that comes to mind. Take out some photos, or other tangible evidence of their life, to make the memories flow back to you. You may even want to do a photo collage, either for yourself or others close to them. There is a release, equivalent to growing wings and flying, just by giving forgiveness to oneself and others. Remember to bless and thank the experiences, as you let them go. Death, eventually you'll accept, is simply a transition of the physical body, as their soul will always be with you in your heart, if you choose.

If your loss has been traumatic as in murder, extensive disease, etc., and not saying that any loss is ordinary, you may want to join a group where other people have had similar losses. This is a mutual healing process, as their feelings are pure empathy of having been there, rather than the limp-sympathy others feel so inept in offering. Truly, the best healers are those who have been deeply wounded themselves. With this learning and letting go of the grief, anger, etc. you may begin to find the path to give memory and sense to the situation. The list of home-grown - grassroots organizations that have come out of tragedy, are extensive over the last fifty years, since speaking out has become more acceptable that suffering in silence.

Other lives can be saved, as in awareness and prevention, even laws written that no one considered necessary prior, like legalized euthanasias. It is beyond someone dying in vain, it is knowing that we are all connected and one life is just as valuable as another. Your own, whole physical demeanor changes when your belief swings over to the positive, as the anger, blame and emotional shutdown is released. It is like supporting peace, rather than fighting against war - fight drains you, but the support spreads positive belief. It never happens over night, but you can be the one who makes the needed changes.

A loss can also be a pet, especially if considered a member of the family or your true, faithful friend. No one should question how much that pet meant to you and how much you choose to honor it. Most of us, that lost pets in our childhood, may not have gotten the emotional satisfaction that we needed to let them go. I had a pet goose named Garfield, who was a wonderful watch-dog in the yard, but eventually became a nuisance to my mother's garden. Naively, I was sent off to the movies to my delight, as my uncle and mother killed and prepared Garfield for dinner.

Upon my return, I was not only expected to accept the situation as necessary, but to sit down and eat him. I couldn't, and didn't forgive my uncle or mother until many years later. There were other ways to handle the situation, but I did learn from it. When my son's ducks - given to him by my mother - got too big and unruly, I talked to him about a farm I had found, that took such pets and they would be so much happier among other animals. We visited them several times after taking them out there, until he had let them go emotionally.

* * * * * *

No problem can be solved from the same level of consciousness that created it. Albert Einstein
The key is that we must keep on keeping on, even in the face of adversity.

# *Who Are You? ~ Part #49*

**Exercise:** Questions to ponder and respond to with time and thought. Who are you? - What are your ethics? - Is your Being - your inner self - happy with what you are doing? - Have you fulfilled or at least working on your goals? - Do you still have dreams unfulfilled? - Who told you they could or couldn't be fulfilled? - How do you want to be remembered? - How often do you have joy - real joy in your life - daily, weekly, monthly, never? - Who or what is stopping you from being what you want to be? Is that from your Past? In reality, *only you* can stop you from being what you want to be.

**Mantra:** "I am more than *good enough* to live a life full of love and over-flowing with my Divinity, as I am connected to Source. I am whole and wholly loved, just as I am." You have to reach high to grow, and seek far to go beyond the limits of who You think You can be. You need to look deep inside to see who you are, as you dream big to be more. The journey is also about the joy that it brings, which is part of the reward of making it. Your thoughts are the only way you focus, or direct your energy for the changes you want in your life.

There must be contrast in your life, for you to see the choices you can make. If you have not experienced any bad/difficult things or misfortunes, then how will you know, or be grateful for what you do have? We must see variety, diversity in what paths are open and how available to you. It doesn't have to be the way it's always been - don't let anyone tell you that you can't have more or be more. You can be as much, or as great as you want to be, no matter who you are. Use your innovation, competition of new ideas and variety, in being a melting pot, as the spice of life is generally looked at in a good way. This is generally accepted as one of the foundations of the United

States and other Democracies, as to one's abilities and dreams taking them, as far as they want to go. Immigrant success comes from not taking what's being offered for granted, as many citizens do.

Even after living in Japan for seven years as a corporate trainer, learning the culture continued to be almost a daily lesson, or slow peeling of an onion - not an easy process. One of the common colloquialisms is *sho-ga-nai* - literally, "There is no other way how to do it" or "This is the way we do it" or "There is no way except that way, so I/we give up." When the "We" is spoken, it stands for 'We Japanese,' as in speaking as to the 'The Way or *Kata*' is done, one Japanese speaks for all. The formal saying of *sho-ga-nai is shi-kata-ga-nai. Shi-Kata* means "The Way How To Do." As the Japanese are one of the most modern, homogeneous societies in the world, the Kata is taught from day one and is sanctified as inviolate, as it literally does affect every part of Japanese life, in the upmost detail to be followed.

To not do something the 'Japanese way' can lead to both private and public expulsion, ostracized, disowning regarding inheritance, ex-communication, etc. Likewise, as the basis of Kata is being of 'pure blood,' it is more important to them than the most die-hard white supremacist in the U.S. It can affect their job, marriage and general acceptance into a group. Stray dogs/mongrels are not accepted in all *sense* of the culture. Kata is another reason now, so many young Japanese leave Japan to find out who they really are, when they know they don't fit into the traditional society at large.

Therefore, it was interesting that the Japanese also used *sho-ga-nai/shi-kata-ga-nai* frequently as an expression, or *excuse* when *they gave up on something,* didn't want to seek another way, or just persuaded themselves to give up. It was conveniently-used when they did not want to accept or try someone else's way of doing something, especially a foreigner, or something that appeared rather new or risky. The only exception to this rule was if the person suggesting the new approach was esteemed with notoriety, or extra education/experience. Luckily, with time, I rose into this last category and was able to make changes I was quite proud of accomplishing - especially for women students/participants with me. But many give up on any individuality, accepted their fate as no choice but to leaving, or often take to much drinking or gambling, as drugs are not widely available.

Which brings me to a more mixed approach. While traditional in Japan for the first son to follow in the family business/lifestyle, it is something that has slowly been released, in your more Westernized or Democratic societies. Still, even the most supportive parents, families in general, try to restrict their children by indoctrinating them into following their traditions. Guilt is a primary method used, as well as passive/aggressive communication regarding "What will people think/say?" or "How could you do such a thing after all we've done for you?" "Doing that will be such a disappointment to (whomever)."

It is as if, parents have their children to either fulfill their own long-lost wishes/dreams, or be prosperous enough to continue to take care of them into their old age. Sort of like having slaves or indentured servants, that *never* are given their true freedom. At the same time here many freer Western people let society/culture - family, religion, money or simply tradition of the related group, control or restrict you from being who you are. Some people are even too afraid to dream, as if someone might read their mind, or see their individuality blooming.

The summer before I left Japan, I was again visiting friends in Brisbane, Australia. I had flown in very early that morning, showered and taken a short nap before meeting them on the Riverwalk for the weekend Market. While we were walking around, I saw a charity march came through, with the wonderful, usual Aussie-mix of people in all kinds of dress, singing, pushing strollers, carrying signs and balloons. As I watched with fascination, I suddenly started to cry and my friends were rather alarmed, as I am not the crying-type.

They asked if it was jet lag, but as much as I had traveled, it rarely bothered me. I finally told them, that in looking at the Aussies and comparing them to how the Japanese would do any similar thing - all dressed identical and walking only symmetrically - made me now realize that *I also was losing my individuality.* I saw I had adapted and assimilated too much, more in trying to fit in enough to not attract too much attention. The decision was made right then, to leave Japan the following spring, as that was when most contracts ended.

I still look on Japan, as the most pivotal experience of my life, as I learned so much about myself and other people/things. It is still a life/lifestyle that I was glad I was able to recognize and move on past, before I had totally lost who I was. Some people working there were/are not so lucky, in their situations of where they are living and the conditions controlling them. When you stay too long, you really can't ever go back home again, as *home* has become the 'foreign' country.

\* \* \* \* \* \*

"Your living is determined not so much by what life brings to you, as by the attitude you bring to life; not so much by what happens to you, as by the way your mind looks at what happens." - Kahlil Gibran

Integrity is doing the right thing, even when nobody is looking.

Empowerment is the inner joy of knowing that external force is not necessary to be at harmony with oneself.

Learning is a treasure that will follow its owner everywhere. Chinese Proverb

# The Change Process ~ Part #50

## A review - with new perspectives

Change starts with the experience of an inner void, or just repeated restlessness. Things that used to draw your full attention, or situations that you got completely caught up in, now leave you empty or uninspired. Somehow, things seem to have lost their usual meaning and purpose, or you feel an extreme effort to do your routine, as to why bother. You may have been continuously looking for outside validation of worth, because of being unwilling to face the underlying inside fear of rejection, abandonment and loneliness. While your consciousness may be in the grip of fear, with the ensuing need to constantly reaffirm itself.

This deep fear and the need for outside reassurance, may long be hidden as the true motive for many of your actions. Your whole life may be built upon them, without you being consciously aware of it. Perhaps you are aware of a vague agitation or tension within. But more often, it is a major event, such as the break-up of a relationship, the passing of a loved one, or the loss of a job. This comes along to invite you to truly examine *what* your life is about. Or, how now your whole life is working for your happiness, or not. You may not even think about joy, as it has been so long since you knew it.

If you are constantly on the defensive, and are always feeling lack, a need for more, but not sure of what, you are ready for change. Yet for some, even when their life is like a black hole that can never be filled, they don't want to go deep into themselves. As if acknowledging a real problem exists, you may have to do something about it. For you know deep within, you feel alone and fearful, as everything seems meaningless, fragmented and incomplete. You may have developed coping strategies: shopping, eating, other vices. But these no longer seem to make life bearable, as well just dealing with problems at the periphery, instead of at the center. In this way, you try to alleviate the inner pain by feeding it with phony outside attention, or even fake acknowledgment, quasi-power, etc. While denial keeps you from the true answer, or solution that comes from inside, your soul has a deep longing for Oneness, safety and love.

**Exercise:** Everyone longs for unconditional love, which must begin with being totally aware and one with your own Divine-Self. In other words, if you don't first love your Self unconditionally, no love from the outside will be accepted or believed. Even the unconditional love of God/Source is not realized, if you think yourself unworthy of it. The first step is the hardest, yet it can be the easiest with the old methodology of repeating something until you believe it: "God/Source loves me unconditionally, therefore I must be worthy of being loved. If God/Source loves me unconditionally, then I can love myself also unconditionally." As always, the key word here is *"unconditionally"* - no strings attached, like if I was smarter, better looking, richer, etc. NO! God/Source loves me unconditionally - 'warts and all' - so I can love my Self-unconditionally.

While you may choose to examine, and then let go of stuff -whatever, or whomever rejected you from your Past, you really don't have to do that. You know you are worthy and loved unconditionally. So, all you actually have to do is acknowledge that they were wrong, for whatever reason. Yet, you do need to Bless and Forgive them and yourself for that rejection you believed. There were many lessons to be learned from this experience and that is what you are here on Earth to do - have experiences that make you realize who you are. If you had not been rejected in the Past, you may not be as loving and accepting of others now. When you have *learned forgiveness* from your own pain and suffering, you will not pass that pain and suffering on to others. It is when people have not forgiven, that they continue to inflict pain and suffering - along with rejection - on others.

The power of forgiveness is beyond your personal experience. Understand, that all of the perceived-evil in the world, is always the result of massive insecurities and fear, so the need of clinging to one's personal power. It may sound so very simplistic, but all dictators, or lesser, more common greedy or powerful people who mistreat/reject others, do so because of their own hidden fear of rejection, insecurities and deep-seated inner feelings of lack. This does not necessarily mean wealthy people, since there is no negative energy surrounding money. There are enormously wealthy people who are phenomenally generous philanthropists, giving and helping unknown millions. In the opposite vein, it can be said for those who perpetuate discrimination, prejudice toward unknown others is only their fear, because they are different from themselves, so must be lower or unacceptable. This separates them from those who know forgiveness and those who do not.

It is not a giant leap, to go from loving oneself unconditionally, and recognizing that we are all One. God/Source does not just love you unconditionally, but all of us, for we are All Spiritual children of God/Source. Therefore, if God/Source can love us All unconditionally, then maybe you can learn to love All others unconditionally. Yes, it is very basic, so think about it. If you loved yourself unconditionally, and you are no longer constantly, fearfully looking for outside validation, then everyone else loved themselves unconditionally also - who would be left to hate? Who would there be to kill, or go to war with if no real fear? If we all loved ourselves unconditionally, there would be no need for outside approval or recognition or competition. You no longer need rely on other people's judgments and you are not edgy about what the people think of you. Then, you could love each other unconditionally, so there could be Oneness and harmony, finally peace - No suffering, No greed, No pain, etc. It really all does start with just one person.

This acceptance of unconditional love is also the first step of enlightenment, or beginning on your Spiritual path. Think of the Dali Lama - China took his country, tried to take his life, destroyed all his temples and killed thousand of his people, yet he has always, only expressed love for China, in hopes that they will see the light of their doing. That is pretty, powerful forgiveness and unconditional love. You do not fight war with hate, you bless it with Peace. It is a whole different paradigm, frequency and positive energy.

With the release of fear, and its other cohorts of negative beliefs, you can live more from your inner inspiration to do what brings you joy, which brings creativity into your life. You feel relaxed and happy without the need to control or mold the flow of your life. This is living with full trust in what life and freedom will bring to you. Now, when you give or do things for others, it is no longer an empty unconscious call for attention, love and recognition from the receiver of the gift. Kindness expects no rewards, as you are no longer hiding from yourself. While you don't need to do things anonymously, there is no expectation of accolades, or resentment if not received. Your true giving or doing for others, no longer has an umbrella of control over it. You are also no longer in a state of Self-denial, or need to be the hero, as your behavior is coming from your heart and soul, not your fear or manipulative ego searching for love from the outside.

With the acceptance of your own unconditional-Self, this empowerment soon builds your confidence and self-esteem. You have no need to contend yourself with what love you might have missed from others in the Past. You have moved on and gotten past that, as you are no longer in fear, or lost and afraid. You are a whole, worthy person who is loved unconditionally, and loves all others equally unconditionally, because you know there is no lack of love in the Universe. This also gives you Divine Power, which means positive energy to do and create anything, and everything that you want that brings joy to all. Just ask for Divine Assistance to receive it.

This new awareness unsettles everything that seemed obvious before, and it awakens emotions within you that you don't know how to deal with. When you start to doubt the benefits of your old ego-based patterns of thinking and doing, a whole new side of you enters your consciousness. A spontaneity of freely expressing your feelings and emotions are the entrance gate to your greater Self, or into your Higher-Self. By exploring what you truly feel, instead of what you are told to feel, you restore your integrity, that part of you which is your inner child. Getting in touch with your true feelings and emotions sets you on the road to liberation from your ego, fear and negative energy.

You ask questions about the meaning of life, about good and bad, what you really feel and think, as opposed to what others have taught/told you to feel and think. These questions need to be seriously considered, as they are very real to you, and they have a direct bearing on the life choices you make. You look at yourself and you think: "Is this me? Is this what I want?" You receive glimpses of who you truly are and can be: your uniqueness, your individuality. You are no longer dependent or restricted by anything around you: your parents, your work, your relationships, not even your body.

But this new freedom has also created confusion, doubt and disorientation which released old psychological wounds within you, which you need to heal. Since these have been buried for so long, you may not be able to cope with this pain. Concentration on loving your-Self unconditionally becomes more important. Also, Do Not blame or judge yourself for any of this pain of your Past. This may lead you to punish yourself with negative behavior patterns: uncontrollable mood swings, addiction, depression, anger problems with communication, or difficulties with intimate relationships.

Self-criticism does not accomplish anything. Yet, many of us fall into it rather quickly once the facade has been removed of who you were for so long. While you may not like who and what all you realize about yourself, it may be difficult to stay positive through this self-revelation. So, you must keep your mantra of loving yourSelves unconditionally, and knowing God/Source loves you unconditionally. There is no need for regrets, as we all made mistakes or missteps in the Past - your lessons learned, and probably more also in the future. It was never written that you-human had to be perfect. Remind yourself of tolerance of all things and people, with acceptance and full meaning of unconditional - just as you are - no bells, whistles, bows or ribbons.

* * * * * *

**Fear doesn't drive change - but it does perpetuate mediocrity.**

# *Change & Pain - Part #51*

**Exercise:** If you need to take each and every pain from the Past to examine where it came from, or what was attached to it, then do so. But you must remember to keep it firmly in the Past, and just because something once was, doesn't mean it now is. Study it well to understand what you learned from it - all pain has a lesson. Then once again, deep breathe several times: Love in - Anger out, bless it, and forgive the attachment to it and let it go. It may have been part of who you were, but it doesn't have to be part of who you are now. One question you do not need to ask is Why? There is no real answer that makes sense, so let it go under the category that people are ignorant, and may not have even known what they did caused you pain. Or, they were more insecure and fearful than you, so they had to strike out in whatever way they could, to hold you down or control you. It is what it was, but doesn't have to be any more. Do not sabotage yourself, or your opportunity to fully make the changes that you want in yourself. This is so very key to moving Past your Past - letting it go, for you to have learned from it.

Something you may not realize is that some of this pain may be attached to prior lives - you are an accumulation of them all, Karma brings them back. So, while some things come up, and you may be confused as it does not seem to relate to anyone, or anything in this current life, it may be a very, old pain that your ego has not let go of. You may want to do some deep breathing or meditation to get in touch with this pain, so you can fully understand it and how it has infected your current life. The same process then of blessing, forgiving and letting it go is done. Included in the pain may be some of your own behavior or traits, or characteristics, that you're not too proud of to have been associated with from your Past. The same process, forgive yourself - who you were, but you no longer plan to act that way.

Think of it, as if once you owned a big gas-guzzler car and now you have an energy efficient, non-polluting, hybrid/gas-saving car. Simply, now you know better. While you may have done those things under the influence of others or to impress others, or some fear, the accountability for those is still yours. The responsibility to change those things is Yours, as it is to let go of them. All things change and even some people choose to. You have made the decision to change, so now allow yourself to do it without punishment, questioning or other judgment on Your part.

You do not need to judge yourself or others, as if right and/or wrong. It is simply an acceptance of doing what seemed the best thing at the time, or having a misstep that you will not repeat, as the lesson was learned. Fear is the most powerful negative thing that makes you do things that you don't want to remember, much less acknowledge to let go of, even for your own good. Love is the only thing that can ever conquer and erase fear, especially when that love is unconditional, the pain can be blessed, forgiven and let go. Again, it is the contrast in life of having known fear, or pain, or suffering that you can appreciate joy and love. If you *only* had a perfect life, where would be the knowledge of gratitude, or the experience of improvement, or the challenge of living life and having a full expression of all emotions? To let go of judgment is to also let go of doubt and have trust in yourself - others, even when you might be wrong. Judgment can lead to perfectionism, which can be very dangerously destructive, as it does not exist in all people. Judgment does *not live* within love, because it is the opposite of acceptance, a basic part of love, which in turn heals all pain.

Change on the outside happens as you are open to it and make the changes on the inside - the thoughts and feelings of - in your heart. Self-acceptance is a part of your unconditional love of yourself. Love is the biggest magnet for positive changes in your life. If you love and accept yourself for who you are, you will attract circumstances and people that reflect your self-love. It's as simple as that, truly. When you respond to the pull from your heart-centered intuition, it all then unfolds, as you are following your heart's desire, which is for Your highest good. You know when you have released all your ego-control, because things you want just flow to you. You don't have to work so hard at making them happen. If something you think you want is not coming to you, then perhaps you need to rethink, deep breathe and sense if it is for Your highest good. The sensation of pounding a square peg in a round hole, should tell you that you are not in the flow. You need to release your resistance and surrender your control to Source and trust in the Divine Will to guide you. Which means let your heart - which is connected to Source - guide You, as it has replaced fear, and being pushed by ego.

Unfortunately, there is no switch to flip, or magic button to push for these changes. The move from ego-directed-mind-controlled action takes time and practice, especially slowing down enough to hear your heart-directed intuition. If your life has been push, push, push, and go, go, go, the noise alone would make hearing that inside voice hard to hear. This is where the written word can assist the verbal, as you take the time to journal. The morning 'dumping' of all of your frustrations, feelings and emotions of daily life gives a real clarity that works better for most people than meditation. It does take some time to learn, so if you have a problem doing meditation, simply start with doing deep breathing - at least three to begin with and then building to ten at a time - with a count of ten per each in/out.

As your breath goes in, you see it connecting to your heart - since the oxygen goes there anyway, this is not a big stretch for your mind to resist. You can say to yourself key words to assist with your connecting to your heart-intuition: Love in - Fear out; Love in - or Worry/Doubt out; Love in - Pain out. Or choose your own words in like Guidance, Direction, Trust and then whatever negative you want extracted out of your emotions or feelings. The great, easy thing about deep breathing is that you can do it anywhere, anytime as you do have to breathe, and most people don't pay attention to your breath being deep or not. I've started doing it at stop lights when feeling surrounded by idiot drivers, that I'm about to scream or beep at. It works for me.

Besides your morning journal, it would be helpful during this tenuous change over period - tenuous because it is new and easy to slip back to ego-directed way of doing things - you might want to take time, at least weekly to write down all that you do want to accomplish, or change in your life. Goals can be deceptive in that unaimed ones never miss their mark, but you do need to know what you do feel - not think - you know you want. Goals can change, they are only written on paper not stone, and it is best to concentrate on only three at a time. The more time you take in understanding the reasons you want them - don't assume here, it is best to write out those feelings - the more you will believe that you will get them. In other words, these desires are more a part of your being, than your doing. Deep desires don't have to be from your childhood of wishes, dreams and hopes. They can be a new something that was just revealed to you.

They are coming to you, you are allowing them into your life, because you desire them and truly believe you deserve to have them. If you still do not love yourself unconditionally, or believe you deserve the things you desire, you won't receive them. Your *heart has to believe that you believe you are worthy* to receive. It is never God/Source saying "No" to you, it is You saying "No, I am not worthy of this," or "This is not for my best and highest good." Your heart must be ready to receive, so you may need more Self-work to accept the abundance that God/Source is more than willing to give to you. Are you still judging yourself and others? Do you still beat yourself up for mistakes or missteps? Ask yourself how much you trust - are you still trying to control outcomes?

If you have a bump or tightening in any of these questions, then take out a piece of paper and write FEAR at the top and really, really dig deep and see if you still have some stragglers hanging on. Pick some of the usual topics of money, job, intelligence, talent, looks, etc. and list absolutely everything that pops-out of your emotions or mind, feelings. New fears come on board when you least expect them, creating blocks or detours, in your positive energy flow of receiving all the Universe wants to give you.

This transformational change that you have chosen to take on for your betterment, is not to be thought of as a conversion, as if one day you are X and the next day you're Y. It is also no reality-show that at the end of the thirteen-week session, a whole group made you over. You do the work on your own, with only your intuition and God/Source there to guide/support you. It is a process that moves along, as you are ready and choose to do so, as it is not easy, but the greatest challenge of your life. As said before, it has detours, sidetracks and backtracks, so you will only go as far as you choose to go in this life. It is your journey, your path. You are only doing it for you and by you, as your choice. Remember, when you life lessons are over, so are you. So, if you're still here on this rock, you still have things to learn.

Letting go is a major part of this change process - that means old habits, people, things, ways of doing stuff. Very little may be the same, and you need to look at that prospect as refreshing, revitalizing and opportunities to explore your Self more. Granted, as your Spiritual energy grows, surrounds you and supports you, the journey may take you places that you never could have dreamed you'd to go. Your true Spiritual essence will begin to permeate all things that you do, then soon Your Spiritual being will be the foundation of everything you are. Change is never easy or quick, but it can be a lasting growth that takes you higher and brings more joy than you ever knew ever existed. Yes, Understanding Oneness, and being part of the perpetuation of the real belief in Oneness, will be part of Your usual daily routine, all in Your Being and sharing Your Spiritual light around and to others.

* * * * * *

Real Peace starts with stopping the Wars inside us. It takes great passion and great energy to do anything creative. Then again, you can make anything you do creative.

# *Past Fears ~ Part #52*

When we experience a situation that has a strong fear-imprint, it may be the energy of fear is associated with a Past life trauma, yet still be a very real part of our Soul journey. This may have happened, or brought to you by some de'ja vu flash, with vivid visuals, or emotions attached that relate to some phobia which you may currently experience in this life. Sometimes people will live in, or be attracted to an area that has their particular fear-vibration. In other words, they have "asked" subconsciously for another life of conflict in the same place. That is why some areas of the world are always in chaos, with generations of people who hate each other, return life-after-life to do battle. It is as if, they are trying to get past that particular fear. To so many in the outside, Westernized-countries, the reasons are not logical - especially when religion, sect, tribal or a caste system is involved. Still the conflicts, even wars that kill tens of thousands of people occur over and over again. These places hold a particular fear-imprint that people return to many lifetime after, to resolve healing their fear.

For some of us, it may have been resolved to a certain extent, but we can experience them again when we visit a place from our Past, or connect with people that resonate with our similar soul-wounds. For many of us, this experience of learning what caused the fear-energy to begin with, can heal it. The knowledge-visual may bring acceptance, forgiveness or release, so that you feel comfortable once again fully in the flow. If you so choose, you may be capable of having been placed there, to heal the fear-imprints for the collective of others also, who have gone through similar pain and suffering like yours. To be a very successful experience may bring a new fearless-energy, for having accomplished an important part of your soul journey.

Earlier in my life, I had very strong claustrophobic-feelings and never knew where they had come from. Some people, through the years, had remarked that I was probably drown, or suffocated in a previous life. It wasn't until my late twenties, when I went to Mexico City on business, then with extra time a trip out to the Aztec Pyramids that it all came upon me. I knew many people had died from sacrificial rituals, so when the erie feelings came over me, I merely thought some ghosts were there. Then as I walked around, climbed and touched so much, de'ja vu flashes started coming stronger and longer, until I was almost knocked down. Later, in the visitor center the flashes came when I would get close to certain objects - like the stone calendar, or read some description of a ritual regarding the medicine man.

At the Anthropology Museum back in the city, again these Past video clips played across my mental-screen, like some tour I had taken. The giant - perhaps six feet tall - stone-carved calendar was the main item drawing attraction for me. To the surprise of my friends, I seemed to know all about it and I had no idea how. Once I got back home, I found a person capable of Past-life hypnosis-regression and learned of a very fascinating Past life. I was the daughter and only child of the village stone-carver, as my mother had died shortly after I was born and my father refused to remarry. By the time, a teenager, my father had taught me how to carve the many temple decorations, as well as the stone calendar. I was serious, very good and dedicated to it.

This angered the medicine man, for they were sacred objects, so their carving could only be passed from father to son. The chief of the village had no real problem with me, but to the medicine man it was somehow diminishing his power and control, for a female to do the job. One night he and some of his cohorts kidnapped and drugged me. They wrapped me very tightly in some blankets and put me in their canoe. They were about to embark on their annual Spring trip across the Gulf of Mexico, where they did trade with the different Delta Indian tribes. Once I woke up, I was told that I would drown if I tried to escape. Since I knew the water was very deep and I could not see any shore, it was either death, or take my chances in a new tribe.

I researched much of the information that was recorded from this Past life regression and found that it was true, that the Aztecs were the only tribe to cross the Gulf, as remnants of their culture had been found in archeological digs of the Delta. I also read many times that there is usually some connection-thread between our various Past lives to the one we currently live. My mother was three-quarters Native American - Choctaw, Chickasaw and Cherokee - Mississippi born, where many of the Delta Indians lived for thousands of years. Also, as a child I never had a problem with a row boat, but I would refuse to go in a canoe, for no real reason and a kayak absolutely freaked me out. Interesting, how little tidbits are salvaged from Past lives. Luckily, my claustrophobic feelings all but left, when I had learned the details of their creation. They only came back once, many years later when I felt I was put into a fear-position of no escape. Actually, my panic attack scared the other person so much, that he immediately fled from me.

**Exercise:** Phobias can usually be reduced, if not erased, by a behavior modification process, where under a controlled-environment you become desensitized of the fear of the action. This is how people with a fear of flying have slowly become accustomed to all parts of flying, in small repetitive steps. I love snorkeling and I would become claustrophobic, as soon as I put the mask over my face. For me, I deep breathed repeatedly, talked to myself, placing the Golden Light around me for protection, reminding me that no one was trying to hurt me. Also, I repeated that I could leave the situation whenever I wanted. I did not want some fear to cripple me or keep me from doing things that I wanted to do. It is rather amazing that mental control from this life is capable of erasing a fear from another past life. Using Behavior Modification is very powerful in helping to eliminate many fears or situations that feel uncomfortable for you. I have worked with many trainees in my work and my Life Coaching to help others recover.

A few years back, I learned from an Akashic Reader of another very old Past life, which had left-over lingerings - most I won't go into - but it was a Past lover. We were from two opposing sides and for my safety, he was trying desperately to get me to return with him to his country that had conquered mine. He said many times how much he loved me, and in leaving, his pained-love the final time he said, "No one will ever love you as much as I do!" Then, in my discovering and uncovering our romance - I did find him in the history books - I began to feel his love-pain had been almost a curse. I wonder if I'll again meet him, to find the love and settled it. And in staying, my head was cut-off as a traitor.

I don't think I've had a fear of loving someone, as I feel I've loved many, but it never lasted. I now consider that some of that was probably because I never thought that they loved me "enough," as that was a word I frequently used. It is not unusual when we are young and romantic, that when our hearts have been broken several times, we will put up a protection to keep us from giving too much of ourselves. This is quite sad, for then you will never know the sheer joy of your surrendering to love, when the right one comes along. Fear is such an ugly, destructive emotion, especially when it is love it is afraid of. You might say that it is quite a conundrum, in that the only real emotion stronger than fear is love. So, I would think it would have to be a very powerful love, that is able to release the fear for surrendering to it.

\* \* \* \* \*

Difficult things take a long time, impossible things a little longer.
You are never given a wish without also being given the power to make it true. You may have to work for it, however. Richard Bach
Not our logical faculty, but our imaginative one is king over us. Thomas Carlyle
We are what we repeatedly do. Excellence, then, is not an act, but a habit. Aristotle

# *New Experiences ~ Part #53*

Everything always happens for a good reason. Good things can also result from bad situations, though it may take a while for us to see them, or realize. If "A" didn't happen, neither would have "B," which was a really good thing. The bottom line is that you are where you are, know what you have experienced, but now you have within your own reality an opportunity to move beyond that. If you insist on that you maintain your attachments to your Past, you will be going nowhere fast. This journey is about living *actively* within your human life, and mastering the skills which can make that life happier, even joyful. If that is not happening in your life, then the plan should be to change that which you have conformed to, or have attached yourself to out of ignorance - not knowing something better is available for you. Then you need to acknowledge that everything - up until this point - did serve a purpose, so there is no need for any regrets, resentment or guilt. You let it go, as you're ready to move on.

**Exercise:** When your life is filled with drama and distractions, you need to go within as your authentic self, your truth exists inside of you. Remember, Never expect your truth to be the same as anyone else's. Honor yours, respect another's, but never insist they follow yours, or you theirs. Once again, simply stop what you are doing and begin to breathe deeply, so you may be with yourself by disconnecting from the outside and being still. Feel the breath going deep within your body and then slowly begin releasing it out. The unconditional love of yourself goes in and fear, doubt are released out of your drama with each breath - over and over. You may focus on a particular part of your body that feels pain, and send it healing White Light to surround it with love. As you continue to breathe deeply, you may even want to do a small meditation, by thinking of some *thing,* or *place* that gives you pleasure. If you are really stressed and can't fathom anything to be happy, simply cover your eyes with an eye-pillow or cool, damp cloth to totally block out the light. Still, keep your deep breathing going. Into this blackness, simply visualize a single dot of your favorite color. Focus on this until you begin to relax and then play with it, change the color, multiply it, play 'pong' etc. It doesn't matter, as the idea is to distract yourself from what is stressing you, by letting go and having some fun, or even laughter with the nonsense. Do work at maintaining this for at least five minutes.

Now you should be able to recall some relaxing happy place, or some experience that has made you happy. Indulge yourself as you engage each of your senses from head to toe, to totally recall this time and fully relax. Remember this scenario, file it away and repeat it to yourself that you will return here whenever you feel any drama, heavy stress, or need a distraction from what your busy life is throwing at you. It would really be beneficial if you could practice your escape daily, perhaps as part of your lunch hour that you take for yourself.

Remember, you only need five minutes, more would be nice, but sometimes it's easier to convince yourself that at least you have done five minutes just for you. The bonus is, of course, that you will be totally revitalized to face your afternoon with new energy. If you have any problems getting to sleep at night, you can program this deep breathing visualization to put you to sleep, simply by asking for it to do so. Thrive, not just Survive - the choice is easy and it's yours. There are many excellent meditation tapes, either for stress reduction or other specific needs - try them, they work.

**Foray:** I joined some friends at the art museum for some free jazz concerts. It was more for visiting the friends and getting out than for the unknown local musicians. Afterwards, it seemed with things that I had been going through, that the music became an analogy for me. While it went off in some wild, even uncomfortable ways at times, direction with the techno-sounds, it finally got pulled all together to make a more familiar, acceptable, enjoyable sound to my ears. It was more than experimenting to some of the listeners, as some people did leave. It was kind of like having faith that while I may wonder off on some happy trail, that turns out *not to be*, I found my footing on the new path. I would never have gotten that experience without the foray, yet how much of a lesson I received, I did not know immediately.

**Exercise II:** I must remind myself also, to accept times of simply allowing myself to take a new path, as that's what the journey is all about. While I may have some definite things I would probably never do - bungee jumping comes to mind - I try to never say never and thus have had some really wonderful experiences in my travels. Ask anyone what they would 'never do' and you might be surprised by their livid answers. Then, ask what they really want to do and have never done - upon their regalement of these things, carefully ask why haven't they done them yet? How many things do you do only because you think they are expected of you to do? How many things do you simply like to t*alk about doing*, but have never actually even checked out what all might be involved in doing them?

Many of us get too analytical about which way we are going and keep plugging on, to what we feel is our true goal. Yet, removing the blinders and letting the attraction of a different destination be a good distraction, might change that goal completely. You never know if you don't try it and the liberation of a different surrounding or view, might be something that can have an impact down the line on your life. While we all know not to judge a book by its cover, we still do it. Some things are not just for 'other' people to do or experience. Or, of course, too many side trips or excursions into the unknown that end up negative or disappointing, may turn out to be procrastination, or a need for attention through self-created drama.

Do you need to re-examine where you're going, or where you are, and what got you here-now? Or can you go with the flow and see if there is some benefit to it all? Not everything is a real great learning lesson, sometimes a trip and fall along the trail is just an awareness of what to avoid. Still, the point is that it is new, maybe just a tiny course correction, so as to not have a repeated safe-thing from the your Past that brings no new experiences.

One of the most important things about new experiences is to not have too many expectations regarding them. Even when these things have come highly recommended by someone, no two people are alike. High expectations can totally dampen what could have been an unfolding of amazing, surprising events. It is always important to go into these situations with a positive frame of mind and you will find it. While a certain amount of planning or information makes it even more enjoyable - you're not missing a demonstration because you never checked the schedule - or if you are going off to a foreign country, do be familiar with some of the culture or customs, so you don't offend anyone. Part of your whole growth is being able to interact with new and different people - even if you never see them again, it can be a lifetime memory.

While not every little incident is a life changing moment, you do need to take responsibility for all that you create. Life doesn't just happen to you, you do create all

271

that you experience, even those little mundane things. Some humans are very good at telling stories about ordinary things, while others are oblivious to key incidents that they should have noted or questioned. However, sometimes you tell your Self things - blame and complain - about situations and other people that keep you in stagnation, or pain. Part of your journey, as your conscious awareness grows, is you do become cognizant of creating *illusions* to serve your 'stuckness,' instead of creating more joy. This is when you need to stop talking and start taking action. Change doesn't happen by just talking, if it means something to you, then take action.

Lifetime markers tell you where you've been and also where you still want to go, so are not just age-markers. Many people and situations have been brought to you for many reasons. Maybe your speaking out, or doing something is the tipping point for a change that others wanted, but just didn't know how to make it happen. Once again as Gandhi said, you can "Be the change you wish to see in the world."

\* \* \* \* \*

# *Victim Story ~ Part #54*

Each lifetime is a journey in overcoming soul-wounds and their lessons from paths we have already traveled. These wounds and lessons are revealed to us in our 'victim story,' which represents the beliefs that we have about our powerlessness, lack of control and ultimately, our disconnection from God/Source. Your victim story plays out in your life in many different ways, through people you meet, situations encountered and events. But, none of them is as powerful as the way in which you re-create your victim story through Self-Sabotage, the deliberate destruction of your dreams through your own efforts. It may also be done through basic lack of effort in you changing things, by accepting them as they are - built in helplessness - or settling for what you think is your *limited-portion* of a joyful life.

Years ago, I worked for one of the largest Housing Authorities in the country as Public Information Officer. Part of my job was seeing that the adults of our 65,000 residents, had an opportunity for job training, so that they may sustain themselves. This was the original idea of setting up the Federal, State and locally supported Housing - *assist people until* they could get back on their feet, on their own. After observing one particular 13 week class for becoming a welder, I saw it had a large drop-out rate in the 12th week. Most of the prior attendees reenrolled for the next class. While the student-residents were totally supported and paid while taking the class, they were cut off from assistance once they got the set job - it only paid $10 per hour. Even back then, it was unsupportable for a family.

When I discussed this with the manager of the largest family development - how we could get higher paying wages for more of the residents, or at least not hit them with increased rent and expenses immediately - his answer astounded me. He blatantly said, "If I get all of them working at good wages, then they'll move out and I'll be out of a job." When I mentioned about the extensive waiting list to move in, he simply shrugged his shoulders. "New people are more of a hassle than those who have *accepted how things are.*" I even took this concern to the Executive Director, to no avail. Needless to say, I did not stay any longer than I needed, to get another more worthwhile job.

**Difficult Exercise:** Self-Sabotage is an unconscious, full manifestation of your victim story, in which you create *proof* that you are unlucky, undeserving, unworthy and not entitled to the blessings that you *may* believe you have access to, but cannot connect to. With Self-Sabotage, you do not need anyone else to take your good away from you, as you do it yourself. And, it basically happens when you are so afraid of losing something that you destroy it first, or so afraid of success or what happens afterwards, that you ensure that it never happens. The symptom of not ever trying, guarantees that you can't fail. Or, the breaking up with the potential love of your life, before they can break up with you, since you believe they will, as you are not worthy of them. "Argue for your limitations, and they are yours."

Think about what things in your life that have "almost" happened, or that shortly after you started that new job, or met that new person, you just "knew" there was no real point in going on with it. Yes, you will say there were reasons, or the best rationalizations for failure or losing out. Now, write about them honestly and *thoroughly,* then let it go to forgive yourself completely. This can be an open forum writing, in that as you are ready to acknowledge more Self-Sabotage on your part, write it down. The more you release and let go, the more you will recognize to *not repeat* ever again.

**Easier Exercise:** Fear is part of every act of Self-Sabotage, and it is a deep-seated fear that you have carried for lifetimes. You may fear success, because you may have once abused power in your Past lives. Or, you fear loss, betrayal, abuse or abandonment, so you ensure that you never move past your basic position in life. Easier to stay stuck in the rut, than pop your head out to see what's going on in the outside world, that *may* make you happy. The source of your fears may be unknown, *you just know* that you are terrified, unable to move forward. The unconscious nature of Self-Sabotage keeps your fears and motivation hidden until you are ready to release your victim story. The 'pursuit of happiness,' we are taught, is our inalienable right - so why aren't you pursuing it? Do you know what makes you happy? Make a list - start simple, chocolate or ice cream or a sunset - etc. Give yourself the smallest bit of happiness everyday, or several times a week, then build up from there, knowing that *you do deserve it.*

You will remain unaware that you are in a Self-Sabotage mode until you accept that you could have made different choices or acted differently. This can either create another victim story, or raise your determination to stop using Self-Sabotage to make your victim story true. The choice is yours and until you are willing to approach your life differently, your victim story will repeat itself in Self-Sabotage. When will you wonder what happened to your life and your dreams, and why they never seemed to come true? This week, look at any areas of your life where you are stuck, check to see if it's by Self-Sabotage. Can you acknowledge your victim story and make a choice to act differently? If you do, you will be many steps closer to living the life you want to live, and releasing your victim story from your Past.

Focus on where you are going, not where you have been. No need to wallow or stay stuck on Past pain or sorrow. Ask, who has you chained to it? If you are not happy where you are, then choose to change where you want to go. Focus on what makes you happy and what brings you joy. Think about what feels good and visualize you having that, surrounding yourself with it all. Every place in your life, where you feel you are undeserving, unlucky, unable to create joy, abundance or love, is a place where you are out of balance with your Spiritual Truth. It doesn't matter how you perceive others feel about you, the Truth is that you are unconditionally loved by God/Source, so therefore you can love yourself the same - unconditionally. This must be practiced until it is accepted and believed mentally, psychologically and Spiritually. Can you look in your mirror and say "I love YOU?"

That is the test, if you have released your victim story, try it - DO IT!

This is the step of how it always starts in the dynamic of the victim-perception role. Change is that point when the victim refuses to accept their worthlessness any more from anyone, including them-Selves. Recognize that others will hang onto their role of mistreatment of you, *for as long as you do not give them a reason to stop*. This is your Revolution within and starts when you - the victim refuses to accept any more mental or physical abuse. You finally begin to take back your power. In all situations of repression, the real moment of External change is when the person decides for themselves: I will not take this any longer.

This is when physical change truly starts to follow through on the mental, psychological and Spiritual change acknowledgment. All of your fears - which of course, unworthiness is a prime part - have some basis in the Past, either in this lifetime or another. While, as mentioned before, you may want to investigate what and where they came from, or simply affirm to bless *them all f*or the lessons learned, forgive anyone attached to your fears including yourself, and let them go, as you no longer need them in your life.

Nothing is more important to *not* being a victim, than having a good education. It is the foundation of everything from gangs to crime prevention, to basic growth of the economy, as well people's personal pride and well-being. Also, the higher educated the woman, the less children she has. The concept-belief of barefoot and pregnant is a male cultural-religious control over uneducated women. No one is proud of a lack of education and usually let their life be run by their ego-fears or insecurities, as they begin to believe what those in power tell them. That's why dictators and religious zealots have their greatest control over uneducated people. As the saying goes: "You either pay for a good education now, or pay for the consequences of its lack later." In the USA alone, over 70% of those people incarcerated, do not have a high school education. No matter, whatever other negative situations in their lives, this alone sets people up in our modern world for failure. We all contribute to victimization - through our discriminatory practice or prejudice, or simple apathy of allowing it to be done.

# *Denial, Delusion and Blame ~ Part #55*

While the whole idea of change may scare many people from even considering it, they may want to, or need to, assess what 'constants' in their life they do keep. Constants can mean: friends/family, significant other, job, where you live, how you spend your money, hobbies, sports, habits, etc. ALL those things that participate in your life, as your choices now. What stays and what goes - and you don't have to decide all at once. Some things are easier to let go of, or more obvious to let go of, if you are serious about any change for growth in your life. It is a process of fine tuning all that you, with awareness, consciously respond to rather than unconsciously react to as living only in rote. How truly, deeply honest can you be about who you are? If you cannot be honest or authentic with who you are to you, then how can your relationships with anyone be real? You don't have to be certifiably-crazy to be delusional about who you are and what you are doing with your life.

Key Question to ask your Self frequently, in this whole process of change: What part does Denial, Delusion and Blame play in your assessment of yourself?

**Exercise:** This is more than a looking in the mirror question, this is a pen and paper inventory, a time-consuming repeated question. So what constants excite you? You are unique, we all are in our own way, so what is unique about you? What do you take positive pride in - not ego-boasting? What are you good at - talents, skills, traits? What knowledgeable information do you take pride in knowing-having? What new ones, of anything would you like to add? If you have not reached the success that you feel you deserve, who do you blame? Do you delude yourself into thinking that those things you felt entitled to were denied you for no reason? How many things-situations have you denied were your responsibility, for having created in your life, as it is? Can you acknowledge the times your were self-destructive or even actually sabotaged your success? Can you honestly say that integrity is a basic core part of your character? Do you 'play bully' to all those around you, because you are in-denial of the state of your life? Where is all of your anxiety, fear and frustration coming from and who are you blaming it on? Heavy? Yes.

Often it is a tragic, or traumatic experience that brings you to this awakening-realization that a CHANGE is needed in your life, or you may not continue to have a life. In reality, some people may or actually choose to let go of their life, than change it. Change is the antipathy to the human tendency to form habits and reliably keep them, even when they are not good for us to have. Denial, Delusion and Blame are emotional habits that many of us develop - consciously or unconsciously - when we get hurt. Yes, every human being gets hurt emotionally, whether physical or other abuse was part of it or not. In order to protect your heart, body and spirit, you may close down parts of your emotional selves. You may develop defenses, Denial, Delusion and Blame, because life is difficult. At times, it appears that you are all alone, and you become convinced that you do not have any personal resources to engage a problem with your full mental capacity, as you have shut part of it down. When you experience a moment of anger or fear, this is especially true as you cannot think straight, if it reminds you of a prior negative situation. Some people say they feel as if their mind goes blank in these moments. This is what happens in trauma.

Many people may tell you and you will probably *not* want to hear it: "This is the Best thing that ever happened to you!" Whether it is the loss of a job, a loved one or personal accident/incident, it can be an opportunity to start over, by reinventing yourself. One of the first steps, would be your awareness of the crutches of Denial, Delusion and Blame that you use out of habit. Consciously recognize moments that the associated words pop-out of your mouth and that they are not true. You, and only you, have total control over what you do in, and with your life. Big shock. Even those self-destructive things, perhaps the "accident" that brought you to this point, was your subconscious creation. So, if you have the power to mess your life up, then you also have the power to straighten it out. No one was raised in Disneyland with perfect TV-land parents. We all have things from our Past that are not pretty, or that we want to remember fondly. Guilt and shame will eat at you like no disease does.

But, if you want a profound healing experience, it will take a great deal of patience on your part, and support from all the people around you. Your part of it, to really get a chance to fully become whole again, is simply to let it go. Rather than walking around with parts of yourself closed off, frozen or fragmented, you release, forgive - yourself and others - and accept the love that has been waiting for you. Never assume that the other you was normal, you were merely surviving the Past difficulties by Denial, Delusion and Blame. Once you have gone through the process of recovery-letting go, your ability to think clearly returns. There are no limits to your mind to come up with creative solutions to what lies ahead and no limits to your heart to see the good in others. You will eventually be able to open your heart, despite the risk of pain. Yes, you may be vulnerable, but you are truly feeling the essence of life as never before, with joy and happiness from releasing the Self-imposed strait-jacket.

Your life no longer needs to be choreographed by your ego, to keep you behind the facade. And, the people in your life, no longer need to dance around you on the eggshells you set out for them. Yes, it will take work and the letting go process will take time, but you will slowly see the limitations, that you had put on yourself and others in relating to you. It will be a brave new world for you, in every way. But for many of you, it did not come too soon, as living with part of your Self frozen, was just no longer acceptable. It may have taken a real tragedy, but that emotional scar will heal, as you have learned to take responsibility for your life, forgive yourself and others for those missteps-mistakes. Where there is accountability, there is no blame.

**The Bigger Picture of Denial, Delusion and Blame:** Most of us compromise every day. We allow minor rudeness to go unchecked, as well as being non-participatory, in even local governmental policies that we actually oppose. This inertia may be fed with: "Oh, well, what can I do about it?" Or worse, we expect a group or organization of our similar belief will speak up, or stop it somehow. If really not wanting to take the time to deal or think about it, you may actually tell yourself that "things will come out all right in the end." It is that sad selective-amnesia that allowed ugly genocides of numerous sizes and variety to become the ilk of Earth's history. Most people truly believe that it will never happen to them, but if they do not speak up for others, who will speak up for them? So goes the ripple in the pool - if you do not step in when one person is abusing another, what will you do when your local, state or national governments do something wrong to others? Never forget - We truly are One.

Don't wait for a ripple to become a Tsunami before you act. Or when you've learned to recognize Blame, Denial and Delusion in your Self you can recognize it in all things around you and help to change it. Something as basic as littering, wasting water or graffiti can be halted when one person speaks up for change.

\* \* \* \* \* \*

It's better to light a candle than to curse the darkness.
Eleanor Roosevelt

It is best to bring the knowledge of Light to all who want it, so they do not return to darkness.

A Visionary needs Action and, having a strong Desire to make it come true.

I know of no more encouraging fact than the unquestionable ability of man to elevate his life by conscious endeavor. Henry David Thoreau

# *Jealousy-Resentment - Part #56*

Think about the words "if" or "why," and if you've ever used them out of jealousy or resentment. "If I had been born rich, I surely wouldn't have these financial problems." "Why was he/she chosen for that promotion instead of me?" If you've used similar statements or questions, how much of it was blaming another, or even the Universe for your situations in life. Are there things that you feel you missed out on - wrong place-wrong time, or never even given the chance? Do you feel angry or jealous when others get that one thing you really, really wanted? How much energy are you putting into these things? Yes, you may be overcome with intense sorrow for the loss of, or not getting your dream-partner-job, etc.

You may even go to bed from the pain and the disappointment, crying until no more tears are left to shed. Sometimes it is good to do total-wallow in a loss for 24, 48 or even 72 hours; it gets the worst of it all over with and out of your system. But, is there a point to continue to sob, huge uncontrollable tears, or be angry, jealous or resentful for a life you never got to live, a love lost, or whatever you didn't get that you thought you were entitled to have? How will you move on with your life, if you don't surrender the *illusions*, and let go of the regrets or jealousies?

Once you have come to terms with the loss, you can begin to heal. Open your eyes and truly look around you, so that you will have gratitude for what you do have - that which was All God-given to you. Eventually, with the gratitude process, you will become capable of even feeling happy for friends and others, who live the good life you always wished to have. You may even acknowledge that the things they have, they truly deserve. You may also realized, that perhaps the life you have is more suited for who you are. Maybe you really would not have wanted to do what they had to do, to get that life. Maybe you see that status symbols are just empty material items. Dreams are not set in concrete, as neither are goals. They can be changed, which is sometimes a good consequence of loss.

With acceptance, sometimes comes reassessment from deep inside, with much soul-searching rather than simply wanting what others have. It can be a huge turning point - albeit painful - in your life. The key as always is that you shift yourself energetically to the present, and away from the Past. Letting go of baggage, unfortunately, is not a one-time thing. You pick up and carry new attachments in life, as if you are covered in velcro, which does not slough-off easily. You sometimes have to stop, reassess what is slowing you down, or taking you in the wrong direction. Then conscientiously, pull or pick it off of you. Thus, letting go once again, of useless baggage.

**Exercise:** How many times do all of you get caught up in the illusion of what you think is expected of you to do, or be in some particular situation? You often form a mental picture of what your life should/would/could be like if this or that was or wasn't as it is. Then, when it doesn't live up to your or others expectations, you are quite disappointed. Who's running your life? Take some deep breaths - love in and fear out - until you are in touch with your Higher Self - your Intuition. This process may be a much longer investment of time than just some deep breathing, to see and understand what your Soul's life-plan may be for you. It is not that often, with your limited perspective, that you can see the big picture, or even be ready to accept it.

In essence, the Big Picture means understanding that you chose certain experiences - difficult and easy - in order to flourish, grow and heal. Being placed in the situations was necessary to achieve your real Soul dreams, hopes and aspirations. When you follow your passion - not what you think or are told by someone else - you usually excel and succeed. You cannot judge your worth and value because past dreams did not come true. Sometimes it is the experience that is the important part, so the disappointments need to be let go. The 'old domino affect' of not being able to accomplish one thing without having experienced the thing before it, whether it failed or not.

You also cannot beat yourself up for the many opportunities that you let pass by, because they weren't what you were hoping for, or fit your perceptions, at the time. We all have regrets over opportunities discarded, or missed chances. Whether they were regarding someone or something, because they/it didn't fit your expectations/standards, at that time. On the other hand, you may have been allowing your fears to limit you from taking a risk, or just trying something new-different. These things need to be examined and assessed, so that the changes that you are making in your life, are going to be effective. How much do you believe in synchronicity - which is a pointed coincidence? You can't win the lottery unless you buy a ticket, but how about something coming to you totally out of the blue? Truth is sometimes stranger than fiction, and the good stuff does come to you when you believe it will - *Self-fulfilling prophecy*. Remember you attract what you desire, when you work towards it, and keep positive thoughts regarding it.

Dreams do come true, in ways you never would have guessed or suspected. You Must Work IT! Too often, it is your own thoughts - even if they are NOT verbalized - that place limitations on what, or how you receive it! Again: "Argue for your limitations, and they are Yours!" Sometimes those dreams or desires are too specific, rather than being open to explore and experience what the Universe wants to send to you. With my requests, I usually tag on "for my best and highest good, and the highest good of all." I also trust the Universe, in knowing that I am Divinely guided, so it fills me with colorful, fun experiences that shape my life with love, happiness and abundance. Always about the journey, and sometimes those side paths can bring more joy, than you've had in a long time. You learn that you are never alone on your path, but it is yours individually, and at some times, there is not enough room for another human being to be with you.

The important thing to learn is that we deserve wonderful things and that is what Source/the Universe wants for us! Sometimes, when you are totally open and grateful for whatever, Source will weave magic into your life, far beyond what you would have ever dreamed. As the saying goes - "Be careful what you asked for." You may think at the time that you want it or even need it, but looking back you can often see it was *not* the right thing at the time. Forgive your-Self for any jealousy or resentment that you may have had for others, curbing in that critical judging, even of those who judged you. When you rise above that, you also raise your Self-respect and always send a blessing to all, for any gifts *they receive.*

This will make you a teacher to others, as they learn from your example. You are continually learning who you are by the path you are on. Not knowing who you are, was when fear controlled and limited you from becoming the New You. This is the the incentive you can share with others behind their change, for growth and expansion in to a whole new unlimited Universe of joy and experiences. Ignorance is not really bliss, it breeds fear, which leads to control and the struggle for power to have more, or being better because of ego-insecurities. This is not a battle you need to fight, as there is no winning; it is against your inner-Self and you will lose.

\* \* \* \* \* \*

To get Respect, you have to give it.

You teach best what you most need to learn. Richard Bach

If possessions are your sole source of evidence of your success, you will be devastated more than most by disasters. You may consider living your life out of your safety deposit box, or just live your life without attachment to material things.

# *Acceptance of All ~ Part #57*

**Exercise:** "God Loves You, and I'm working on it!" Acceptance of others, as they are - warts & all - continues for me to be a challenge. I have a friend who says: "God loves you, and I do too, as I let you go in peace - and go as far away from me as possible." **Repeat:** Acceptance is NOT agreement with those you have a problem with in any way - Freewill and choices for all, and accepting someone as they are, does NOT mean they need to be your new best friend, or marry into your family. As part of the Step Process, of bringing change into your new life, Acceptance is one of the hardest steps, as far as I'm concerned. I will NOT be a doormat, nor Not speak out if someone is being rude, and it doesn't have to be to me. I will question, if someone or thing - as in job or attitude is wrong. If you have not created a list of everyone who ever caused you - in your mind and heart - pain, hurt or even disappointment or betrayal, then you need to do so. The list also, should include everyone who you think or perceived stood in your way, or caused you suffering, as *they* played a part of your life lessons.

Remember, as you review the list, that it is not a hit list for retribution, for you are moving past that to forgiveness. You might want to consider a little mantra like mine ("God Loves You, and I'm working on it!") to get you past the acceptance hurdle. Just catching yourself being critical, or maligning someone will help you to catch yourself sooner next time.

The key here is to once again look for the Big Picture, as to how these pains were contributions to your growth and learning. You needed them and in reality *you asked* to experience them, as part of your life path and journey. As we are an accumulation of all that, you could not be who you are today without them. Therefore, you need to give the alleged-perpetrators the gift of acceptance, tolerance and then forgiveness to let them go. Most people you are involved with are part of your Soul Group, which means that they have been with you before in other Past lives, and some many times. You have all voluntarily interacted and exchanged positions-relationships with each other for the fulfillment of your Karma, or life lessons. In more basic terms: playing the good/bad-negative/positive role for sake of the experience - jealous lover-forsaken wife, etc.

I know for many of you this may be very hard to swallow, as the experience may have ended in your death - as I recently found out about a Past life. But, to put it bluntly, these Past experiences must be *memorable* for you to learn from them, as you progress through each life choice you have made. So, with that awareness, look at them and the *knowledge* these people gave you, as this gift of love for who they truly are/were - understand their pain, suffering, doubt and fear. Within their own insecurities, see where they were often more afraid of you, than you may have been of them. Realize also their knowledge of the Karma, they were creating it for themselves, as they helped you along your path and the part that their fear may have played in their actions.

From this point on your path, acknowledge their contribution in your life, so *by giving them acceptance you closed that connection.* In this way, you may release any negative energy that attracted them. You then begin the process to forgive them and forgive yourself too, because you created this life with responsibility for it - meaning then everyone and everything in it. By giving acceptance and forgiveness, you also release them from their Karma, so they can do other things with their life. This releasing is also for you to move on and do the other great things that you were meant to do with yours. Yes, those of you that had both physical and emotional abuse - it is through the acceptance of forgiveness that you will not repeat the vicious circle. No, this is not easy and may take time with professional help. As with most positive action, there is a positive response.

The benefits that arise from letting go of judgments - whether directly connected to you or not - about what someone should or could have done, instead of what they did, truly was their choice. Once we stop questioning their actions or motives, and remember these choices are all part of *Their* life lesson, that they are learning, or still need to learn. They are not where you are on your path. They have Their Own Path. Source/Universe only desires for you to be happy and that can occur when you are aware of your choices, your path, so thus your lessons. You can not be rescuing others, especially when it may interfere with them learning their lessons. Yes, a word to them of warning from your own Past is acceptable, but if they choose to not heed it, then let it go. Send them blessings, love, peace, joy and a guiding light, but do NOT judge them, for you have no idea where they are on their path.

No judgment, truly is giving the gift of acceptance. This can release them from your personal expectations and you from more exhaustive energy, that should be spent on moving yourself forward from being haunted by your Past. If you are still here on this rock, then you still have things to learn, as well as to continue to create a life of joy and given limitless abundance in all things. You have chosen your path that leads to the life that you want to live, and you need to accept that others have chosen theirs. Accept also, that there is No One Right Path. What works for one, may not work for another, and you have the Choice to change your path, as long as you are here, in this life time.

Tolerance, is said to be the rock foundation of acceptance, as it is a huge, broad-based word. It is not just a liberal, open-spirit toward opinions and practices that differ from one's own. It is one's personal control to endure without repugnance of the actions. Key is again that tolerance/acceptance does not mean agreement. This was a lesson that became embedded into me, with not only my seven years in Japan, but my travel to many other countries that allowed things that I definitely did not agree with, much less like. How many times my new trainers remarked how something was done differently in the United States, and I quickly reminded them to accept it, as they were not in the USA.

Culture, traditions and societal actions vary even in the States from region to region. In foreign countries, this is multiplied according to how close their relationship is similar to that in the States. In other words, Canada would be more similar than Mexico and Japan more similar than China. Different doesn't make it wrong or bad, it's theirs.

Yes, we are All One, in essence as children of God/Source, yet just as we each have our individual paths, we have our own ways of doing and saying things. We are still All Spiritual Beings now having a Human Experience - uniquely your own. As I've said before, God/Source gives us Freewill to live our lives, we need to learn to give it to each other. Each country has their own laws, customs, culture, etc., just like each State has theirs. If you don't like those things or how they do them, then leave. Tolerance and Acceptance does not mean you *have to stay* around those people you don't agree with. Just as forgiving someone of a Past hurt, doesn't mean you have to become best friends with them, or even do the forgiving in-person. No one has a right to mistreat you - you put yourself in that position, so you can also remove yourself from it. It is your choice, as always. Think about these things and ponder them carefully in your heart and mind.

\* \* \* \* \* \*

Prejudices, it is well known, are most difficult to eradicate from the heart whose soil has never been loosened or fertilized by education: they grow there, firm as weeds among stones. Charlotte Bronte
If only we could all accept that there is no difference between us where human values are concerned ... Liv Ullman
Sometimes the people who are crazy enough to think that they can change the world . . . Do!

# *Responsibility - Accountability - Part #58*

Some may think Self-responsibility or Accountability is the answer to many of our personal and collective woes. Placing blame on another, does not get to the source of the issue of why so many people do not want to take control of their own lives. In the most despotic situations, you do have choices as to what you believe, even if you don't have many choices as to what you can do, if Self-preservation is primary. Self-responsibility empowers the individual to learn from any situation and take a step into a higher level of awareness.

Choosing to be a victim is a choice of inaction - which is still a decision - as it places the power of one's experience in the hands of another. To some, it is easier to have others direct their lives in avoidance of making those decisions and being accountable for them. "It's their fault; they did it to me. They made me do it." That is a cop-out, a blindness to one's creative abilities in every moment - situation. The question may be, how great is the fear of screwing up your own life, in that you'd rather have someone else do it for you, so you can remain free of the accusation?

**Exercise:** Who influences your thoughts? Why? Look at it from the perspective of choices you have in a your daily life. A belief is really only a thought you keep thinking, or someone you consider important keeps telling you. Stop thinking it, or listening to that person and your belief will change. It is as if, you only listen to one set radio station day and night and they speak with such authority that you must believe every word they say. How can you not, if that is all you ever hear? Change Stations for God's sake and get other perspectives!

It has been estimated that a human being processes somewhere between 12,000 and 60,000 thoughts per day. Taking an average of 36,000, the typical mind entertains a thought about every two seconds, even when you are dreaming. So, why have you given another person control over your thoughts, which means power over your life? The most important thing to remember always, is that you are the creator of your own reality. Whether you accept that or acknowledge it. You are where you are, because you have created that experience in your life. Granted it may have been created subconsciously, but your own consciousness brought it into fruition. It may not have been a cognitive choice, but it was your choice of a life experience to have. Likewise, most people will not accept that any bad things that came into their life was from their own focused thoughts. It's still easier to blame others for the bad and take credit for the good.

It is all a process and you have the power to focus on where you choose to be in that process. Who is pulling your strings and where did the strings come from? If you are not happy, you can simply focus on improving those feelings - what would make you feel better? Your mind probably wouldn't accept feeling ecstatic, so you need to move slowly in feeling better. Say you're walking along, tripped and fell - do you get angry and upset like someone pushed you? Or go into blaming, like you have in the Past? Is it someone or something's fault that you tripped and fell? Maybe the sidewalk is cracked or broken, and the city should have fixed it. You know the city has budget issues, are you going to sue them because they made you fall, though not really hurt? Or perhaps, you will blame yourself for being clumsy or not paying attention and verbally beat yourself up, as some people saw you fall, so you're embarrassed? Or, do you simply focus on rubbing your knee or elbow, or whatever part struck the sidewalk, then say, "Better pay attention more, so I don't really get hurt," and move on?

In other words how you handle any situation - action/reaction or rational response - has to do with where you focus your emotions and attention. If you have been working on feeling better, happier in your life and taking responsibility for your life, you do not get angry immediately or blame others for those things that happen to all of us. While you are Special in many ways, you are not Special in that the Negative or Positive Only comes to you - unless that is what you do believe and then Focus on it.

Yes, you can choose what comes into your life - so why would you choose the negative, and then blame others? Choose the positive energy emotion you wish to dwell in, and move on with your life. You can take pride, even accountability, for the happiness that happens to be in your life as you chose it, you practiced focusing on it and thus created it in your life. The positive energy - happy, grateful - also means you are moving on, while the negative - blaming, angry - means you are still stuck in the Past.

How you respond to any situation should be focused, not a reaction from your Past stimulus. While no one has a right to mistreat you, you also don't just hit someone if they bumped into you. Road-rage is usually very ego-centered, as if it was damaged, even if there was no damage to the vehicle. An apology (responsibility) - whether you truly mean it or not - is a social gesture that can eliminate most confrontations, especially with strangers. Ego-based emotions are the most difficult for most of us to move past and takes diligence through situations with focused practice. Along with this, cognizance is usually coming into Your prior negative thoughts, so often puts you in those confrontational situations. What better place to expel pent-up anger than road-rage? It is not difficult to seek out, likewise angry people.

**Exercise II:** So, what can you do to help You focus? First as always - deep breathe to take in love - release out anger/ego/fear - you'll know when its gone enough that you can interact with others. Plan ahead for your commute, if you are still learning to let go of anger-ignitors - leave for work earlier, take public transportation at least part way, or van pool where you are not the driver! There can always be a Plan B to avoid participating in having your small buttons pushed. Still being stuck in the Past, means subconsciously you are choosing to put yourself in situations where you will have drama, confrontation and the opportunity to blame others. There is no part of Self-sabotage that brings more happiness and joy into your life. Stop to look at the Big Picture of your Past life and how often you have consciously or unconsciously sabotaged happy opportunities from ever coming into fruition.

Yes, we all are like onions in letting go of our many full layers. What major lifestyle changes you need to make may be like putting a price on your happiness and joy - what is it worth to you? If you need to think about how long it's been, or how much joy you've recently had, you really do need to make some real positive decisions now. Do something just for you - it doesn't have to be expensive or really time-consuming, start small so you don't create guilt. Be sure that you do take the time to savor the joyous moment, so you will know it is worth it. Now, how much of the rest of your life do you want to have similar moments? What are you willing to give up on your own - no one else to blame, this is your choice? Who or what is controlling your life - job, partner, location, friends, relatives? Life truly is too short to not live it with joy.

Physical exercise - take five minutes and go out doors with bare feet. Even if you feel water droplets coming down, five minutes; the rain will not hurt you, you will not shrink. It will all work in your favor. Just go out doors and stand on the grass. Allow yourself to draw in the energy of holy Mother Earth. Trust me, it will make a difference in your whole day. I had a friend who brought all of his colorful, fallen leaves into his house to walk over and feel the crunch barefoot or with shoes. Sure, the vacuuming after was a chore, but he loved nature.

In autumn, most trees and plants let go of their leaves, it is a natural growth process. If they didn't, these old dried leaves would stunt their growth and eventually, the trees or plants would die off. Likewise, is the energy of letting go or moving on the elixir of life and also, Self-preservation. It is not pushing something or someone away, it is letting go of what no longer serves you. Letting go is a healthy and beautiful feeling, so just let go to be open, to be free.

When each individual is able to give themselves permission to embrace their feelings, they can then take accountability for what they need. You embrace yourselves as being perfect, to join life according to your happiness. Most of you were told long ago that you were not as good as you really are, or what all you did or did not deserve and therefore you stopped having fun. At its core, the question of fun as you move along your journey will always be personal accountability, and the courage to stand up for what you need in your life.

At the same time, it's the courage to allow one another to all pursue their own versions of happiness. It is thus your responsibility to create your own happiness, so whenever those that you enjoy spending time with decide to move on, there will still be happiness in your life. You cannot depend on another to give you happiness, or to make you happy. It is neither their job or responsibility to do so. Have the real courage to see what you need to pursue your happiness, while still allowing others to celebrate their own pursuit of happiness, with or without you. Trust that you will not be alone as you increase your own love of self, for who you are, so you will be surrounded by loved ones.

**Note:** There are volumes of psychological, sociological and anthropological research that has been done on the theme of "Built-In Helplessness." This is where some agencies, or various government programs, have created generations of people who have had all their ability to choose and decide eroded. They have been funneled into programs, that in the essence of "helping" these people - and under the assumption that they could not help themselves - have become totally dependent on the helpers. It is the whole repeat of the story of feeding people a fish rather than teaching them how to fish, fearing that if they all learn how to fish, then the "helping people" will not be needed, or will be out of jobs themselves. While related to this topic, it needs its own understanding of how your Past controls you. Your Independence, making your own choices and learning from your own mistakes is *empowerment,* which give us pride and joy in what you can do on your own. If we are ALL truly One, then there should be no Entitlement of someone to be treated better than another. If you believe someone or something owes you - as in government hand-outs, then you've truly already given up your individuality and power.

\* \* \* \* \* \*

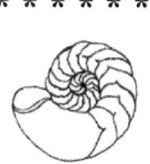

298

# *Growth Assessment ~ Part #59*

**Exercise:** There is something rather definitive in writing out one's true feelings, as to changes made and those still in process. This should be continuous.

**My Personal Thoughts and Assessments** - Perhaps similar to some of yours. I release the regrets of all the people that I have hurt in my lifetime, or often thoughtless things that I did or said to them. I do release and forgive myself, as well as others for those things done and said to me over my life, for whatever reasons. Those actions did not come from the God/Source, that I know now is within myself, nor the God/Source that was within them. I truly forgive both my parents, they were probably doing the best they could and then forgive myself for my resentments towards them. While I was raised under judgment and criticism, I know they felt, and believed, it would make me a better, stronger person. Likewise, unfortunately, I passed some of that onto my child, and I am glad to have a better relationship with him now.

Also, I'd like another opportunity for a wonderful, loving and accepting relationship with a like-minded man - giving and sharing, so many things we'd have in common. Those things that I did not have in my previous marriages, as I feel now capable of unconditional love.

Open, honest, trusting and loving. No one is perfect. I do not expect myself, coworkers, friends, relatives or lovers to be so, either. I am learning to accept others as they are - any changes have to come from them, because they want to do it. My growth and changes for me, myself are My choices, I've given to myself. They have not been easy or quick, so I need to respect in others, if they choose *not* to make their changes. I wonder why I lack patience, or simply wanting what I want immediately, despite who or what is around me? Patience is more than a virtue, it is a well-honed practice of understanding time. I see and do understand now, that those things that I often criticize in others are really those same bad habits of myself - either of Past or still present. I need to be more genuinely kind to others, whether I feel I know the person or not. I, too often question the deeds and actions of others, when it is many times myself that I am questioning. I am accepting and love myself - usually unconditionally - and I do take pride in myself, my accomplishments. I do not need to prove or explain who I am, or what I can do, as I diligently work on keeping that ego in check. We are all struggling with our insecurities, so there is no need to cover them with any created facade.

I am as I am, and am accepting me as I am. As long as I keep my connection to Source and keep the old stuff cleared out, my path is good and smooth. I am happy in my work that Source has brought to me, and having everyone be accepting of me in the work I do. I am worthy on my own. I see myself as happy at doing great work, often inspiring others. I have learned so much in all that I chose to change about myself. I know that as I open up, I can share more of myself, of what the changes can do and have done for me. I see myself speaking before crowds and sharing those experiences to change people's lives. The years and work on releasing all, has been exhaustive and I truly cannot say it has been totally eradicated. There is no longer a need to do things the way that I've always done them. There are new ways that are better.

I still instinctively will strike out when I see injustice, or in my opinion, a 'wrong' has been done. I guess I need to focus on all the content, or extensiveness of it. Perhaps a concise, basic statement as to my disagreement, or personal opinion, as to what was said or done should be learned and practiced. Then let it go - drop it - release it. These things, while they may sound basic or simple, are not that easy for me. I say that I have a strong sense of 'right and wrong,' but I'm still working on it all. We all are really a work in progress, as long as we choose to change and grow.

Now your turn to write, reveal and release. Don't forget to always acknowledge your accomplishments in growth-change so far.

**Awareness and listening** - key steps to be learned and practiced. We never know who our teacher will be, or what we might learn when we least expect it, from the most unlikely source. God does work-create mysteries and the journey is what life is all about. Some days we are the student and some days we are the teacher. We may never actually know which days are which, when we are open to all those around us.

\* \* \* \* \* \*

Vision without action is a daydream. Action without vision is a nightmare. Japanese proverb

Example is not the main thing in influencing others, it is the only thing. Albert Schweitzer

Be ambitious for the work and not for the reward.

If you don't like something, change it. If you can't change it, change your attitude. Maya Angelou

Change will not come if we wait for some other person, or some other time. We are the ones we've been waiting for. We are the change that we seek. Barak Obama

# *Thoughts, Affirmations & Musings - Part #60*

Gathered from numerous, noted sources - use as you choose.

"Treat each other with the greatest of respect, for you are looking in the eyes of God. Nurture one another every chance you get, and as your path becomes difficult, share that with others so that they may soften their path. Know that it is a beautiful game you are playing here on planet Earth, and play well together."

From the Group - Steve Rother - Lightworker.com

You can't move on and cling to old ideas at the same time! Your future happiness depends on your ability to leave the Past behind you.

If Patience is my ally, and Patience is my friend, Then I am cool, calm and patient. Everything is in the flow.

Do you truly want to see yourself for who you are? Then release and let go - surrender - You do not need to be in control - Be in the flow.

I am releasing and allowing pain to be released and let go of, as I forgive all from my Past, including myself. I surrender it all to God/Source, as I am not alone and I am loved unconditionally.

I am learning to discern what is truth from illusion - at all times and places. **Illusion:** Perception is Everything! Don't confuse me with the facts in Black & White.

Think of the endless possibilities that we are given to chose from every day, in every way, regarding every thing that passes through our mind, and in front of our eyes.

Life is not measured in the number of breaths we take, but in the moments that take our breath away. Breathe deeply and enjoy life.

People rarely get to know, or take time to know, those who are very good - as if they can not get past the outside "good" veneer. Is it that they can't imagine being like them?

Practice compassion and acceptance, as you may not always agree with someone, or their choices, since you may not know what they're going through that influenced them.

The world is full of people with opinions, *who don't have to* change theirs to make you happy. Get over it and accept it, you are not going to change everyone's opinion to agree with yours. It is OK to have your opinions, it is NOT OK to Distribute them unwanted.

God gives us freewill to choose, we need to remember to give it to each other. We have the freedom and power to choose what we want to accept and reject, so does everyone else.

"You make a living by what you get. You make a life by what you give." ~ Winston Churchill

**Old Souls-Giving:** Some Souls come into their Earth-life with more Light enveloping them from their entrance moment. These souls are very old, and rare with many life times of experience, as well as some of a *Lemurian* ancestry. For the past few decades we have referred to them as Indigo, and recently as Crystal children. We are fortunate to have them, as we face so much change - circumstances to stay out of Past darkness and they keep moving us towards the Light. These Light-Bearers/Pathfinders are often our Poets or Writers and Teachers, who often lead us. They show us the way to Truth, in some of the most *unexpected and incongruous paths* to get us back on course.

The joy of giving generously and the ability to receive gratefully, is a reciprocal cycle. When we give generously from the Spirit, we partake of the consciousness of prosperity and abundance. Therefore, the more we give, the more we not only receive, but our capacity to give increases.

The Adult Bully Profile is one who's ego is filled with massive insecurities, which must be masked by being loud and not open to another's opinion. He is totally ego-controlled.

Most of us understand that when the student is ready, the teacher will appear. The teacher, no matter how anxious to train the student, cannot make him willing and ready to listen, or accept the teaching. People have to want to learn, just as they have to want to change. It is frustrating to us teachers, but it is still the student's choice. That is something we must be aware of accepting.

"When you want more for the other person than they want for themselves - you will be frustrated." ~ Richard Bach

**Dreams of the Past:** If you continue to revisit your Past through your dream-state - people and situations popping up, or old memories resurfacing - there is no need to re-live the pain related to that Past. These dreams tell you how far you've really come, in that you can let go of them, whether an old belief system, or a painful experience that prevented you from moving forward. The Past will show up to remind us to forgive others and ourselves, as we release the fear, or sadness that we held onto for so long.

**Positive aspects:** Feel good about you - say often: "I adore me - I appreciate me." Look for reasons to appreciate yourself. Critical of others is criticism of Self - for subconsciously we see our faults in others, and don't want them seen in us. Look for your value in all things -

Feeling good about me attracts positive energy. Look for positive little things given, or brought to you to appreciate.

**Becoming your Authentic Self:** Exercise knowing who you are gives a clarity and understanding of who you thought you were - even the good stuff - and that you can totally become so much more! Question what really motivated you before, or what your new motivation is.

**Karmic Burden:** The releasing of the need for power in any way must be done to receive Light, and help others on the path.

Actively connect and share - generosity - a sense of abundance - pooling resources.

Breathe Deeply Often - Ease into Everything - Be Aware - Be Present

The Balance of Power is responsibility. You are responsible for your own well being, your happiness and finding joy on this planet.

To increase your power in any area, increase your responsibility.

Find the commonalities between each person you interact with, and honor them.

The collapse of negative power leads to waves of turbulence that cause a tense void, which leads to new awareness of what power should really be.

When you change the way you look at things, the things you look at change.

Whether tis nobel - to be or not to be. The level of living beyond everyday is Self-actualization. Integrity is doing the right thing, even when no body notices.

Forgiveness opens doors, for what we give out does comes back to us usually multiplied.

"What we have done for ourselves alone dies with us; what we have done for others and the world remains, and is immortal." Albert Pike

Take responsibility of where you are - not blaming others - then you have the power to release it, let it go and move on. Fault is not outside ourselves.

My path is all about me, as your path really has to be all about you. If we don't take quiet time to contemplate ourselves, we will not get to know that New person inside us. As we travel on our paths for growth, we need to recognize that the person inside may not be the same one with each additional introspection. Even the busiest of us, need to take a few minutes to deep breathe and ask for guidance.

Plan ahead for a few hours without any outside stimulation - phone, email, DVDs, etc. As your personal worthiness increases, perhaps you will even give yourself a few days - it is one reason some people go off to spas or retreats. Amazing decisions can be made in solitude - listen to your inner voice. When you are alone, your deepest part will tell you things because you are listening, and it is often speaking of your Self-preservation.

As you become best friends with your inner person, there is a freedom that builds courage as you realize what a very accomplished and experiential person you have become. You have an understanding now that we are all one, as you have reached a certain level and thus awakened to this enlightenment as it is. You also have an awareness of what you are doing here, and that you are connected to everyone. You are capable of coming into a right relationship - love and acceptance with an end of judgment of those you interact with - an acceptance consciousness - no criticism of another's choices. You have awakened the presence of love within you and others, yet you have discernment still in your freewill of choice without attachment.

Understanding the process of letting go and release is a step process of putting space/time between you and whatever/whomever is no longer serving you as a positive purpose. There is no need to be cruel, or rude, just slowly move away with a separation that eventually will be accepted as part of your changing.

**Exercise:** Now, jot down some of your Thoughts, Affirmations & Musings you've picked up so far. Things that have stuck with you, or that you like saying - using. These are your little support-steps that you can fall back on to use when you need them.

# *Love ~ Hate ~ Part #61*

Some say the opposite of Love is Hate, others say it is Apathy, as it has no emotion. Even hate has some emotion attached to it. I believe the exact opposite of Love is Fear, as it freezes all feelings with its negative-vibrational energy. When you are in a Fear mode, you cannot express Love for anyone or anything, especially not for yourself. Love is the strongest emotion and power that you have available to you. It can truly conquer anything, if you simply believe you are love, loved, lovable and loving. Love can erase Fear, once you can accept that no matter what the situation, you are always, always loved unconditionally by God/Source.

The True love you experience from others is simply the reflection of your shining light of the love you have for yourSelves. "You complete me," which may sound romantic, subconsciously says that I am incomplete, not whole; at its most base level - "something is Wrong with me." It needs to be transformed into "You reflect me." In other words, we are equal, just different as in how Yin/Yang match each other by reflection to fulfill their destiny. The linchpin is, as always, that one must love oneSelf first for it to work.

**Note:** I must say that in the process of my growth so far, I am now totally uncomfortable with writing the word 'hate,' much less the saying it. I have been dutifully practicing for sometime to not use the word, even in the most innocuous way, such as expressing negative feelings for something like hot dogs or rude drivers. In this way, I'm working at keeping any and all negativity out of my positive energy field. I continuously look for the positive and usually find it, which of course, makes me happy.

**Exercise:** Erasing Negativity: Visualize yourself as having a giant eraser and every time any negative idea or feeling pops into your head, whip out that visual-eraser to eradicate it thoroughly. Just like any good exercise, when you do it repeatedly, it becomes an automatic habit, so the eraser eventually dissolves negatives instantly. While it may not work on negative people, then put the Golden Light around yourself for protection against them. Without being rude, remove yourself or make a blanket excuse to avoid interacting with them. They may get the hint. It not, just let them know that the activity or people are 'just not what you're into any more.' You truly do not have to explain yourself, as that is giving away your power.

The unresolved fears that created the negativity will no longer have control of your life, as you created a visual power that erases them before they develop any influence. Follow the erasing with deep cleansing breaths to heal any old wounds, and surround yourself with unconditional love. It soothes like a magical-salve. There is power and strength to endure, as confidence is built up with each successive eradication of a fear. You are becoming really empowered. Take pride in your accomplishments over fear, and have profound joy fill in the vacuum of the space that fear dominated.

Once you allow the Universe to point you towards healing, you need to surrender your control and resistance, so your energy will be unblocked to flow and move forward. The Light then carries you through your lessons of healing, to allow the positive energy to flow for your release of pain replaced by peace. The surrender will also allow you self-love, that guides you into the flow of miracles and unconditional love. When you surrender, you replace your will with Divine Will, and trust that you are Divinely guided in all you do. This process replaces Fear with acceptance of your connection to God/Source. Ask for Divine Assistance if needed in Healing and clearing, with releasing, while finding opportunities of Light, or

Beauty in the darkness - which means expecting a miracle and then receiving it.

**How to love yourself:** Stop all criticism of Self and others. Stop scaring your Self! Fear from your thoughts - Make a list of all you fear - Now which can you control? They are Your fears - you CAN control all of them. Love is the most powerful thing in the Universe, so logically you can change negative into positive by loving it - totally - completely.

Choice is taking charge and as you take action, it gives you more energy. If you're not happy with your choice, then make another choice. It's yours - you can change your choices at any time. If you look for it, you all have a Yellow Brick Road leading to your heart, as you continue to see through the illusion of fear. Remember that Love conquers Fear, so just visualize, or breathe Love into your Heart, and Fear will retract out! Nothing is by chance, there are no mistakes or coincidences, as everything happens for a reason. Your Love for your-Self rescues you just in time, it is Synchronistic! You face the most intimate relationship you have, which is Love with yourself in all its glory. You can't run, you can't hide and learn you can no longer keep projecting your fear and pain or blame onto others. It is only, and will always be about love.

This Love transition includes every one of us, and so is not something we wait for others to do for us. The relationship you have with yourself, at the deepest level must be understood completely. You can then have great relationships with others, and finally have a real sense of peace in who you are. In your state of acceptance-love, judgment disappears. This then brings you new beginnings, which involves aligning, as well as disconnecting from the old beliefs. It is not simple or easy to undergo the whole step process of letting go. Some ugly Past stuff has been with you for many lives, and many stuck belief systems that you have been holding onto, so tightly for so long. Take it all one step at a time, and praise yourself for each and every accomplishment of ridding you of your Past!

Bless all those who push your buttons - thank them for the awareness, and then let them go. These people give you reminders of your own deficiencies, for you would not be reacting if they weren't true to some extent. Blessing them allows your own self-love to fill in the space they have vacated, and makes sure that they don't return. Do not repeat what was said, or beat yourself up for doing it, for that keeps them within your energy and your attachment to them. You want something - anything - totally and completely out of your life - don't hate it, but love it and let it go!! Thank whatever the thing was for its lessons and then Pouf! Enough! In this way you free yourself, as it is time to stop the cycle. It is so simple, most people do not believe it is true - if you don't like what is happening outside of you, change what is happening inside. Then watch how your disengagement affects the outside world. It works both ways, and this is how you sort out what to keep and what to let go.

Take a moment to give thanks for every challenge experienced, for every tear shed, for every moment of woe, or grief and sadness. It is those dark nights of the soul that you have endured, are experiences that you came here to learn from, so they are to be loved, not hated or feared. They have made cracks in the defense walls of your ego, and burned through the veil's illusion, as they erased ignorance to reveal your inner wisdom. Now, you must trust yourself, and the aspects of your Divine Self that have guided you. You are protected, as you reach out and share your gifts with others, so they may learn to love as you have. When you learn to love the Divine mystery in all things, you will have an understanding beyond this world.

\* \* \* \* \* \*

Every great dream begins with a dreamer. Always remember, you have within you the strength, the patience, and the passion to reach for the stars to change the world. Harriet Tubman

Don't compromise yourself. You are all you've got. Janis Joplin

Progress is impossible without change, and those who cannot change their minds cannot change anything. George Bernard Shaw

Only I can change my life, no one can do it for me. Carol Burnett

# *Being of Service ~ Part #62*

Money and material things do not fill the void within us and do not show real love, most of time when given to us. Insecurities and lack of self-confidence may be masked by expensive things, but they cannot replace unconditional love from another or yourself. You will not be remembered for the "Bling" you wear, but for the Service that you give to others. "You get all you want in your life by helping other people to get what they want in their lives." What you may have been told or seen in your Past, usually only feeds inner-conflict and the feeling of self-doubt of who you are and can be. When you can no longer accept your strings-being-pulled like a performer from a circus act, Self-exploration may be required to change the direction of your life's sojourn. The giving of Service can bring real Bliss, which beats out Bling once you've experienced it.

**Exercise:** Clarity does not come easily for you to see who is really in the mirror, when your friends - entourage - keep it smoked over. It is time for another real 'stare-down' of yourself in the mirror. Spend at least ten minutes looking into your eyes and who you see in there. Just removing the mask for most of us on the Spiritual Path is the first not-so-easy step on a long list of changes. What remains is often a more complex ego and doesn't appear in an easy to understand form. Think octopus with its tentacles deeply embedded, to keep you totally clutched in its power. What changes have you already made? What changes do you still feel you need to make? The choices are not so clearly defined, as to the changes needed next for you to grow and to discover your Divine Destiny.

These are *not* loaded dice where every chance is a winner, as it is no longer just about you. Being of Service means that you know that what you do will serve others, through the highest good for all. What talents can you really share? Is there still a dream that you have yet to unleash, or at least develop? Fear and avoidance doesn't work here for long. Sometimes in avoiding our destiny, by taking another path, we run right into it. This is your truth of what you are here to do and when you accept that discovery, you are clearly on your path to some great achievements! It is showing appreciation to God/Source for all your talents, by sharing them with others.

Your belief in your Self does not need to be confirmed by others, for you to be who you are. It is only necessary for you to believe in yourself, and those beliefs which you live by every day. Yes. Breaking away from your Old Beliefs for your new growth and support usually brings pain, because you're separated from others you've moved beyond. You will soon meet more people of like-mind, as you demonstrate who you are now. You learn to understand that you can share the world with others, without sharing their same world-view. Kind of like when you've forgiven someone, it does not mean that you have to be best friends with them.

How you view the world from a 'fixed' perspective or flexible one, represents how open or exposed your world is to other situations or possibilities. How far back do you need to step to truly clarify your goals, so they reflect your vision of the Big Picture? In all things, there are blind spots, simply because we do not have 360 degrees of sight; we barely have 180. There will always be things that you do not know, and if you did, that knowing might adjust your view. Life cannot be lived under a magnifying glass, nor with binoculars. It needs to be lived face to face in real time.

A break-through of acceptance is when you are willing to change your mind or your goals, once new information is brought to your attention or awareness. To proceed forward when you know there are blind spots, is a fool's folly based on ego. This would be similar to making up a story based on few facts, but perpetuating it to be true. Like using the child's 'telephone' game as a basis for an important decision, or in defense of an error regarding an accident that could have been prevented. You need to take time to check out the facts. Just as no one is perfect, no one knows everything, even when it is related to something that you've done before. Few things remain the same for long. As they say, "You don't need to be a rocket scientist to know."

Communication is more than the language that we speak. True communication means that there is a speaker, as well as a receiver(s) of the message. The receiver's perception of you has great influence on how your communication will be accepted, or interpreted by them. Many marketers and retailers have learned that lesson the hard way. Likewise, how you perceive others will influence how you speak to them. We all may have an information overload at our finger tips or ears, yet miscommunication or misinformation is also rampant without discernment. Progress is understanding we are All One and connected, accepting that without judgment is a process. Letting go of Your Past interpretations of others will make the steps easier.

We are all linked in and connected to one another, yet this is sometimes easier to understand when you stay in your comfort zone. Once you get out of it, where you are among more people who are very different from yourself, confusion can prevail. This is especially true if we take the time to try to understand regional customs - beliefs that in our own country feel foreign to us. But, actual foreign travel is the very best experience, even if it is only to our neighbors north and south. Of course, passing through like a tourist simply for the well known sites or shopping, is not the same as staying a few days to know the locals and their customs.

As long as your mind is open and you are willing to try new things - you don't have to like them, but you won't know until you try them - it will reduce any prejudice, or narrow-mindedness that you might have. Awareness comes in all forms and from all people, if you are just open to the opportunity to receive it. Lao Tsu: "He who controls others may be powerful, but he who has mastered himself is mightier still." Your ups and downs can be a real, thrill roller-coaster filled with Past baggage, or an enjoyable, freeing, rolling-hills kind of ride. It is, as always, up to you and your choices.

We learn to be more of service, once we experience which of our skills will be most helpful to others. Most of us have talents that are unknown to us, but can and should be seen and appreciated by others. Keep the Past out of the Future, so it is open for new creative invention. You cannot move forward with new ideas, when your feet are stuck in old ways of the Past.

**Exercise II:** Think in a way that you have not thought before - how far out in left field can you go for an original idea? When you do look for the positive, you will find it. Likewise, it is also with the all negative. Being positive/optimistic is like being a magnet. Remember: You always teach best, what you most need to learn. Human Beings are the only creatures on Earth, that can consciously choose the choice for direction of their actions with *reason.*

To be truly of Service, you need to be Authentic and Original. This means to be truly authentic in all you say and do, so it must come from your Heart. Being original, acknowledges that there is only one you, so make what you say and do represent you, not a copy, or what you think someone wants you to be. This means you are in a state of acceptance of you, so judgment disappears - it is a release of the ego, which frees-you up, to be who you truly are. Service is a generosity of Self, or the act of giving freely because you desire to, not with the idea of receiving a reward or gift in return. To be truthfully-generous means you want prosperity, abundance and wealth for all. It's both the joy of giving and the ability of receiving - they are different facets of your same blessing.

Some find it easier to give than to receive - if so, they may want to question their feelings of Self-worth. *You* are taking away the joy from another in refusing their gift. Generosity is motivated by love for all, as well as the individual. As it must come from the heart, true giving cannot be forced or fulfilling an obligation. In most cultures, giving is wanting happiness for others and happy for them receiving it. Celebrating another's happiness is a gift of bliss for all involved.

# *Transformation ~ Part #63*

Transformation is the giant step in the change process. There are many ways you can change - physically how you look, mentally how you think and even emotionally how you feel. All those changes stem from who You were, but no longer want to be. Yet, if we say that a person has totally transformed, it is as if they have no relationship to who/what they were in their Past. Like the true amnesiac, they have no known Past that they have escaped from, to be this new person. Think of the word metamorphosis, as in the funny looking, small caterpillar transforming to the beautiful butterfly. This is no Cinderella story, as she knew from whence she came and would return - a Past existence. The light, airy pretty butterfly has no memory of any Past life as a lowly caterpillar, and simply enjoys flitting around doing its job of flower pollinating. But then, as controlled by instinct, it will lay the eggs which go into the larvae, then the caterpillar and finally a pupa, or chrysalis becoming the butterfly again, to repeat the cycle.

We could say that the butterfly has 'no baggage' of its Past life, or even related to its life stages. So there is nothing to speak of, to hold it back - pushy mother, neglectful father, poverty or lack of education - just the self-made butterfly, its own persona. Not quite the same for us humans. Even the child adopted from birth, may later question where they came from and why their birth parents gave them up. This may be a whole revealing, growth quest, or an obsession that holds them back from becoming who they might have been, with all of the advantages of the new parentage they were given. Or, think of the music or movie stars, who go from oblivion to crushing-celebrity, no privacy in the occasional overnight sensation situation, they cannot handle.

While one may be instant and the other a life-growth process, much has to do with one's attitude and behavior in how it is handled. No matter how much you may have wanted the success or questions answered, being prepared for the reality is not something you can actually do. Not even the caterpillars crawling on the ground, can then suddenly decide they want to be in the sky flying as butterflies instead. As humans, our instincts are more limited in telling us what we have to do. You have choices - though you have a pushy mother - and you have the process of reason to help you make those choices. But, you often still choose mistakes or missteps. Remember, there are no wrong ones - they are all experiences for us to learn lessons.

**Exercise:** Even with a good life education and a positive direction, finding one's true path to making the changes needed for a full transformation, can take years with more slips or missteps along the way. Think about it and write down what missteps you have had along the way? How has your life changed? What have you learned from them? Did they seem positive at the time? Thus, a major part of taking on the *mantle* of real transformation has to do with accepting yourself as who you are Now. Which you can do, if you've completely let go of your Past, or released it to being just that - a Past life. There may have been many battles - personal or public - and most of us give a rousting applause to those who have overcome demons, or other addictions, to fulfill their destinies of success in whatever field. Some cocoons take longer to complete the growth change than others, so we may have to return to the cocoon for another start.

These things have usually made us stronger, although there are also those who failed to find the support from within, or without. An important cautionary part of this tale is that not all people, especially those from one's

Past, will accept the transformed you. Ask reformed alcoholics, or addicts, as they're not usually accepted by their 'using' friends. Their belief in who you now are, is not necessary for you to be who you are. So, just keep believing in yourself and know what your beliefs are, and that you live by them every day. Do not try to change their perceptions, they may eventually accept you from your actions, so move on and spread your new wings to fly your own way. And, you can share the world with others, without sharing their world view.

Change is threatening to the ego - yours and others around connected to you. Ego believes security comes from clinging on, or attachment to the old ways. Any change you make, which is aligned with your inner truth, is always a healthy improvement. Think of your first high school or college reunion, where usually the largest physical transformation may be noted in each other. Reunions start out at every ten years, then as we age, are moved up to five years or less. Refuse to go into judgment with yourself or others, when you see either haven't changed enough to your liking, or they simply haven't noticed. What positive qualities you may have developed, could be totally different for them and their Belief Systems. While you may have moved way past the big money, title, job or even address, their insecurities and egos may still cherish these things. Actions speak louder than words, so show compassion with others who have different values. You may be planting your useful seeds, which will germinate when those things become shallow, and no longer bring them joy, or even satisfaction, as they thought they should. You are now allowing for their Universal Laws of Cause and Effect to run its course.

There is, of course, no need to rescue or preach, as you show love to yourself and others, especially when they have known you to be harsh and critical in the Past. You are no longer connected to that old paradigm, with negative views or messages to the world. You are in the process of revamping and erasing your Past conditioning, as you have set your intention to be more awake, to any limiting-negative thoughts. Then, you are accelerating the shifting into new positive vibrational energies for full transformation. You have become more conscious of what negatively impacts your present, so you will have more power to alter your future. You are now fully cognizant of creating your future by how you respond to life today. You do not allow gloom-and-doom thinking of others, to color your world with negative bleakness. The "Mute" word is worn off my remote control button, and that is not just for commercials. I enjoy listening to the news, but since Negative and Fear "sell," I don't allow it to creep into my being, even by osmosis.

I believe that the real Truth comes from my God/Source heart connection, which gives me inner peace. Yet, I understand that, since I live in the reality of the real world, this involves connecting a balance with my truth. Still, I believe there is no truth in the negative, or fear-mongering approach. Don't bring it up, if you don't have a suggestion to fix it! Simply talking about something creates a growing negativity, or vicious circle of Self-fulfilling Prophecy. That is not part of my now journey, or the path connected with my heart, as I am also intuitively guided to my transformation.

The group consciousness will either grow with a positive awareness, heralding new creative inroads of expanding into joy, or continue its trek into negative-muck and mire. This does require you stepping-out of limited thinking, and of Not repeating the sad, old stories from the Past. Yes, the world contains much pain, abuse and greed, etc. But, if we focus on liberation from these thoughts in the Now moments, we are no longer allowing the Past to hold us back. That is real transformation, and can be had by any who are willing to work for it.

As you disengage from what no longer represents who you are, fear may be stirred up. Again, as recommended before, use your real breath, to deep breathe yourself back into focusing on your heart, with the love coming in, and the fear going out. As you continue to deep breathe, repeat other positive thoughts, such as what Gandhi said, you can "Be the change you wish to see in the world." There is no secret ingredient in life, no fast-forward button, quick fix or short cuts. We have lessons to learn, to grow and to move forward on our path. The Transformation will come, as you Believe in your heart Truth, as Love creates your Power to manifest, to realize the waiting magic - miracles that abound in life. And, if you question when your work is done here on Earth and you are still breathing, then it isn't.

Most of you know and accept, that you opted to be here at this moment for your own evolution, and to share your Light with others who want it. You can not save the whole world, as the whole world is not ready for you to save it. You are here to *serve* the world, as much as you can with your talents, yet you are also here for the sheer joy of living life. Hopefully, you have learned that there is no need for your suffering, others - themselves may need to relieve themselves of their own suffering, you cannot do it for them. You can simply-only be the Wayshower, and the Lightworker by your Transformation, away from all that is negative.

\* \* \* \* \* \*

Worry often gives a small thing a big shadow.
Swedish proverb

When You change, so do your perceptions, therefore everything around you seems to change.
There is no indebtedness with gratitude.
Poverty has no power over the abundance of God.
We cannot change anything until we accept it.
Condemnation does not liberate, it oppresses. Carl Jung

# *More Manifesting ~ Part #64*

**Regarding Manifestation:** When people ask us how long does it take for something to manifest, we say, "It takes as long as it takes you to release *your resistance.* Could be 30 years, 40 or 50 years. Or, It could be a week, or even tomorrow afternoon." It truly is up to you and your belief of *acceptance* of what Source/God wants to give you. Abraham-Hicks

While tons of information has been written about manifesting what you want, most of it has suggested all you truly have to do is to snap your fingers and voila! When it doesn't come true, most people just blow-it-off, as another airy-fairy thing from the woo-woo people. What they probably didn't mention, since they are trying to reach out to the *uninitiated,* or people who have Not been studying Metaphysics/Spirituality, is that it takes work - *to work.* And more involved, there are rules. Actually, they are the *Universal Laws,* of which there are twelve (see back section). An full understanding of each is required, to comprehend just how complicated manifesting can be, when you may be *violating* basic Laws, that you are not familiar with at all. Since they are all tied together, they also involve manifesting your requests. While it is not a question that Source wants you to have all of the abundance you want in the world - as it is unlimited - it is slightly more complicated than "Ask, and you shall receive." I have always preferred: "God helps those that help themselves."

**Exercise:** These are the Twelve Universal Laws - which they affect all of us without judgment, whether you believe in them or not. It is your job to look them up (listed in detail at the back of this book & the internet has them) and read them until you can at least, basically understand them - following them may be another thing. They are, as they say, rather simple, yet therein lies the difficulty to comprehend them fully and *their power*. The Law of: 1. Divine Oneness; 2. Vibration; 3. Attraction; 4. Abundance; 5. Action; 6. Cause and Effect (Karma); 7. Compensation; 8. Correspondence; 9. Energy; 10. Relativity; 11. Polarity; 12. Rhythm. This is very Key: You must read them ALL, not just the ones you think you need to know. They ALL *work together* for manifesting, as well living your life more smoothly.

Also, you need to be in a relaxed state, prior to doing any of your affirmations or intuition manifesting. If you are anxious or just nervous, your energy will absorb, or process your feeling. So, take 3 - 5 deep breaths with Love-in and Fear-out, then begin at your head and move throughout your body, down to your toes visualizing-releasing, letting go of all tension, fear, guilt, anger, sadness, or whatever old limitations you have within any part of your body. Once you've gone from head to toe, now begin again visualizing-infusing love, peace, happiness, joy, safety and serenity into every part of your body down to the cellular level. You will not only be surprised at how good you feel, but how positive you will feel about your manifestation coming into fruition quickly.

The next misconception most people have is not understanding that God/Source does not wear a Timex, or have a clock or calendar. Time is linear, as created and thus controlled by man. Divine timing is fluid and not linear, like man's time. So, you need to keep in mind Divine timing, when asking the same request over and over. I include also, asking for Divine Assistance in bringing forth what I'm asking for, as well how it helps others. I also may add Now, or specific event.

While saying affirmations or chants may be good for you, in convincing yourself, that you truly deserve what you want - especially with a lot of emotion, it is not the most productive approach to God/Source. Once, if stated with that strong, deep emotional desire, is sufficient. A Universal principle is that truths and desires are revealed at their appropriate time, and not a moment sooner. Trust me, you were heard, but you, yourself, may not be ready for what you are asking for, or it may not be for your highest good. You all know the saying: "Be careful what you ask for." These may be those lessons brought to you that were very painful, and you may even end up blaming God/Source for cursing you with what you actually asked to have - repeatedly.

The thing that you wanted, may have been pushed further into the future because of a host of factors, some of which may have little or nothing to do with you. Or God/Source knows you're going to learn this is not what you really want or need Now. For another thing, what you wanted may be configured in a different way for your highest good. Perhaps it will manifest, but may take you a while to recognize it. Or, it may also be a much more wonderful version coming your way down the road, once it's invented or revamped. These may sound like confusing excuses, but things aren't always simple or easy.

But most importantly, being able to manifest or bring forth what you want, requires that you are *in alignment* with what you say you want and desire. That is to say, in that you truly believe you do deserve or actually want it. In other words, if they are only words, not true emotional feelings of your deepest desires, the Universe/Source doesn't bring it forth. Any negative doubt, fear or worry will also negate your manifestation. So, if your belief of worthiness of receipt counters your desire, it will not be manifested. You need to carefully examine both your verbal and thought requests with what deeply does resonates within your heart and soul, so it will be manifested. If beliefs from your Past limit your worthiness, you'll only get say $100, not $100,000. So, You need to do some examination on it.

Releasing the attachment to, or the expectation of a result is important for the situation, to be kept freely flowing to you. As soon as you instill any control, you are also putting limitations or restrictions on the request. If you are going to ask Source for something, you truly MUST surrender and release all of your resistance to being the one in control of the results. If you think you can do it alone, then do so; or if you think you can do it better, then do so! But if you are going to Ask for Divine Will or Divine Guidance, then don't give Source the map or directions You want it to take. You must have faith and trust in turning it all over to Source, to bring forth what it is that you are asking to be brought forth. Otherwise, you are putting up blocks, roadblocks, walls or even speed bumps that will slow down or restrict the flow of all of the positive energies of joy and peace for the miracles to be brought forth. Check - ask to make sure the positive vibrational energy coming into you is free and clear, so it is flowing through and around you.

To be in the flow, You must allow the flow to be, which means not interfering or controlling - let it Be-let it go-Thy will be done. You will truly see things shifting in your life as you release your ego from controlling. Know that what Source is bringing, is for your highest good and will guide you on your path for the highest good of all. It's usually when we experience something that we don't want, that we get clarity on what we do want.

You must believe that you are truly moving toward your heart's desires. You must believe you are in synchronistic flow for all of your heart's desires to come to you. Balance - Patience - synchronicity of Timing - if you didn't get what you thought you would within the time frame you expected it would arrive, then let it go for now. Understand Synchronized-timing is for 'your best and highest good, and also the highest good of all.' Freedom from time - happy to know it will come when it is best for it to come. Therefore, no worries, no dramas, no anxiety. You must have absolutely no doubt that whatever is expected will appear at the best time for you. Remind yourself and Source that whatever abundance will bring joy to you, which is doubled when you share, which you plan to do.

Intention is not something we do, but something we connect to in the Universe through Source, as Source is Intention. Everything is intended - all things come from God/Source - we are all connected. It animates all life - how well we are connected to Source states how we get those things we want. When positive thought and positive emotion come together - "mountains can be moved." What reasons you want something with emotion, and why you believe you will get it, is your mental state of being and what attracts things to you. Know, You are a complicated being, so you need to also make sure that all parts of you - your Spiritual, Emotional, Physical and Mental feelings are in alignment for your desires.

The act of focusing your consciousness is an act of creation. Consciousness creates all you have, all the power you need to create all the changes you choose. The focus of your awareness becomes the reality of your world. To simply say that you choose a new reality is not enough. Feeling as though your goal is accomplished, with much gratitude and appreciation that your prayer is already answered, is key. These are feelings created without ego and judgment. This is believing 'as if' you already know 100% that your request will come forth. This means you need to do whatever it takes to convince yourself of this, there can be no doubts or hesitations. Every goal, wish, dream, or intention needs at least 30 days to see it into fruition. That means, 30 consecutive days - do not miss even one, or you need to start again!

I knew a woman who could do the most amazing intention requests and affirmations, and so be in the flow with her emotions - then after completion she would giggle or laugh. I asked her why she did that, and she admitted that she didn't really believe she deserved any of which she had just asked. In talking, she shared her extreme negativity from her childhood. Obviously, that Past stuff - and it is just that - needs to be cleared first. Since she rarely received anything asked for, I wondered why she bothered. She said she hoped that as Source did give her some things, that she would come to believe that she deserved more.

It may not be just this life's beliefs that are holding you back, but also Past lives where having any kind of abundance was not ever acceptable to your belief system. If you lived in a caste system of some sort, or a communal life where no one could have more than another or your mental belief was of limitation. If you desire abundant money, you may need to be specific that it is now, in this lifetime with abundance to spend and give away as you choose.

There is no need to give up your dreams, just because your parents - or whomever - didn't have their dreams fulfilled. There is also no need for you to feel guilty being happy, if others from your Past weren't. When you are 'right' with yourself, you are allowing all abundance to come to you and you have great appreciation for it, in having brought it to yourself by believing that you truly deserve it. Appreciation is true love for yourself, God/Source and ALL things - it is also absence of doubt or fear, or Self-denial - or any hatred of others. When things don't seem to be moving in your life, make a list of all the positive things in your life. Look for things to love and to appreciate, as you are open, willing and allowing for even more that God/Source brings to you with continued great Love-Appreciation. Take nothing for granted, except that you are loved unconditionally.

If your thoughts and beliefs are not in alignment with your intention - your desire, then it cannot not be manifested. In other words, if you merely doubt you won't receive it, much less say it out loud, it will not be manifested. You do need a good understanding of the Universal Laws and how they work in tandem with each for the manifesting of what you want. Yet, most importantly is that you are practicing them and that puts you in the right vibration to receive what you are asking for. Our vibrational frequency - the higher the better - is in direct correlation to how much we have moved from fear to love, and our connection to Source. Yet, again not just in our lives for ourselves, but how much we practice it to others.

As always, it is a step process of moving towards the positive and no longer being afraid, doubtful, disillusioned, depressed or angry, which are fear based. The moment you move into unconditional love for yourself and others, this energy leaves you open for manifestation of miracles to be brought to you. What you cannot manifest today, you may do so tomorrow. Your prior failure or mistakes in the Past, are not held against you. You are always given another day to experience a new joyful life, with peace and abundance in all things. Greed in all of its non-sharing distinguished characteristics will stop any of your manifestations. Karma balances when you least expect it to do so.

# *Past Pain ~ Part #65*

As previously mentioned, on the Spiritual path things or situations will happen that jerk us back to our prior Past, freezing us in our tracks. I have mentioned several different processes, to help get you started again, depending how deep or hurtful or fearful the past memory was that attacked you - which is what it really did. First of all, there will always be people, places, or things-situations that will surely remind you of your Past. As said, no one was never raised living in a Disneyland, or if your parents were overly protective, you were not that prepared for the real world. Bullies always exist in all arenas and jealousies raged in junior/senior high school much like they do in your adult life. Yet, that knowledge does not make the situation easier, or more acceptable. Some pain, no matter how much you deep breathe it, talk to yourself, or even examine it to forgive yourself and others are involved - still hurts. Some pains also come back to haunt us, period.

**Exercise:** So lets look at some steps to take to release you of those truly painful memories of the Past. Reoccurring pains come back as there is some definite fear or ego attached, that wants to hang onto you. As soon as it happens, you need to start examining your situation that brought it back. How was this similar to the original? Who, what, where was/were involved in the original pain? What was your reaction at the time? Was fear involved? Did you at the time talk to, question or confront others involved? Have you since? Even if the people involved are now deceased, you can still speak to them effectively.

Have you gone through the Forgiveness Letters - even though not mailed, sometimes are more appropriate than doing it in person - including a letter forgiving yourself? Did this pain leave you with a physical reaction - stutter, tick, fear/phobia, etc.? Have you ever had counseling, or talked with someone you trusted with your feelings? Can you accept and believe, that you are no longer that person who received this pain? If you can take the time to journal, or write down some of this information with truthful answers, it will help the pain let go of you. Somehow, the process of pen-to-paper releases so much of your pent-up emotions and painful feelings.

No matter how adult you think you are, when dealing with all feelings/emotions, do not waste your time to attempt to apply logic to releasing Past hurt/pain. It is simply apples and oranges. Look at the Reality TV - how can they become so manipulative, etc. when it is only a game? It is life in a microcosm and you need to accept, that real life is still a game. Or, take for instance, young star-struck fans who scream, yell or faint. Sure, at 13 we accept it, but what do you call an adult who stalks a celebrity? We certainly cannot see any logic, but there is also, truly a lot of emotional feelings being expressed and then painfully rejected.

Your feelings connect to one another for the best and worse reasons, which does not make them bad or good. It is still better, to have the feelings than go through life apathetic. Following and trusting your intuitive feelings is about as close to logic, that you can ever be expected to get from them. Again, it is better to have real, true feelings you do believe in, than put forth fake ones to please others, or not act as your mother may have said, "unacceptable or inappropriate."

Your emotional feelings are what make you human, so if you repress them you can take much of your humanness away from you. In extreme cases, people have become sociopaths or even psychopaths, hurting strangers for no apparent reason, as they reminded them of something/someone from their Past. It is healthy to release pain, at least to yourself, if not to another. It is no longer considered a sign of weakness, but of being human. So, don't let the ego keep you bottled up and becoming humorless, rigid or poisoned on the inside. No one goes through life without some pain, yet it is personal and individual.

Thus, it is an inadvertent-discount when someone haplessly says, "I know just how you feel." You want to say, "But, you don't! It's my pain and I'm feeling it!" Yet, you know they are merely being kind, or trying to make you feel better, or they really are discounting you, because they don't want to be involved in your problems. If you were walking around smiling or even being blissful all the time, then people would definitely call an ambulance, or report you to Human Resources, as an itinerant employee about to go ballistic. So, damned if you smile too much, and damed if you don't cope with it all.

Your painful feelings are a problem, in that they are slowing you down from the new life you want to have. Some of these are basic anger, fear, or simply situations which have left you with feelings of inadequacy, that are holding you back from success. Knowing the real source or root cause of a pain reveals it, acknowledges it, or brings it to light for what it needs to heal it. Truly, that light in your previous, scary-darkness brings enlightenment, that often dissolves the power of the pain. It sometimes has to be mentally/visually re-experienced for you to see it for what it was, to no longer have the power over you. Recognizing what kind of pain is triggered to come back to you, is necessary in being able to release or neutralize it from stopping you in your tracks, and impeding your growth. Read the following list - any words that bring a "ping" to your emotions or feelings needs to be written down and thought about: Anger - Clumsy - Disappointment - Dread - Embarrassment - Envy - Fear - Fear of small spaces, heights, water, insects, other

- Guilt - Ineptness - Inadequacy - Jealousy - or Physical Pain - Sadness - Scared *of what* - Shame - Too fat/thin - Ugly - Unloved - UnWorthy - Worry - What else? Not good enough?

If the source or root of this pain is not immediate, approach it from as many different angles as possible, as you may have buried it really deep. This is like toxic-material that has begun to surface, so its removal is the only way to keep it from continually infecting you. Be prepared that once you do discover it you may be shocked, for if it was from a really, early age. Perhaps it was a misconception or something totally misconstrued like still being angry at an older sibling for telling you Santa wasn't real. It may also have been something that you just overheard, not only not meant for your ears, but not even referring to you. A child, overhearing adults referring to a parent who would never find happiness in marriage, but the child took its meaning upon to be themselves. Some painful feelings may have contributed to habits you developed to counter them - dread may lead to procrastination; maybe ineptness may have lead to being indecisive, so not making a decision as you may feel you can't make any mistakes.

**Note:** If you have a strong emotional fear of physical pain, you may want to seriously consider professional therapy, as the trauma of buried-abuse may be ready to come forth. None of these processes are meant to replace professional help in any way, nor will you ever be "pain-free" from your Past situations. What, hopefully, will happen is that you will be able to turn them into small blips, that may cause you to miss a step or two, but then tell yourself - "That was then, and this is now. I am no longer that person." And, continue to work the path. Some pains will be released enough to eventually fade away, or no longer have the affect, and control over you, as you have truly grown beyond them. It does take time and much work to be pain-free.

Others may take a retreat of 24 to 72 hours to kind of wallow totally and thoroughly in that lost Past of pain, or hurtful memories and feelings. This satiation will sometimes give the pain - especially if connected to that child inside you - the love - recognition that it needs before it can let go of you. Yes, there may be screaming, yelling, some crying and beating of pillows, but if that is what it takes to be released, then you need to do it. You may also get to know yourself more and/or better, than you ever have before. Afterwards, freer and self-accepting, ask for the presence of Grace to enfold you with Golden Light of your Forgiveness to surround and fill you, and others involved with the Past pain. Be sure to fill that vacant pain spot with Golden Light/Love.

Some pain, as in losing a loved one, some people don't want to let go of, so they don't have to return to living life on their own. Even when they feel at fault or guilty for some reason, they can also learn to visually move those lost-love feelings to a special corner of their heart and mind. There they can then stroll down memory lane with all their good, happy and personal times they had with that person, any time they wish, or need to recall them. That is very healthy in that you, the survivor can continue on with life, yet keep that loved one with you. It is important to remember that no one, NO ONE dies before their time - even in disasters, accidents or suicides. Their soul made a real contract which they agreed to, prior to their birth regarding their death. There is a purpose or reason for how someone dies, as to the affect-effect it has on others. Eventually, you will see and accept, that Good ALWAYS comes out of something bad - everything as a lesson. We are ALL One and connected - accept this or not, it is your choice, but it is one of the principles of Metaphysics and Universal Law.

Don't forget as mentioned before, you may be carrying pain from a Past life or from generations past in this life, that you are not really aware. You may need a good healer who has worked with these situations. Or, your Chakras need a really, good clearing/cleansing which pain indicates. Karma, whether from this life or others, can bring in some physical pain in your bones or joints, and that speaks of deep aspects needing to be cleared. The more often that you do Chakra - energy clearing and other body work, the more you will be capable of warding off any of these Past pains to invade you. This is why your regular physical and emotional Self-assessing is so very important.

**Exercise II:** Forgiveness is also letting go of the attachment of the negative energy of the other person. This releases all that negative energy within yourself. It is that negative energy which makes the pain reoccur within yourself. Depending on how deep this pain is, which either has to do with how long you've had it, or how powerful the old incident. Then the forgiveness may need to be multilayered and you will feel some release after each session. Along with that, you may be visualizing what part of your body is affected most. If you are having a problem finding the part, just concentrate on your heart. See your dark spot dissolved as you release it. Working with deep breathing - Love in - Pain out; Forgiveness in - Pain out; Release in - Fear out; or any other words that feel right to you. Forgiveness is all about your love, unconditional towards yourself and all others involved.

# *Karma Law ~ Part #66*

While the Universe does not test us, per se - though you often think you are playing the part of a modern day Job, from the Bible. It does give you opportunities to express your beliefs, or do the right/best thing - in other words "practice what you preach." You probably don't think of the little things as being Karma *collectors* and only those big things that others (bankers, profiteers, politicians) do that clearly spell out: G-R-E-E-D. Yet, even the small things - like keeping the wrong change - set up the Cause & Effect Law of Karma, that puts results or consequences into motion. These little "dings" can cause delays, or do permanent stoppage on an intention you want to manifest. They can change the vibration of your positive energy, which needs a certain frequency for manifesting things in your life.

So, if you're not getting what you desire, you may want to look back on some of your actions, messages or negative thoughts. Just because your Past taught that "a white lie was OK," or "possession was nine-tenths of the law, or finders-keepers." It doesn't mean it was best or just. That would be like someone catching a shoplifter and making them share their bounty, or they'd turn them in - actually knew someone who did that. 'Two wrongs never make a right.' Many think that the missteps of Karma are the "shit-happens" of our everyday life. Yes, probably so, but what if it didn't have to happen? Be aware of your car horn and patience or rudeness to pedestrian and other drivers. I have no problem with pedestrians, but I'm still working on drivers.

While I was living in Japan and traveled often throughout Asia, I had the opportunity of buying pirated tapes, CDs and videos. At first I took advantage of it, feeling the big producers could afford the loss, but often the material was not what they had said, and rarely worth the price I paid. But Karma being what it is and was, I could not scream, but I did cry when my own copyrighted material was stolen, and then offered to others. Bingo! With awareness, when later offered real ivory and tortoise, I refused it, though others said it didn't matter, since the animal was already dead. I knew it did matter to the future animals, that would be slaughtered to replace what was bought. Nowadays, I do see this as the equivalence buying some cheaper Chinese made goods instead of American made, or a real hand-made art/craft items.

So, much of what we do is done not out of any actual harmful purpose, but without awareness or actual stupidity to open your eyes to the consequences of your actions. This is truly what this law of Cause and Effect is all about - stop and think what your actions, or negative energy is doing, that will be boomeranged back to you in multiple amounts. I am all for Capitalism, because I believe that its foundation is competition. Yet, some players won't play by the rules of ethics, as they are greedy and just after the money.

**Exercise:** So, fully understanding all of the Universal Laws can help you to comprehend why certain things may befall you, when you think you've been a 'good' person, not cheating anyone out of their life savings, etc. People don't trip over mountains, it is always the pebbles along the path, that can send you over the edge - literally, as well as figuratively. These Laws do not make judgments, they simply create *an effect* for every cause. Think of them as computer oriented - they can only respond to what has been programed in, so there is no special treatment or exceptions for anyone or thing. If we do positive things in helping people, donating, or act in responsible ways in gratitude, forgiveness; the effect or results is returned to us exponentially. Think of it as Lady

Justice NOT blindfolded, but having 360 degree eyesight at all times, everywhere. Those scales are out there measuring and weighing everything we do or say. The Law of Karma is working to teach us or bless us and surprisingly, sometimes both almost simultaneously. Don't forget, even your thoughts, beliefs and energy have an affect on those scales.

While no one can play 'Goody-Two-Shoes, Pollyanna, or Hero' all the time, you can be a far cry from the bully or egotistical "It's ALL about me, shallow person." Yet some people, who are very career-driven, don't realize how insensitive or inflexible they are, as justified with being fair - 'just honest,' as in not being compassionate to anyone. I'm a little OCD and sometimes more blunt, so try to catch myself if it slips out. Some do not understand loyalty or appreciation, in that efficiency is everything, when people are paid fairly for the job they do. Some are perfectionists, expecting others to have that flaw, as it is. These are the classic "ends justifying the means," as long as they don't technically break any human laws. They usually don't consider themselves as cruel or even a mean person, just doing what *they think* is right, or expected of them to do.

Most of us are not aware of the energetic vibrations that we are putting out, but others can quickly pick up the negative resonance in a room, or even single-out the source. What is most fascinating to me as referred to before, is that this negativity all comes from Fear. If this idea of fear was posed to that person vibrating it, they would think you were crazy, weird and probably offensive. If you wanted to freak them out more, just tell them that it can be cured or removed *by love* - the perfect transformation would be if it was unconditional-love. But, of course, we know that is not going to happen, as the person has to want to change, which starts with awareness and acknowledgment of their flaws. Then again, you can offer an opinion, that being more accepting of others is a start and go from there.

The best situation, as stated before, is to lead by example. So when someone notices how positive and happy your life is, you simply tell them that you work at staying in a positive vibration of love. If you haven't lost them in your directness, you can add you are continuously working at letting go of anger, doubt, fear and any negative actions or thoughts. The magic starts when they ask how and why you've done this as you move onto unconditional love, and how the positive energy creates miracle-manifesting. You do not need to be such a passionate-cheerleader that it comes off as, "I'm better and more advanced than you are," or even intimidating, as if you belong to this exclusive club that isn't accepting any new members. We are not reformers to the end extent that convert to your obsessive ways and beliefs, or die. This would not make us that different from the above described "ends justifying the means," people. It's always a choice for people.

Think of the Crusades and how much positive they did Not accomplish - there is still War in the Middle East. We don't want a zealot that eventually burns out, or addiction that alienates all who are not on a par with our feelings. Passion, like heroism has its place and purpose. But the middle-road is always best, as fully acknowledged that we are not perfect, and it is not what you are striving for on this Earth plane. We appreciate the happiness of your success, and offer the choice to others to find their paths. Their is a contentment-satisfaction of doing what one loves to do, with the bonus of positive feedback.

Acceptance is a key part, in that what you see inside another person is often what is similar or don't like within yourself. You point it out in another, so they don't notice it in you. If we are All One, then acceptance and tolerance is the foundation. Also, acting stoic and/or feeling that you have to suffer to be rewarded is not part of Karma. There are no evils in wealth, as long as you've earned it by your own talents and not Past ancestors through their graft or greed. Then, it's important to share it with others, so you will also receive back more abundance in kind of what is given.

\* \* \* \* \* \*

Remember that not getting what you want is sometimes a wonderful stroke of luck. Albert Einstein

I get everything I want in my life, by helping others get what they want in their lives.

Intelligence is the ability to adapt to change. Stephen Hawking

When you forgive, you in no way change the past - but you sure do change the future. Bernard Meltzer

# Soul Groups ~ Part #67

Understanding Soul Groups is much like accepting as true the idea of intuition, synchronicity, reincarnation or even the manifesting something, as basic as a parking space during busy times. It all begins with the Metaphysical/Spiritual concept of us all choosing our parents and family for the experiences which they will give us, related to the lessons we need to learn in this particular life. The size of your soul group varies from life to life, depending on what you need and they in return need from you. It is sort of like a giant jigsaw puzzle, where just when you seem to get the pieces to fit, it is time to start over in a new one. So, your current family, relatives, friends and so-called 'enemies' probably have played the life-game with you multiple times before, but usually in various positions, as you are here for the new challenge. Portraying the more 'ugly-parts' may actually speak of how much they love you, as they contribute to the lessons that you need to experience. While conscious in this life, you rarely have glimpses of who or what, you were in Past lives together. And, blips may come out in dreams, or hypnotic past-life regression, or Akashic readings of this knowledge may or may not be real helpful to you in this life.

Think about the truly talented actors you admire, they love to play the more challenging parts to expand on their own experiences, or referred to as 'against usual type-cast.' Consider Meryl Streep or Al Pacino, they can and do play about every kind of character out there, and been rewarded for doing so by their peers. You, too, have played the 'baddie' for other members of your soul group, but those memories may not be as recurrent to you, unless very life-changing. We usually remember those most prevalent lifetimes of our 'staring-roles.'

Currently, you may have healing contracts with certain other members of your soul groups, sort of like Karma clearing. This may mean that prior to your birth, you agreed as *part of this life journey* to complete those contracts. If you've had a problem or separation from a parent or sibling and that irritation keeps coming back up, you have not healed that Karma as hoped. They may be expecting your help to heal, but you may no longer want to deal with them, as their energy is so awry to yours. You may hope, or help them to find other teachers that have more patience for their healing. Yet, your moving on may leave you feeling guilty, or sad, as you don't really have an acceptable solution to your contract. Still, is it fair that you are so uncomfortable dealing with them, because of being out of a vibration? Unfortunately, your strong emotional DNA ties to your soul group, may tempt you to delay your own growth, because you feel their pain and/or fear. This is true of why my non-association with my older sister, unfortunately she has no interest in changing, so I've let her go with many blessings.

**Exercise:** This is where you need to examine your natural tendency to help them, just because that is what you have always done. Perhaps, this is the life where you are strong enough, or ready to say, "No, I'm not going to delay my growth and movement. I have helped you so often before, and enough is enough. I cannot complete the your contract if you are not willing to cooperate." If many others in the soul group have given them one more chance repeatedly, for them to 'see the light' for the completion cycle of their healing, then it may be time to let go for this life time. If this is what you believe, then the choice for you is obvious, to continue your move into your higher vibration and experience your reality from this new level. I am without qualms.

We are all given the opportunity to complete our cycles and move into higher levels of being, to accept our new vibrations for ascending. But, not everyone is ready, nor willing to do the work that is required for their completion. Who you are becoming is not who you've been and, no one has the right to hold you back from your Divine Destiny or happiness. Family may be blood, but such not a life-saving match to you. It may be part of their game to see how long they can hold you at their level. As they say, about rejection in your own hometown, it would be more so in a family rejecting bold, brazen stars showing them all up.

If in this life time, this related-person may not have had to be responsible or accountable for many of their actions, because of the parents or spouses, or even children taking care of them. Then, they often cannot face the painful choices we've all had to learn, to heal and grow without our hands being held or our feet guided. Your choice has to sometimes be self-preservation and what is best for your own soul growth. You must then disconnect energetically from those others in your soul group to allow them to perhaps find their own power, for their healing and ascension in their own way, perhaps in another life. You can only guide everyone to the light, even those of your own soul group, but that final choice is theirs. So you can then gently disconnect from your contract and release yourself from the commitment of their healing. Hopefully, as you complete your cycles, you are allowing for them to develop their empowerment and divinity on their own, without sacrificing your own soul growth in the process. Remember, it is still a singular path. There are no lessons learned, if you are carrying them and making the decisions for them.

If your mind has slipped outside of accepting unconditional love, which we all do from time to time, your immediate loneliness makes you feel its need to assert power and control over your own situations. This is, of course, without acknowledging that on its own, this mind has created this reality. The ego, along with the insecurities of fear, quickly denies that *its* clever mind took part in any of your Self-sabotage resulting in your suffering, injustices, or betrayals being experienced. In its avoidance and fear of being judged harshly for its mistakes, your ego immediately projects those errors on others - ones usually in the soul group - rather than judging itself. This human-mind has forgotten the attributes of the Divine mind, where knowing it is loved unconditionally is basic. All kinds of emotional - psychological patterns emerge from simple procrastination - not making a decision of action, to passive-aggressive - where one moment blaming oneself to the next of blaming everyone else. Usually, the target of each of these reproaches is someone within Your soul group. There is a safety of non-violence for the bad behavior, yet resentment, as these people know your deepest secrets more than anyone else.

Perhaps the most revealing story I could tell of my mother is the day following my father's funeral, after the relatives living within the area had returned to their homes. My hapless-sister and I had to travel together - at my father's prior request to get us to reunite, which didn't really work - but we were staying a few days at the house. So, I went to the grocery store to get some basics and stuff for sandwiches for my mother and our road trip. My father loved the Deli section and I picked up most of what I remembered that they both liked, including a fresh loaf of Jewish Rye bread. Money had not been a problem for them, though both living off retirement for many years. I came in with all of the fixing and proudly announced them to my mother, trying to please as usual, as I entered the kitchen.

My mother always managed to find errors, a long time thing for us, which I truly thought I had passed, especially by moving far away and her out of my daily life. Sitting at the table, she looked up at me and said, "You know I never really liked rye bread, I just ate it because your father loved it so much." I plopped down in a chair and just stared at her, amazed. They had been married over fifty years and she'd not hesitated to chastise him or speak her mind. Also, I distinctly remembered us four kids, having several different kinds of bread in the house all the time. Choices - availability of food was not a problem.

My mother's favorite game was stoicism, and often moved up a notch to rescuer or even martyrdom - "Look what I've done for you; I was only doing what was best for you;" or her favorite, "How could you do such a thing to embarrass me so, what will the neighbors say?" When I finally questioned her as to why she would eat bread that she didn't like all those years, she again simply said how much my father liked it, as if her eating it made him happy. I then commented, that I doubted that he could have cared less whether or not she ate what he ate, as their taste with many foods varied. I think my final comment, as I should have remembered there was really no use in arguing with her, was something like, she just enjoyed punishing herself and blaming others for it.

She started to cry, asking why I was still so mean to her. Which meant, of course, as an adult I had accused her of her game-playing, stoicism, etc. about ten years prior and she literally had a stroke. Not my finest hour, but then I had put up with all her badgering of me for about thirty years - including almost killing myself. I left about six months later to freedom and a new life far, far away from her. Having it all then come sweeping back to my memory was *my fault* for being *pulled back into her game*. I was still being controlled by that child inside wanting to be accepted by her. Thankfully, I did release her.

I share all this with the reality of the reoccurrence, of painfully understanding Soul Groups. This telling acknowledgment and eventual acceptance of it was more difficult with the premise that *we do choose our parents, siblings, etc.*, as well as our birth order. Yes, had my older sister and the younger of my older brothers, really been playing their designated roles of hapless-twits in this life for me, my lessons? Sadly, true. When younger, I could only relate more to my oldest brother, but then even that faded over time. I kid you not, I had often been asked if I wasn't secretly adopted. If it had not been for my closeness to my father - physically and emotionally - I would have considered it.

Though I admit, my position of unexpected, late-last child, played a major role in my non-acceptance and treatment in the family, especially by my mother and sister. Now, I've often wondered how many lifetimes we all had been together? And, what positions we played out for one another, to have the lessons - experiences to be learned in those lives. I eventually believed that I had created some whopper of Karma in those Past lives, that totally got dished back to me in this one. These are the major forgiveness patterns that we all need to recognize and process. This life is a learning-game, it has been hundreds of times over for many of us. Now, think of the people you chose to play with you - those you love and did love you in playing it.

On the other hand, consider those distant relatives or cousins that many ethnic groups, races, etc. that have been fighting each other for eons. You shake those family trees and we know they are related. Some of those have chosen to keep hatred for who-knows-what any more - politics, religions, cultural traditions? It may have started with jealousy, resentment, or simply fear of one having more power or even being more successful than other. If asked, most would not even know why they war and kill each other, as it is an old belief system from their Past, that was told to them to believe and follow. So, we might say, that some Souls as they are returning, rather than grow/change by choosing new families, want to return to what they know best. Sad, very sad indeed and also makes my family, not so difficult anymore to accept, as my choice from my Soul Group. I do believe that I am a Spiritual Being having yet another human experience. Fortunately, I think I'm getting a lot more of it right this time.

* * * * * *

The bond that links your *true family* is not one of blood, but of respect and joy in each other's life. Richard Bach

Make the decision to let go of small-minded people - even friends or relatives.

The only way to make sense out of change is to plunge into it, move with it, and join the dance. Alan Watts

They always say time changes things, but you actually have to change them yourself. Andy Warhol

The first step toward change is awareness. The second step is acceptance. Nathaniel Branden

# *Past Lives ~ Part #68*

As previously said, along the path of your journey, blips and flashes of Past scenarios run across your mind like an old film, or they may come up in very, vivid dreams. If you have not yet, perhaps you are ready to more thoroughly exam some of your Past lives, especially those that have left you Karma-burdened. We've talked about the Past Pain and some Karma, but it may be time to totally release yourself from any negatives that you've been carrying *again* in this life. You may find yourself tapping into what you would consider your Past life experiences, as you question why you did or said something that the New You would not have done. You don't really need to ask where did that come from, as you know - a Past Life snuck in or popped out to throw you off course. Kind of like your lips were moving, but what you said didn't come from your current mind.

**Exercise:** In reality, as you allow your consciousness to move through your "I Am Presence," you can draw from the multitude of previous experiences that you may have had. How much you need to know about that particular Past Life is up to you. Usually, unless it is a rather fascinating story, I only want to know enough to find out what "thing" or Belief System, is tripping me up in this life. So, your key – any time if you find yourself in confusion, or out of Your heart-energy – take those deep breaths, focus on your heart/soul and know that you are protected and connected to Source. See your positive Heart Chakra whirling, activated in bright, Green light and feeling totally protected.

That will be your key, the deep breathing and feeling protected and connected to Source. After several deep breaths, ask your Higher Self to release you from Any and All negative energy, from Any and All Past Lives with Karma attached. You love it, forgive it and thank it for whatever lessons it gave you, as You are ready to move on. Ask your Higher Self to replace that negative energy with Golden Light-positive energy, as that is what you want in Your life now and forever. Keep breathing deeply, and be sure that you visualize the negative-Karma energy going out, so the Golden Light-positive energy comes in. You may need to repeat, or continue the process until you do feel a lightness. You can visualize your Heart Chakra filled with both its own Green light and the Golden Light. If you need to prior see that Karma energy as a dark spot, then ask to do so, to make sure you see it gone.

It truly doesn't matter what happened in your Past, you have no need to totally relive the trauma - either done to you, or by you. You're already Here - repeat frequently that you are protected and connected directly to God/Source. This is liberation of your Soul, you do NOT need to suffer any Karma from ANY Past Life! Always invoke the power of Grace and Harmony, visualizing your connection to Source with Positive energy surrounding you, above, below and within you down to cellular level. Because we are all out there in the public, we pick up negative energy from mass-consciousness, just by our own interactions or osmosis. I do a clearing regularly of any negative energy in my emotional, conscious, subconscious and unconscious energy, replacing it with Golden Light-Positive Energy, as stated prior. I also do a balancing of my male energy and a balancing of my Vibrational Frequencies for good health and happiness.

It is just that simple, though not easy to do: Remember, take a deep breath, truly know that you are protected and connected to Source. Then, Liberate yourself - Free yourself - Choose for yourself - No more suffering. You – YOU – have to make a choice that you're going to be the New You, that you're not going to let all those Past negative, ego energies feed off of you anymore. It is a choice-process to do it.

There is only choice to grow and while that sounds wonderful, it requires a tremendous amount of personal responsibility. You can be anything that you want to be, as long as you do love yourself. And, in loving yourself, you'll understand yourself. No matter who you were in the Past - good, bad or in between - it is/was your Past. So, You no longer have to pay, feel guilty or have punishment/suffering once you have let it all go with forgiveness and love. There is NO bad luck, that is a cop out, a game - illusion you have been playing on yourself. It's an experience, which you can stop, as soon as you experienced it -ENOUGH. There is nobody pulling any strings, but you. I encourage each and every one of you to step up and take responsibility for your life = Freedom. You have lived many lives upon our Earth, many lives in the Universe - now live a happy, joyful one - here, now.

Granted, most of you have been given certain Belief Systems, programming or controlling you over many lifetimes, that you didn't think you had a choice. It may take a little bit of practice and a little self-confidence to choose your choices. And, there are varying degrees of perception available to you right now, one may be Self-preservation by rejecting old Belief Systems. You need not know exactly all the circumstances, you need only know the essence of the Past, that does not work for you anymore. These new positive energies assist you in creating a greater, more stable foundation for where you are within your life. Breathe in that which balances the knowing, that you can BE all that you want to Be, and DO all that you want to Do.

If you feel the need to know more details of a Past Life, there are Earthly Guides who can help you with that. I need to add, that you should choose someone who has been recommended to you, so that you will be surrounded by your Guardian Angels protecting you in the process. If Trauma is/was involved, you may not always like what you have done, or who you were in your Past. Still, if it is seeping into your current life, it does want to be released and forgiven.

If there is a lot of unresolved emotional energy left over from countless lifetimes of unfinished business, it will take time to be able to find closure with your Karma, or complete healing cycles. If in each new lifetime you take the opportunity to resolve this, you can avoid getting into a Karmic-cycle which stops the learning, as repeating the lesson over and over again. Using this step-process, you can get some understanding of why your situation, or the other recurring person isn't changing. Awarenesses have been received in this life, that with clarity and releasing, you can move onto the next relationship or interaction, with your changed energy resolution, and NOT get stuck in the illusion of the outcome, based on the Past.

So, you then have a celebration, not the repeated life-cycle challenges, a sad story over many lifetimes resolved, as this is what you have come here to change in this life. You have grasped the power of the Present, as you realize that you can and must change the Past. Don't wait for personal issues and blockages to tell you that something is seriously wrong. You may even have a sense of great fear or panic, claustrophobia and paranoia in crowds, as a traumatic re-enactment of a Past life bleeds into your current one. It can be something like an electrical charge in your spine or a recurring energy surge. So, if that probable Past is faced and deliberately changed, you have re-scripted your Past, and any fear from it then eliminated.

It is as if the trauma never occurred and that is exactly what happens. You have the ability to remove trauma from your Past at anytime. God did not bring you to this planet to suffer. Instead, there's the expectation of that magic-moment, when you'd have the epiphany: You are a part of God. You are not just a Human Being, but a Spiritual Being having a human experience. You are God's Perfect Child, loved unconditionally for who you truly are - inside and out.

\* \* \* \* \* \*

When you come to the end of your rope, tie a knot and hang on. Franklin D. Roosevelt
We have four kinds of Sight: - Insight - Hindsight - Eyesight - Foresight. How many do you use daily, if not at all?
When we are no longer able to change a situation - we are challenged to change ourselves. Viktor E. Frankl

# Chaos Theory - Part #69

Chaos Theory - a briefly-simplified, wide interpretation: The name signifies what may be apparently-disordered, but with thorough investigation shows there is underlying order, in apparently-random data, or related contributing parts. Or, when things seem in absolute chaos, there is actually an *orderly foundation*. But, most importantly, regarding your transition, is that you find in the chaos and maintain certain tendrils, or connections that keep you going in your positive direction. Key to this would be, your anchor to God/Source, with the unconditional love that abounds around and eventually within you.

As much as most of you on your journeys are letting go of your Past, still there is the recognition that you are a true-accumulation of your Past. Meaning, much that has made you who you are, is exactly what you are trying to shed. Do you see the dichotomy here? While discipline or punishment may have made you strong, or have fortitude against difficulties, then ONLY the pain needs to be let go of, in order to put positive-focus on future choices of a better, happier life. The continuous confusion may come from holding on to, all those positive things that you have turned around from your Past, while releasing their negative roots. The blaming has been replaced by forgiveness, and responsibility to move on to live in the Now, free from any chains - visible or invisible - that bound you before.

The vast majority of humanity, still allows others - personally or through the media - to define their life for them. Various groups -organizations profit from this relationship. They use fear to promote their agenda - they manipulatively preach doom and gloom, if You don't do or believe as you are told. It is much like the pharmaceutical companies creating new faux-diseases to get you to buy more drugs. This plays on your embedded belief, that your life can be much better protected with a pill, rather than having a healthy lifestyle, as that may be too much work. It will take a lot of patience, to allow your human brothers and sisters to wake up from accepting this long time scenario. Fortunately, many alternative therapies and natural remedies are rising above the negative control of the FDA and other government rulers.

Subliminal suggestion plays directly to one's Past beliefs or prejudices, suggesting they don't need to take responsibility, or share the wealth, or be accepting of those who are different than them. We are ALL One - Equal - as we ALL come from the same God/Source. Those easily sucked into these various prejudicial-propaganda need to discover a type of Self-love that has been missing from their world. Many from the generations that spoke out for Peace/Freedom in the 1960s and '70s have continued to contribute to the shift in humanities' consciousness. For many, it was part of their service-contract to fulfill in this lifetime, of their acceptance prior to coming on Earth. Many have now realized that they truly are Angelic Beings, having a Human Being experience, and so allow joy to guide their positive choices.

We all know that many people are just now waking up and participating more in things like New Energy, protecting Mother Earth, Spirituality or metaphysical groups. Some don't have all the overlays from years of mandated religious beliefs, or maybe political turmoil. So they're very open to any freedom and coming forth, involved in the idea of personal choice. The release of control-structure, to break free and have that liberation, at times was/is chaos. What you have learned so far on your path is similar, in it is a blessing, And curse, at the same time. But this chaos has caused you to look at it from more than an organized, linear perspective. Once you have seen the forest for the trees, or the other side of the coin, you learn that it is not chaos, but freedom with a myriad of potentials to choose.

In this New Earth Energy - Spirituality is eclectic, it doesn't require Group structure. You can personalize it to your preferences or needs. Your belief systems are based on who You are Now and in your choice future, not someone else's dictates of how you must live your life. The more you learn from your positive actions, the more It is always giving back to you, as God/Source is limitless in its abundance. With full acceptance of this gift, you are rewarded with what you need showing up through things or people to guide, direct or give you what you ultimately need or desire.

So, as you're discovering that your New Energy can/does have chaos associated to it, there is always a giving nature that defies its structure or logic, unless You make that as part of your ownership on it. You are progressing, albeit sometimes the hard way, but as usual those times have catapulted you into looking at things in a whole new way. You no longer let anything and anyone define things for you to do, or be who you truly want to be. Spirituality is definitely more than a religion, even one that you may say has been personalized just for you. Spirituality is Your direct connection to your Divinity and you allowing that Energy to flow through you, as often as you choose. For some it's on a daily basis, some it's hourly, or others it's on a moment-by-moment basis. Once you've gotten comfortable and accepting of your Divine Energy flow, you don't even have to think about. Within your heart and consciousness, it is simply always there.

When you have this surety of who You are and how strongly you are connected to God/Source, you don't have to convince anybody about anything. "I am who and what

I am." This brings harmony and balance to your space, as this truth controls any chaos you might feel. This is a strength that needs no defending, as well as an acceptance that everyone has a choice in their beliefs, and that in no way changes or discounts Your beliefs. Granted, if someone is irritating in their need to have you convince them regarding your beliefs, then step away, or do whatever you need to disconnect from them. You may want to work within yourself, as to why you would allow another's opinion to influence, or question you to prove yourself or Beliefs.

When you know what is in your heart and mind is true and you love yourself as you are, then it is merely accepting that as your own reality. Yes, it is a process of Becoming who you truly are and that is part of the confusion, the chaos which includes questioning. Prior, you may not have been capable of making many of your own decisions. Accept that you are no longer engaged in this duality with other people pushing and pulling you. Know you have moved away from that. You are no longer caught up in the right and wrong or whatever, you've let go. You are Now true to yourself and, who you know you are to be.

**Exercise:** Do your deep breathing - 3 - 5 deep breaths - as often as needed with Harmony-Balance in-breath - Chaos-Confusion out-breath. Do it until you feel lighter and your Energy is grounded. Also, remember that whenever a person pushes those 'sacred-cow' buttons in your life, bless them as you let them go. That is their role at that time in your life, until you learn the lesson they are helping you to overcome. Through your awareness - questioning yourself - you can learn how to respond differently. I usually just throw up my hands and say, "Whatever. Everything's a choice - you make yours and

I'll make mind." Just, Never question that you are loved, especially by yourself - Know that you are.

\* \* \* \* \* \*

There should be no end to your imagination. Usually the more experience you have, the less likely you are to experiment - so open up!

Concentrate on your breathing, as to who you are.

Music can change the world, because it can change people. Bono

Vision without action is merely a dream. Action without vision just passes the time. Vision with action can change the world. Joel A. Barker

# Simple Truths ~ Part #70

The only thing for certain is that things will change, how we handle that change is as always our choice. Obviously, by now one would hope that you have learned how to go with the natural flow of positive energy. If you always look for the Positive in all things and all people you will find it, then it will make your life and others more positive - even joyful. Of course, if you look for the Negative, you will find that also. Is that what you want to choose - to have negativity in your life for depression and sadness? Do you have a need to be really dissatisfied with something, so you suffer? Do you need to take on the affects of things that are non-consequential to your life, just because they have negative energy?

I am not saying that one should not be empathic at all to the problems of others, but taking on those problems as your own - or rescuing - is neither healthy for you nor helpful to those others. Think about it - being Positive is your choice, granted one you may need to practice, or even "fake it, till you make it," but still a personal choice. You can learn to cultivate joy in the midst of challenges. Simple joy can fill your heart, your entire being, as in Joy there is Grace. And, through Grace there is the realization of Oneness, of wanting to help another because you can - yet, do so without attachment to them or their situation. We are All One, as we All come from the same Source.

Return to basics! You can take loving care of yourself by You staying calm and not allowing anxiety into your life. Know that you are never alone and nothing is ever as bad as fearful-thinking makes it seem. Even, Ask for help - Divine Assistance - from your Higher Self or Source, that is there for You always. By thinking loving, positive thoughts and feeding your body loving nourishment, you can become positive energy. You, only you, choose what you allow to influence you from your senses. If it is disharmonious stop immediately, do your deep breathing - positive key words in, and releasing words out.

Walk to keep your physical body moving, so that your energy stays positive, as your awareness of nature surrounds you with feelings that all things are effortless and easy. Call on the Golden Light to now encircle you, as you allow it to flow naturally through you, so you can receive its protection, giving and sharing with others. You can trust it that all is well, as you are blessed and full of Grace. This positiveness is more than magic, it is knowing that it simply is Your birthright, as a child of Source and loved unconditionally.

This return to basics is important to your commitment and to focus of your journey on the path. There is no time for getting far off track, as you will be called upon to assist novices in how they need to stay positive in those coming times. To be a good 'leader by example,' you have achieved the basics with a confidence without question. Your own missteps are accomplishments in that you mastered them, so no matter how long it took, or how many detours were involved. This is not a fastest-time marathon, this is Your life. However long it takes to learn what works and what doesn't, is what's most important.

If your experiences of growth were half-assed or half-baked or even faked, what kind of a leader would you be for those novices? No, this is not about perfection, it is about knowing at your core, what all flows well and is harmonious to your being, and what does not. This is not glitz, glamor or success acknowledged from those outside of you, it comes from within you first. So, if there is still any disharmony coming from any residue or sludge from entrenched old beliefs fueled by fear, they obviously need to go.

Objectively you need to regularly observe-visualize inside your heart/soul to see if there is anything at all that is not working, or other causing any unrest. You know from your positive, vibrational energy if there is peace within. Set your intention to become more truthful about topics you thought you had mastered. The ego can play tricks on you at any stage of awakening, putting you into illusion. So, be willing to cover what seems like "old ground," learning on a deeper level than before. There is no sense letting even the smallest tangles from any of the old ways, that no longer serve you, back into your realm. The secret here is that only you can change you, so focus on yourself. Once you have your own Self back in order, then you can be that leader/guide to others, with love and care through true authenticity from knowing yourself so well.

It all starts by your Being your own Truth and then radiates out from there to whomever is ready to listen, accept and grow. Then they will know that their journey will be as long as it has to be, from their choices for the lessons to be learned - painful or arduous or whatever. The greatest lesson you may tell them about, is what is meant by you listening to the still, small voice within. How much they choose to believe you, will be part of their path. It usually does take time to learn to focus on the truth, that is found in one's own heart. You are your own torch-bearer, holding the light to discover your own truth.

It is understood in the depths of your heart that the truth of your journey is the very simple knowing that you have achieved enough compassion to allow another to just BE Who They Are! A compassionate-heart allows the complete understanding in the truth of there never being a judgment of yourselves either. When you flow effortlessly from one right action to the next, you are establishing a new level of Spiritual-morality, a code of ethics for all of humanity to live by. There is something about you finding your own truth, that puts you in deep communion with yourself. These realizations help you to release the Past and to experience love in its truth, because love is full of truth. In that way, you know that anyone who places a condition on love is not expressing true love.

Anyone who judges or criticizes others - including themselves - is not expressing true love. No one needs to be this kind of victim, as it usually comes from fears of others, in an ignorant conscious-state. You have the power to eliminate that fear permanently and set in place the foundation for truth and love to exist. The more empowered and self-aware you are, the less you have to fear. A basic truth is that Fear is the number one paralyzing and self-sabotaging force. It causes you to feel negative, burdened, inadequate, useless and worthless. Unlike natural fear in the form of survival or being alert to some danger, this fear is usually created by the ignorance and greed of humanity - one person trying to control another, by putting them down.

**Exercise:** To determine for yourself what true love means to you, write down all of your belief systems regarding love. How have they changed since your journey began? Are there any of them that still come from Past programming of your parents, friends, teachers, or society in general? Study each one in detail, deleting any that in truth no longer come from the very core of Your being. This can be a very powerful releasing, as what is left is therefore Your-truth about love. It can never be explained simply or even permanently - it is too vast and too intertwined with most everything in Your life. Revisit the topic on a regular basis, especially after you have had some related experience, where You may question the presence, or truth of love.

\* \* \* \* \* \*

The ego never wants to be corrected or changed when it's winning. And, it never wants to acknowledge when it's losing. That's why it's the ego, it always thinks it's right.

Knowledge is not power ... wisdom is. Real wisdom is an experience felt ... not a knowledge that is taught.

Growth is painful. Change is painful. But, nothing is as painful as staying stuck where you do not belong. N. R. Narayana Murthy

Find joy in everything you choose to do. Every job, relationship, home. . . it's your responsibility to love it, or change it. Chuck Palahniuk

# Epilogue ~ What I've Learned So Far

Before journeying on the path, many of us may have been afraid to ask the question, "What is Happiness?" Or more succinctly, "Am I happy?" But now, I hope and for myself, I know happiness is all about love - as everything else falls into place after that. And, "Yes, I am happy." I do affirm my happiness everyday along with my good health. Though admitting that I felt inadequate prior from my Past, as most of us have those residues from our parental controls or personal traumas. It is amazing what negative beliefs of others and ourselves we can overcome with age and perseverance. Middle age can prove success over the fears of failure during our 25 - 35 age group. Many of us were trudging on so, to not face pit-of-our-stomach nagging fears.

Some best successes came under the duress of tragedy, or the hardship of staying afloat emotionally. Though each of our travails differ in context and content, truly how they were handled marked the results. Easier problems failed by not having sufficient experience, or not knowing how to deal with them. Some were horrendous situations, another succeeds only because there's no other alternative. As a very adaptive child, I generally knew I had to please my mother for peace and do things for myself, as I rarely any supporters from within my family. Other than my closest friends, that got our divorces together, I lacked confiding my needs, aspiring dreams and desires to others.

While true depression is a chemical imbalance in one's brain, many psychologists consider general depression a defense mechanism. It's deployed by not dealing with what is bothering you, usually from the Past. How many millions choose drugs over processing? In the 1970s, it was Valium that was the trendy-pill to pop whenever you had any stress. Maybe that is when we became so accustomed to taking a pill to make us happy. With that, many are in a combination of lostness and over reaction to their current life from their prior family dynamics. It is difficult for many people to grasp maturity, much less decisions to succeed or face reality. The wounds of anyone's younger years can be healed and released. We sometimes need to learn the self-preservation trick of tying a knot at the end of our rope - so we don't give up. It is most amazing how some depressed, wall flowers and others bloom in their later middle age. I being one during my time in Japan. If only more humans could produce pearls out of irritating situations, the way that oysters do. While wisdom is not guaranteed with age, it is often developed after surviving major, life-challenging bouts. Obviously, the earlier you can release your Past demons the more happy a future time.

There actually have been a number of studies that have proved that a positive/optimistic attitude and general point of view is healthier both physically and mentally, than a negative/pessimistic-depressive one. This is like saying that someone drinks because of they've had a difficult life. No, once again research shows that any addiction comes from some sort of repressed feelings. Get that out and released, then amazingly the addiction is usually gone. The good and bad of all of your relationships, whether of those related to you or not, will define how happy and gracefully you age. The bottom-line is and always will be the various kinds of love you have felt, especially for yourself.

While reality may be defined quite differently by most of us, love in its myriad of flavors has a solid base of happy and feelings of worth. If it is needy and dependent, or you respond by rescuing, you are giving your power away, or even worse, being sucked from you. Competitive jealousy also sucks your power. Continuing to change is the male consciousness of being told they are superior, as women get more comfortable in succeeding in almost all things. Most importantly, true love has never had the requirement of money, education or social standing. Also crucial, is to gratefully come to some point in your life where you do Not respond to someone's expectation of you. It is about simply being loved for who we are - the 'warts and all,' again.

While it is true that my trusting in others sometimes puts me out on a limb with disappointment, I remind myself and accept, that 'winners risk' it all sometimes. For others who fear being hurt, they may die never being able to accept love, or other acknowledgment of a happy life lived. Still, happiness like everything else is a choice - and loving yourself is preeminent to love from another. It may be said that while passion may drive the young, it is compassion that comforts you when older. I guess there is an adjustment to one's life, and I want to go out of mine having sung, danced and played every last note of my music - no unfinished symphony for me. They don't have to all be great and never expected to be perfect, but the lines on my face will be from laughing and smiling, not sadness or worry. Unfortunately, most of the men I loved and who loved me, were never able to truly express or show that love to me. I do not look back on any of my relationships with any bitterness. As I totally accept them, as with other friendships, they come and go into my life, as meant for my best and highest good.

What I needed and learned, was when it was best for me to move on, especially regarding my marriages, my parents and relatives. I had put on facades for all of them for so long, they really had no clue and were rather shocked when I left. They didn't understand what *true freedom* I was talking about and how it affected my happiness. Taking leave of a lover or others, is not something we're taught how to do, as it's selfish, if for happiness sake. The idea of *not* being responsible for another's happiness, nor them for yours sounds foreign, if not bizarre to many. When the concept of trying to please, or make your parent or partner happy has been your way of life, the new idea that "*you* cannot make another person happy, it comes from inside *them*," sounds like an amazing revolution. We all do change, but for most of us, just not at the same time or rate as others. I have finally learned my change is not something I need to apologize for, or even try to truly make amends to anyone. I've given up my adapting a thousand different ways, and still usually not succeeding. I've tried to let go, or leave while I could still look back on some positive experiences together, and maybe be kind, somewhat of friends. To be happy is to be healthy, and it all comes from being loved, of course, by yourself first. Truly, there is no secret ingredient or magic wand. It is a step-process. Either you do believe it and practice, or you don't. There is no punishment, there are only real lessons to learn and the rewards of unconditional love.

# *Appendix*

## Breathing - Visualizing Exercises -

These can be done anywhere, in portions of as much or little as you want, so you don't have to have a quiet space or a lot of time. I often do quickie breathing exercises prior to meetings, when stressed, or just need to relax. You can do them any time you are a Passenger - not a driver, though you can always do quick, deep breaths at a stop light, but do not close your eyes. If you do them before going to bed, be sure to stretch and shake out all negative energy as much as you can through your arms, legs and body. I prefer lying down on the bed, so I don't have to get up to get in bed, that way I can just drift off naturally.

I do water aerobics daily during the week with walking-squats, so do my breathing and affirmations at that time using Divine Assistance.

Make the breathing - meditating/affirmations yours, own it for what you need and want at the time. Visualizing what you want and where you want to be, are the most powerful tools in manifesting and using your empowered, creative energy. You are in charge. It is always your choice to replace the negative with the positive. Breathing is the most natural thing that you've got to do anyway, so make it work for you, in so many different ways.

Begin by taking a series of deep, relaxing breaths - build up to a count of ten in and ten out. If you are working on a specific problem or situation, include Positive words as you breathe in and the words you are releasing, on the out breath. Example: Love in - Fear out; Healing in - Pain out; Harmony in - Confusion/chaos out, etc.

    1) Visualize the breath coming in through the top of your head and moving down slowly like a wave, or sparkling clean water washing through your

body and out your hands and feet - each toe/finger squirting out little streams. As it flows through every little gap or crevice, it takes all of the released tension, pent-up stress, repeated negative thoughts and unnecessary worries out of your body and into the bare Earth. Repeat until you feel a shift of lightness in your body.

2) Next visualize the breath coming up from the glorious, green Earth, through your feet - each toe sucking the vibrations in, through every part of your body and out the top of you head. This scented breath enlivens all the cells in every organ and blood stream in your body with the healing aromas of nature. It is wafting like a fountain from your head, that over flows surrounding the outside of your body, soothing and relaxing. Repeat until the pungent smells of these breaths fill your nostrils. Use your favorite essential oils - see list later. My favorite healer is lavender, but choose what works for you.

3) Now, for the ultimate spa treatment, visualize the breathe coming through both your head and feet at the same time. As these energized, powerful breaths meet at your center, you need to direct them to get the most affect from their transformational capabilities. You can send them to your heart for healing, or your solar-plexus for strength - confidence building, or to your throat for communication clearing. You can choose any chakra to receive this cleansing-clearing power or even multiple chakras. Your body from top to bottom - inside and out - is momentarily hermetically sealed, as the breath is whirling around and through every cell out to your finger tips and toes. You feel your body becoming more

fluid and malleable as every joint, muscle or bone pain is released. Keep your five senses focused, as they are heightened. Again, use essential oils for special healing if wanted.

If any images pop into your mind, don't try to figure them out, just go with the colorful fantasy. This is not the time to let your logical -analytical mind question what the images mean, it doesn't matter, just enjoy them.

## Bringing in Your Intuitive:

Your Intuition is that small voice inside - Your Higher-Self directly connected to God/Source. Resting and relaxed, listen for that voice to answer your call - ask for Divine Assistance for clarity in order to hear your Angels speaking/guiding you. They are there and they are waiting for you to ask for them. Trust me, keep asking and they will come. You must trust yourself in being worthy and loved.

This can be particularly helpful prior to sleeping for dreams or co-creating. While continuing to feel your body and staying aware of your breathing, you may want to bring into focus some situation you are trying to receive clarification on, or a person you are conflicted in how to handle. You want harmony in all aspects of your life, so in this most relaxed state you are more open to options that you would not consider when upset or stressed. Also, if working on a manifestation, use your visualization to focus yourself into that picture of what you desire most. You are now so much more in touch with your feelings so positive as to what you deserve and the happiness that it can bring. You can co-create the synchronistic experiences - opportunities of people and things that match what you desire to come into your path. As you send a message to the Universe, of what you want to create in your life with a visualization of it. How will you share your gifts?

This same process can be used if you need to make a choice - continuing to feel your body and staying aware of your breathing - visualize those choices one at a time. Look at them closely, then put yourself in with them, touch them if you want, talk to them in your mind. Then, open yourself to what you need to know for that decision. Move from choice to choice, asking for help from your Higher Self, (Intuition) until you receive a vibration of your truth, as to which choice is best for you. Once you allow your Intuition to assist you, your access is easier, until you simply call on it in your mind for the answer you need, for whatever situation or decision. Don't let your logical-analytical mind question this process, as it will evaporate.

**Activation of Abundance**

If you asked for abundance, it is on its way, truly - if you were totally prepared for it. There's part of you that has to have a flushing out, a releasing of your old belief systems. Were you expecting it to just appear as a pot of gold on the floor in front of you? There is an entire process that involves clearing every aspect of you, that has ever been in lack of any abundance. You need to go through transformation to raise your frequencies to have an integration of any abundance.

**Basic Principle:**

True, deep resonating desires are always more powerful than recited, repeated rote-words. Follow the Basic steps for speeding up activation of Abundance in your life. Always maintain some sense of humor. Love and Laughter are great healers and always remember that your Journey is about finding Love - being Joyful. If things go wrong - missteps - these are your experiences, your lessons, without humor the Spirit shrivels. A happy soul has been through a hundred lifetimes, so an advanced, wise soul. It knows not to take any of this game too real or seriously. It really will work out for your best, as that is what we are here for - to learn. There is work involved, so asked yourself again, do you really want it?

**Step One:** Look into a mirror, make eye connection with yourself, and say "I love me" as many times as possible during your day. These three magic words help you maintain your self-respect and extend more respect to others, to all life. And, the basis of unconditional love.

**Step Two:** Write the following affirmation and repeat it over and over again to yourself: "I am whole and perfect, as I was created by God/Source!" The greatest secret of self-esteem is to appreciate other people more - any fault you see in them, is a fault you see in yourself.

**Step Three:** Examine and assess if there are any more limiting belief systems that need to be addressed. Look for past judgments of others and yourself. Ask Spirit's support in releasing this. Commit yourself to take the steps in manifesting to experience prosperity consciousness.

**Step Four:** Set clear intentions with your Higher Spirit - you feel you truly deserve/want this. Begin to work with them. Affirm to yourself and all others that you matter, I Belong, I am Worthy, I am Deserving of All the abundance that I desire! Your frequencies must allow it.

**Step Five:** Remind yourself you're never alone and unconditionally loved. Meditate to stay in conscious contact to Source, which respects you. Keep awareness high, your five senses active to detect changes.

**Step Six:** Set goals for yourself to make sure that you don't have any residual anger, resentment or other negative feelings towards anyone that may bring in any Karma-blockage. By radiating forgiving energy outward, you will have positive energy flowing back toward you.

**Step Seven:** Ensure your goals are achievable in accordance with your Divine Destiny. Do not set goals out of your reach, or setting you up for disappointment or sabotage. No room for fear or doubt, nor hesitation of your desire or worthiness. It all must be positive energy.

**Step Eight:** Use gratitude/thanks for overcoming/completing the whole process. Appreciation for all you have been given from Source, along every step of your life path, for it to run smoother and quicker to achieve what you desire most. This positive raises your frequencies.

**Step Nine:** Take action, you must physically participate in bringing your intention into fruition. Also, surrender the goal of your plan to God/Source, as you actively do all you can with an open heart/mind. Ask Spirit to guide you as to any other action or changes. And, so it is.

**Step Ten:** Final step - celebrate the experience of Abundance in your own life on a regular basis and rewarded with fruition, as no lack in the Universe, and God/Source wants you to have your share of it all.

Remember there is no linear time in the Universe, but if you feel your request is not being met, perhaps it is not time for you to receive it. Let it go, or rework it, or simply add: "This or something better." I was told that a relationship I was asking for was being put off, as it would be too distracting for other work that Source wanted me to complete first. You will see things from a different perspective when new good, positive things come into your life totally unexpected. Laugh at it all, yourself for ever doubting, and know you have overcome a small fear. I've always asked for what is for '*my best* and highest good, *and the highest good of all*,' I know it may limit some things I've asked for. Know that Source embraces you and you finding new ways around things - where there is a will, there is always a way.

Allow your soul to become full of Love-Light, to allow the Spirit of God/Source to work and move through you and to be *at-One* with you. As positive energy continuously flows through you, many people are smiling at you, because you realize you are smiling at everyone. Don't ever take anything for granted, except that God/Source so loves you unconditionally. Pay attention so life shows you that Abundance is possible in anything. It's about having a positive attitude, a perception about you deserving all things you truly desire and are a vibrational match. Any negative doubt, fear or worry will negate, interfere or delay your manifestation. A compatible desire will resonates within your soul and it will be manifested.

I have pulled from my own experience and many sources for the above steps. Though there are numerous books out there that offer direction and guide to manifesting, I would like to suggest the truly magnificent books by the entity *Abraham* and the channel Esther Hicks, along with Jerry Hicks. Again, be sure any intuit or teacher that offers manifesting teachings, is *personally recommended* to you. Their manifesting may only be about themselves, or take the money and run thing.

## Seven Chakras Basic Information

There are many intricate parts of one's body working together to bring about balance and harmonizing all of you. Seriously important for supporting and contributing to your Mind, Body and Soul are your seven levels of your Chakras. Your Mind, is where the conscious and sub-conscious are brought together. Your Soul is involved, as it rises to a higher level or your Higher Self, with the clearing of negative energy of Past and subconscious. Of course, the physical Body receives all the results of invisible energy-vibrational transformations, as you change, grow and process. This is the tangible results seen in the accessing and acceptance of higher truth or cosmic consciousness. While you have been creating this happy new person, who no longer contains any old, negative, restrictive beliefs, your body through your chakra openings has been flowing positive energy into your physical being. As well as learning, to access specifically your sixth and seventh chakras, to then become incredibly intuitive to avoid allowing any negative or Past fear energy to return. Also, another benefit of all of this, your left and right brain have become more balanced, so you are now both creative and analytical, thus capability of wisdom. A lot to take in, I know.

**Basics:** Thought is based in top 3 chakras - Five, Six and Seven - Emotions in Bottom 3 (One, Two and Three) - and brought together in Heart center - love feeling (Four).

The following is a general summary of the physical locations and the elements associated with each chakra. There are some minor allowed discrepancies between how different people define or interpret each chakra. The colors and locations of the chakras in a straight line have always been consistent. To be noted also, the base chakra does extend down - for grounding purposes, and the crown chakra extends up - for direct connecting to God/Source, or the influx-flow of positive Light Energy. The chakras in between have vortexes, or general small areas encircling them, as well as being affected both to the front of the body and from the back. There are many wonderful books that give you a more detailed description and explanation of your chakras, please do check them out. There are also many wonderful meditation tapes to develop a more personal understanding for use of your chakras, as well as processes for a more thorough cleaning of your chakras. Being in the flow of positive energy is key to your new Spiritual and physical growth and happiness. Be sure to keep the Golden Light around you.

**Clearing or cleaning your Chakras:** This is a visualization process as you deep breathe, to see each chakra with its color brightly glowing and moving in a circular motion. If so, then your chakra system is all balanced. A blocked chakra is dull in color and not moving because it is filled with residual energy. Then your physical and emotional health can be affected. This occurs as the result of the return to a negative belief systems, fear, etc. The effects of your good - bad habits, beliefs, feelings, thoughts and desires can be directly found in your chakras. So, if you feel sluggish, off-centered or just irritable, you might want to check into each of your Chakras, to make sure they are glowing brightly and spinning. If not, ask your Angel Guides to assist in the clearing of any Chakra's blockage and fill them with a positive Light Energy flow. Each chakra is said to have its own core energy, so think of that energy while clearing. As you become more familiar with each chakra's lesson and what causes its imbalance, you will know what prevention is needed, or problem that may exist, so as to not repeat it.

**First - Base Chakra Color Association Red Sanskit Name Muladhara Location Base of spine, coccyx**

**Lesson Survival** – The right to exist; controls fight or flight. Deals with tasks related to the material/physical world, governs physical dimension - understanding of it. Ability to stand up for oneself and security issues, and is the energy center.

**Imbalances** Anemia, fatigue, lower back pain, sciatica, depression. Holding on to negative thoughts and energy. Frequent colds, or cold hands and cold feet.

Base/Root Stimulants: Physical exercise and restful sleeps, gardening, pottery and clay. Red food/drink, gemstones, clothing, bathing in red, Using essential oils: ylang ylang or sandalwood.

Core Energy of Letting Go - correlates with the Base/Root Chakra.

**Second Chakra**

**Color Association Orange Sanskit Name Svadisthana**
**Location: Sexual organs - ovaries or testes**

**Lesson Creativity** — The right to express feelings. Connected to our sensing abilities and sexual/relationship issues to feelings. Ability to be social and intimate.

**Imbalances:** Eating disorders. Alcohol and drug abuse. Depression, resentful of others or what they have, feelings of lack. Low back pain. Asthma or allergies. Candida & yeast infections. Urinary problems. Sensuality issues, as well as impotency and frigidity.

Sexual Stimulants: Hot aromatic baths, water aerobics, massage. Embracing sensation and different food tastes. Orange food/drink, gemstones, clothing. Using essential oils: melissa or orange.

Core Energy of Gratitude correlates with the Chakra of Creation.

**Third - Solar Plexus Chakra**

**Color Association Yellow Sanskit Name Manipura**
**Location Above the navel, solar plexus**

**Lesson Personal power** – The right to think. Clearinghouse of emotions, balance of intellect, self-confidence and ego power. Ability to have self-control and humor.

**Imbalances:** Digestive problems, ulcers, diabetes, hypoglycemia, constipation. Nervousness, control issues. Toxicity, parasites, colitis, poor memory.

Solar Plexus Stimulants: Taking classes, reading informative books, doing mind puzzles. Sunshine. Detoxification programs. Yellow food/drink, gemstones, clothing.

Using essential oils: lemon or rosemary.

Core Energy of Surrender correlates with Solar Plexus power center.

**Fourth - Heart Chakra**

**Color Association Green Sanskit Name Anahata**

**Location Center of chest**

**Lesson Love** – The right to love, be loved and feel lovable. Love, forgiveness, compassion. Ability to have self-control. Acceptance of oneself and one's worth.

**Imbalances:** Closed Heart, Chest pain and breathing disorders. Heart and breast cancer. High blood pressure. Passivity. Immune system problems. Muscular tension.

Heart Stimulants: Nature walks, time spent with family or friends. Green food/drink, gemstones, clothing.

Using essential oils: eucalyptus or pine.

Core Energy of Love correlates with the Heart Chakra.

**Fifth Chakra**

**Color Association Blue Sanskit Name Visuddha**

**Location Throat region**

**Lesson Expression** – The right to speak, communication and judgment. Learning to express oneself and one's beliefs. Ability to trust, be loyal. Organization and planning.

**Imbalances:** Thyroid imbalances, swollen glands. Fevers and flu. Infections. Mouth, jaw, tongue, neck and shoulders problems. Hyperactivity. Hormonal disorders,

PMS, mood swings, bloating and menopause. Resentment and revenge feelings.

Throat Stimulants: Singing, poetry, stamp or art collecting. Meaningful conversations. Blue food/drink, gemstones, clothing. Using essential oils: chamomile or geranium.

Core Energy of Forgiveness correlates with Communication Center.

## Sixth - Third Eye Chakra
**Color Association Indigo Sanskit Name Anja**
**Location Forehead, in between the eyes.**

**Lesson Intuition** – Right to see clearly. Consider our Spiritual nature and insights. Develop psychic abilities. Have Self-realization. Release hidden/repressed negativity.

**Imbalances:** Learning disabilities, coordination problems, sleep disorders. Depression, defensive victim and blame feelings. Thyroid imbalances, swollen glands. Fevers and flu. Infections. Mouth, jaw, tongue, neck and shoulders problems. Hyperactivity. Hormonal disorders, PMS, mood swings, bloating and menopause.

**Third Eye Stimulants:** Star gazing. Mediation Indigo food/drink, gemstones, clothing.

Use indigo essential oils: such as patchouli or frankincense.

Core Energy of Apology correlates with the Third Eye.

## Seventh - Crown Chakra
**Color Association Violet Sanskit Name Sahasrara**
**Location Top of head**

**Lesson Knowingness** – Right to aspire to integration with God. Dedication to the divine consciousness and trusting the Universe. Developing Spirituality and a higher intelligence. Integrating consciousness/subconsciousness into super-consciousness.

**Imbalances:** Headaches. Photosensitivity. Mental illness. Neuralgia. Senility. Right/left brain disorders and coordination problems. Epilepsy. Varicose veins and blood vessel problems. Skin Rashes. Feelings of denial, blame and disillusion.

**Crown Stimulants:** Focusing on dreams. Writing down one's visions and inventions. Violet food/drink, gemstones, clothing.

Using essential oils: lavender or jasmine.

Core Energy of Responsibility correlates with the Crown Chakra.

Many healers work specifically in helping to cleanse or clear any problems in your Chakras. Be sure to have one recommended. Important after any extensive Chakra cleanse/clearing or of your energy, take a cleansing soak bath with 1 cup sea salt and 1 cup baking soda for at least 20 - 30 minutes to release residue of negative energy.

* * * * * *

**Ram Dass**: ... everything is 'grist for the mill.' Absolutely everything—a traffic jam, an illness, a theft, a noisy neighbor, a flat tire—becomes an opportunity to learn, discover, progress, repent, rejoice, unveil, awaken, love more, and wonder. The smallest detail of life, every single encounter ...

Think about it.

### The Twelve Universal Laws

The Universal Laws are rather simple, but as they are viewed as guidelines, it is their simplicity for your behavior, that makes them so complex and difficult to employ into your daily life. They are all about *truth,* which we all know is sometimes hard to swallow, or even accept. And, I might add, it is your choice to do so. You may be more willing to accept them after the completion of this book, than at the start. Of course, just knowing them provides keys to understanding, as they do enhance our physical, mental, emotional and Spiritual growth.

The Laws also bring clarity to your God-given empowerment for ruling, controlling and directing your life, including your power of creation - manifestation for living effortlessly. The Laws work equally without judgment of anyone, no matter if you understand or do accept them, they are still affecting your life. This is why it is so important to learn them comprehensively, as *what you don't know can hurt you,* and you'll wonder why. The Laws all work inter-relatedly, so just reading what you think are the most important is a huge error on your part.

The basic cognizance is that Every Thing in the Universe is made up of energy, no limitations here, us and absolutely everything of, in, above and/or below. This includes not only tangible, but the intangible - your thoughts, feelings, words and actions are all energy in various forms. This is why what you think, feel, say and do every moment returns to you creating your realities. This springs back to you being responsible for your life, for which you are accountable - if not to others, then to Universal Law. When we talk about someone giving off a 'vibe,' or someone seeing another's aura, it is that real Universal energy - be it negative or positive. In reality, you are all in a whirling mass of energy, surrounded by more constant, numerous other energies spinning rapidly on our Earth, within our Universe and Cosmos. Thus, being comprised of this energy, is therefore why you are all intimately connected within our atmosphere, in this whirling sea of energy.

All of this energy moves in a circle, so naturally, *what goes around does comes around.* Those combined thoughts, feelings, words and actions of everyone on the planet intertwines to create our ever collective consciousness, and the world we see before us. Again, that can be mass-fear when a catastrophe happens, or a positive love with something beneficial that affects more than one country, or group of people. In our electronic world, the exciting or shocking news is then instantly broadcast about everything to everyone. You have seen that single fact alone has the power to create chaos, or a world of peace with harmony - abundance around you. It is not only essential that you learn to control your own thoughts and emotions, but how, or if you are being influenced by those of others. Understanding, observing and following the Universals Laws help you to do this.

## 1. The Law of Divine Oneness:

This helps you to understand that we are All One, and All connected to the same Source, so All connected to each other. Our lives have the same purpose of growing, healing and becoming aware of our Spiritual connectedness. While you all have individual, unique lives, you all belong to the human family. Because you live in a world where everything is energetically connected to everything else, all that you create affects everyone else. At the same time, everything you do, say, think and believe affects others and the Universe around you. Therefore, to judge another is to judge yourself, as there are no differences within the family of humanity. To treat others in a way that you would not accept being treated, would be a violation of this law. It is all about equality.

## 2. The Law of Vibration:

This Law states that the energy of everything in the Universe moves, vibrates and travels in its own vibrational patterns. These same principles of vibration in the physical world apply to your intangible thoughts, feelings, desires and wills. Each sound, thing and even emotion has its own vibrational frequency, unique unto itself. Things/people/experiences, etc. that are within the same range of vibration are attracted to each other, and those that are in different vibrational ranges, repel each other. When you choose to grow or change what you are attracting, or not attracting to you, you need to change or raise your vibrational frequency. This comes as part of your Spiritual growth process on your path. You need to understand that once your vibration has been raised, certain things and people will no longer be attracted, or of interest to you, you *must let them go*. The Positive feeling of Love and the Negative emotion of Fear are the strongest influences.

**3. The Law of Attraction:**

This Law is applied in order for you to attract or manifest all things - people, events, experiences, situations - based on your vibrational frequency, either for the positive or negative on Earth that comes into your lives. Your thoughts, feelings, words and actions produce energies which, in turn, attract like energies. Negative energies attract negative energies and positive energies attract positive energies. Therefore, you must be fully aware of all emotions that you engage in your actions and that they support your preferred thoughts, dreams, emotions and words. The strength of your belief, along with your words and actions used, make this a very powerful Law which strongly warns, "Be careful what you ask for!" Your life can be an effortless flow of miracles, joy and love, or if misconstrued - endless suffering and pain.

## 4. The Law of Abundance:

This Law simply states that there is abundance in all things, everywhere. There is no lack of anything, yet it does depend on your vibrational level as to what, or how much you are attracting to you. Again, this applies to tangible and intangible, so whatever success and happiness, or problems and poverty that you have, depends on your vibrational level for attracting it to you. This law works closely with the Law of Attraction, so you need to pay attention to what you do want abundance of, which again can be anything in the Universe. *If you focus on what you don't have, rather than what you want, then that is what you will have* - the Self-fulfilling prophecy. You must also have a deep desire of what you are asking for and truly believe - be aligned - that you are worthy to receive it.

## 5. The Law of Action:

This Law refers to how we manifest things and movement of energy for any action to be taken. So, you don't just ask for something, *you must do something* to make your dreams come into fruition. If you don't know what to do, then ask for some guidance (as in Divine Assistance), or if you've learned to tune into your Higher Self-your Intuition, then listen to what that voice says. While your words have a vibrational energy, action has a higher vibration which the Universe will respond to quicker. While all energy is moving, you need to give it the direction you want by the action you take. Otherwise, it keeps whirling around. Focus strong beliefs in alignment with emotional feelings, writing them down in detail, along with your actions and you will see the creation/manifestation process unfold before you.

## 6. The Law of Cause and Effect:

This Law states that nothing happens by chance or accident outside the Universal Laws. Every action has a reaction or definite consequence and we "reap what we have sown." This is also called the Law of Karma, as it is *usually returned ten-fold - good or bad -* and if not in this life, then in the next. Some extensive Karma is carried for generations. While the Universe doesn't really test us, it does give us *opportunities* to 'do the right/best thing.' So, depending on your action the response will be likewise. If you did not learn from one lesson, you will be given more. *The Effect may not be returned in the same energy form as it was done.* So while you may only reference it as to bad luck, or an accident, but No such things actually exist in the Universe and, you can accept that or not.

**7. The Law of Compensation:**

This Law works in tandem with the positive side of the Law of Cause and Effect applied to blessings - abundance that you are given -provided with for you 'doing the right/best thing,' either on your own or when offered. The visible effects of your deeds are given to you in gifts, money, inheritances, friendships and blessings. One might say, that it is tangible-proof that you will be rewarded for what you give and those positive things you do. It is all about giving and receiving - the more you give, the more you receive. This law also increases your vibrational frequency and involves one's good works, actions and energy. Key is that there is *no attachment to the giving -* it is without expectation of reward or return.

**8. The Law of Correspondence:**

This Law is based on the principles or laws of physics, that explain the physical world – energy, Light, vibration, and motion – "As above, so below; as within, so without." Everything within your inner world is reflected in your reality and everything in the physical world is also reflected in the Universe. Everything that occurs in your life has a corresponding thought, belief, word, action that is associated with it. Nothing can exist in your outer world, without a corresponding basis in your inner world. And, most importantly, nothing in your own material world can exist without a corresponding basis that is in the Universe. Essentially, everything is a mirror of everything else. It is a reminder that any one thought, word or deed can create an avalanche of chaos or joy in your life. This is how you are continuously creating situations in your life, and even on the planet with what you think, do, say or believe. You do have the power to affect humanity and even the Universe. Because we are All connected, our energy and vibrational energy affects All.

**9. The Law of Energy:**

This Law states that nothing in the Universe is static or stays the same, so all persons have within them the power to change the conditions in their lives. Since energy follows thought/action, at any moment you can transform your reality by changing your thoughts and beliefs, thus raising your vibrations to attract new and different people, situations or experiences. Higher vibrations consume and transform lower ones; so, each of you can change the energies in your lives by understanding the Universal Laws and applying the principles in such a way as to effect change. If you consciously or unconsciously try to block energy, change or transformation, you will feel stuck, depressed and immovable. Everything - all in the Universe changes from the sun, moon and stars to every living thing on Earth. It is easier to go with the flow, than to fight this natural law of change.

**10. The Law of Relativity:**

This Law states that each person will have a life experience that reflects the lessons and soul growth that you have come to Earth to learn. This is solely your lesson for the purpose of strengthening the Light within you. No two people have the same lesson, so they cannot be compared or compete with one another. No matter how difficult you feel or perceive your situation or lesson is, put everything into its proper perspective. There is always someone who is in a much worse position. It truly is all relative. You must consider each lesson to be a challenge and remain connected to your hearts, when proceeding to learn from the experience. Always have compassion for others and their life situations. Do not judge others, as to their handling of their life, and be grateful for your own life lessons.

## 11. The Law of Polarity:

This Law states that everything is on a continuum and has an opposite. The two strongest vibrational energies in the Universe are love and fear. Every other energy is a derivative of these two, which of course, exist as polar opposites - light/dark, good/evil, forgiveness/resentment, etc. The Law is nonjudgmental, it does not state that these are either good or bad, they just are. We can suppress and transform undesirable thoughts by concentrating on the opposite pole. Thus, where your concentration of thought is, that is where the nuances of that aspect appears in your life. It is the law of mental vibrations. So, as you raise your vibrational level, you move from all the aspects of fear to all of the aspects of love. So, you may slip back, until you reach the aspect of unconditional love and then never have to know fear.

## 12. The Law of Rhythm:

This Law states that everything in the Universe vibrates and moves to its own certain rhythms. These rhythms establish daylight/night, seasons, cycles of birth/death, stages of development - sadness to joy, and fear to love and patterns of lessons, understanding, as well growth into Spiritual evolvement. Each cycle reflects the regularity of ebb and flow in God's Universe. There is always a new dawn to learn the lessons, to know how to rise above negative parts of any cycle, to create a new reality through your wiser, creative-consciousness. The challenges continue, as long as you have new experiences to learn.

* * * * * *

There are many excellent books that get into specialized studies regarding the Universal Laws, be sure to check them out for more detailed information. There are also guides and healers who work specifically using the Laws and can assist in helping to clarify any problems that you might have. Be sure they are recommended to you.

## Dowsing - What it Does - How it Works

"I know very well that many scientists consider Dowsing as they do astrology, as a type of ancient superstition. According to my conviction, this is, however, unjustified. The Dowsing rod is a simple instrument that shows the reaction of the human nervous system to certain factors which are unknown to us at this time." ~ Albert Einstein

Dowsing can be defined as a communication with one's Higher Self, or the world of Spirit, using a tool - pendulum, L-rod, Y-rod, bobber - or your physical body, with a desire for an accurate response to a statement, question, or request in regards to information, ideas, inspiration, or for help in some regard. Dowsers are seekers of truth, wisdom, peace and healing. The possibilities of what a good one can do are truly endless, transformative and magical.

Dowsing is also your Natural Sensitivity - which if you're not using you can develop - as it enables you to know things, to seek for and locate things which you cannot know or do by using the day-to-day brain. This

Sensitivity does not come from mere, basic learning or experience, but by fully using the five-physical senses which you were born with. Dowsing, with practice, can be done from any distance either by verbal or mental connection to the person, place or thing you are connecting with to assist or find.

Once you have developed your dowsing skills, by practice and perseverance, your individual talent can be applied to a wide variety of fields, basically unlimited. The traditional talent of finding water, or later oil and gas, have expanded way beyond the scope of ground related things to lost articles, animals and people. With some directed inclination and training, your dowsing can be used to clear negative energy, balance frequencies, help in healing - locating specific pain areas and dissipating stress.

Understanding how dowsing works is not by any real scientific standards, yet it is used by many scientific industries. Dowsing is the connection between you, your Higher Self/Intuition/Source Power and the Universe - including all things in and on it. It is a Natural instinct, that like your belief of being directly connected to Source - in no need of any religious *intercedent* - has been condemned and rejected by religious groups as dark magic or worse. Yet, for many of us who have learned to use it, we know it is communicating from Universal Mind and is a God-given talent and only to be for the good of humankind.

Like all things, it is a choice, should you choose to learn how to dowse. It is open to you to accept the gift and put in the time, also energy, while building confidence in your abilities and powers. You really won't know its power until you try it, as we all have the energy running within us, it only needs to be given a direction. Let all the skeptics have their laughs, while you know how much good you can do for yourself and others.

You may want to read a book, or take a class to learn the essentials, and what tool you prefer to use. They give the same results once you learned how to use and read them, as they do not have to be expensive or complicated. Like everything else, you can find a Dowsers Group on-line any where in the world. Based on information from Shirley Runco, Professional Dowser: President of the East Bay Dowsers Group; www.dowsersofthewest.org and dowsershirley@hotmail.com

\* \* \* \* \* \*

## Natural Essential Oils

Throughout the history of humankind, many different cultures, belief systems and religions talk about using Natural Essential Oils. Many of you have already been exposed to scented oils from aroma therapy, incense, or even aromatic sprays or diffusers for your homes. But, Natural Essential Oils are so much more, as they are usually placed directly on the skin or ingested for healing, or improving all of your emotional feelings.

Uplifting, protective, calming and regenerating essential oils are a unique gift from the natural world. Often referred to as "nature's living energy," they are the very essence of plants, trees, roots, bushes and seeds. They not only determine the plant's aroma, but are vital for plants to grow, live, evolve and defend themselves from many insects, disease and environmental conditions. Today, research shows when used aromatically, applied topically or taken internally, essential oils can calm, energize, balance, purify and rejuvenate the mind - body.

**Medical Science:** We have a gland in our brains called the Amygdala Gland. This gland is where all memories, emotional trauma and all emotions are stored and released from. The only way you can activate this gland, is through *your sense of smell*. This is where the phenomenal essential oils come into play! When you breathe an oil in, the tiny molecules go into our olfactory neurons then into the limbic part of your brain. The essential oil molecules will stimulate and bring the uptake of oxygen to your hypothalamus gland and your pituitary gland. They will then activate your human growth hormone gland and stimulate it to open your Amygdala Gland.

So, when a master blend of an oil says, Forgiveness, Highest Potential, Abundance, or Magnify Your Purpose etc., they truly do support this to occur. Your job is to open the bottle, put the oils on, or diffuse them and breathe them in. The tiny molecules also bypass the blood-brain barrier, so they may have great effects on supporting any neurological diseases. The oils also digest all the chemicals that gets lodged onto the brain receptors from using petrochemicals in everyday personal care products like shampoos, dish and laundry soap, other household cleaners, deodorants, toothpaste etc. These chemicals that lodge on the brain receptors are a main cause of what is called "Brain Fog," or loss of memory, lack of clarity.

From perfumes and aromatherapy to cooking and medicinal purposes, essential oils have been a vital part of everyday life and sacred ceremonies dating back to 4500 BC. After having personally experienced the many benefits of essential oils, I wanted to suggest to my readers to explore them also. Again, it is important to have them recommended to you, as there is a significant difference between essential oils that simply smell good and those that are *pure enough* to be called a therapeutic grade. I was given Young Living Essential Oils, and found them to be exemplary in healing, as well as their whole rigorous Quality Assurance requirements for purity and potency.

They have over 140 single, essential oils and unique, essential oil blends, along with the world's largest community of dedicated and trained wellness-people making them available. Enjoy, my day does not go by without having put a drop or two on my body.

\* \* \* \* \* \*

## SpiritLibrary and other References

As I've said, I've been a student of metaphysics for more than 30 thirty years, from John Randolph Price's *Super Beings* in the 1980s to Abraham-Hicks, still going in 2018. I've read numerous books and was taught by many teacher/guides. But my focus changed to more specific Spirituality when my Dowser guide Shirley Runco emailed me SpiritLibrary.com. My world amazingly opened up and expanded, as the almost daily newsletter came with a wide variety of over fifty writers into my computer. Many names I'd previously read and others unknown. Though all had a different style, most messages overlapped and I felt myself changing for the positive. I was inspired to write, as much of my growth was processed. Then my Angel Guides pushed me to put what I was learning into a blog to share, then this book.

What they say about themselves: "SpiritLibrary was born from a strong desire to make easily accessible in one website, the wonderful abundance of inspiring and empowering messages available on the internet. We wanted to combine our passion for Spirituality with our passion for technology to create a virtual library of messages updated each day to assist people in finding their personal Alignment …"

They introduced me to Spiritual Astrologers, who were so amazing combining the two perfectly and for me foretelling of myself. I've found a variety writing about so many like-minded subjects, that made me feel totally supported in what I believed and wrote. And, so much more to be discovered. It is free to sign up, donate, learn and to grow happy. The answers are out there and readily available.

**Exercises: Your Tools: Breathe - Visualize - Write - Listen - Dowse**

**Key Processes:** Love - first and always! Unconditionally Yourself and others - Acceptance - Forgiveness - Letting Go. It really is all about You! Take care of yourself first, so you can't guide and support others on their path.

**Five things you can do daily, using your tools and processes to progress rapidly:**

1. Begin by acknowledging your direct connection to Source. Monitor your emotions, thoughts, and body for pains or anything feeling out of balance. Visualize your Chakras for color and movement, as well as your energy level. Each will give you very helpful clues about what is out of balance and why. Learning the most from each obstacle will help you to avoid the repeating of painful situations and/or toxic relationship patterns.

2. Set specific intentions and utilize any obstacles as opportunities for growth for what you want to have, be and do. State these intentions in a positive way, rather than negative. Example: "I am feeling more and more confident, empowered each day." You are really a Spiritual Being living and having a human experience. Connect with that knowing and allow it to fuel your next thoughts, words and actions.

3. Take action on those things you want to create in your life. Act on one thing at a time, allowing your intuitively-guided wisdom to help prioritize

them. Even if all you did in one day was to take the walk you intended to, acknowledge yourself for doing that. Procrastination or indecision have negative energy - no decision allows the world or ego to control you. Approach your physical world as a sacred home, being patient and loving to all.

4. Use your Tools along with other simple practices to help you open up more of your awareness. Try out yoga, meditation, tai chi or other mind-clearing exercises. The important thing is consistency, finding something you will do daily that gets you out and away from your routine. When new or repetitive things about your Past come up, try to process them immediately. These things may be triggered by people you run into or just something that reminds you of them. Process letting go of it all, so you can be in the moment of how things are at present. Do not chastise or get angry with yourself. Many of these Past feelings and beliefs have been hidden deeply in your subconscious, or stem from your family's lineage, or your own Past lives. It may take years to clear them all away. They may also have been absorbed from some mass-consciousness that you didn't realize had attached itself to you. Focus your energy on clearing these negatives, so you can more quickly move more fully to embody your light in this life.

5. Begin and End each day by thanking God/Source with some positive and loving thoughts, which include those of gratitude of what all you have or was brought to you. Your inner-state determines how you experience your day, and it will, as well affect your sleep-state. Be unconditionally loving

towards yourself, as that allows the growth over time of an energy field within and around you, broadcasting positive energy from you in all directions. This love-energy attracts fortunate circumstances, opportunities and love from others in your world. Work to expand your wisdom, regarding your intentions and becoming more truthful with yourself about the life you are living. When something unforeseen happens, use your tools to learn more about what your thoughts had mastered. The ego can play tricks on you at any stage of awakening, putting you into illusion. No one is exempt. So be willing to keep learning on deeper levels all the time.

**General Daily Remembrances:** Always do keep the Golden Light around you for protection and the White Light for guidance in front of you, as you continue on your journey. They guide you to stay on track, in the moment with life and connected with your heart. You are always surrounded by unconditional love and blessings from God/Source.
The only person who is educated is the one who has learned how to learn and change. Carl Rogers
Sometimes it's the smallest decisions that can change your life forever. Keri Russell
You must take personal responsibility. You cannot change the circumstances, the seasons, or the wind, but you can change yourself. That is something you do have charge of. Jim John

www.ingramcontent.com/pod-product-compliance
Lightning Source LLC
Chambersburg PA
CBHW070900120626
46546CB00001B/68